To Cathe[...]
Happy 40th
with love and best wishes
Charlotte + Alan

HOME AND GARDEN

"In room decoration with flowers, the old tight pudding-like arrangement of many flowers crammed together is happily no longer seen.... One can hardly go wrong if a bunch ... is cut with long stalks and plenty of its own leafage and especially if it is cut without carrying a basket. I cannot explain why it is, but have always observed that no intentional arrangement of flowers in the ordinary way gives an effect so good as that of a bunch held easily in the hand as flower by flower is cut, and put in water without fresh arrangement. Rosa Alba Queen of Denmark.

HOME AND GARDEN

NOTES AND THOUGHTS, PRACTICAL AND CRITICAL, OF A WORKER IN BOTH

BY

GERTRUDE JEKYLL

*With 53 Illustrations from Photographs
by the Author
and 16 Colour Plates and comments
added to the 1982 edition*

ANTIQUE COLLECTORS' CLUB

ISBN 0 907462 18 9

First published by Longmans Green & Co. 1900
Published by the Antique Collectors' Club 1982
Reprinted 1984, 1986

Published for the Antique Collectors' Club
by the Antique Collectors' Club Ltd.

British Library CIP Data
Jekyll, Gertrude
  Home and garden
  1. Gardening
  I. Title
  635   SB450.97

Printed in England by the Antique Collectors' Club Ltd.
Woodbridge, Suffolk

CONTENTS

CHAPTER I   page

HOW THE HOUSE WAS BUILT   13

CHAPTER II

A WOOD RAMBLE IN APRIL   40

CHAPTER III

A GARDEN OF WALL-FLOWERS   50

CHAPTER IV

TREES AND LANES   59

CHAPTER V

WILD HONEYSUCKLE   83

CHAPTER VI

BRIER ROSES   92

CHAPTER VII

MIDSUMMER 101

5

CHAPTER VIII page
ROSES AND LILIES 117

CHAPTER IX
LARGE ROCK-GARDENS........................... 133

CHAPTER X
SMALL ROCK-GARDENS........................... 142

CHAPTER XI
THE WORKSHOP 157

CHAPTER XII
THE KINSHIP OF COMMON TOOLS................. 173

CHAPTER XIII
CUT FLOWERS 179

CHAPTER XIV
CONSERVATORIES 205

CHAPTER XV
THE MAKING OF POT-POURRI.................... 221

CHAPTER XVI
PLANTS FOR POOR SOILS 237

CONTENTS

7

CHAPTER XVII
GARDENING FOR SHORT TENANCIES . . . . page 261

CHAPTER XVIII
SOME NAMES OF PLANTS 278

CHAPTER XIX
WILD FERNS 288

CHAPTER XX
THE KITCHEN GARDEN 302

CHAPTER XXI
THE HOME PUSSIES 322

CHAPTER XXII
THINGS WORTH DOING 342

CHAPTER XXIII
LIFE IN THE HUT 360

INDEX 369

PREFACE

THE favourable reception of *Wood and Garden*, published a year ago,* has proved that there are many who are willing to receive such suggestions as my many years of work as a practical amateur have enabled me to make. It has further encouraged me to put together in the present volume some more notes and reflections, for the most part also on garden matters, though this time grouped with allied home subjects.

The interest which has been aroused in readers of my former book has been very gratifying, and I hope that the present one may succeed in inducing others to work out for themselves some such results as in some cases I have been fortunate enough to obtain.

In thus again offering my suggestions to the public, it is but just to myself to say that, with my very limited reserve of strength, it required some resolution to face the very real fatigue involved in the execution of my task.

8

* Reprinted by the Antique Collectors' Club, 1981.

PREFACE

May I go one step further and say that, while it is always pleasant to hear from or to see old friends, and indeed all who work hard in their own gardens, yet, as a would-be quiet worker, who is by no means over-strong, I venture to plead with my kind and numerous, though frequently unknown friends, that I may be allowed to retain a somewhat larger measure of peace and privacy.

G. J.

Publisher's Introduction to the 1982 Edition

This is the second of Gertrude Jekyll's books and was written as the result of the popularity of her first — *Wood and Garden*. Then as now her books found a sympathetic audience for two clear reasons. Firstly, her subject matter is based on careful observation of simple elements of nature; things that we all see but fail to examine: the woodland ramble, wild honeysuckle, winding lanes and the making of pot pourri are all acutely observed. Secondly, her straightforward style with detailed comments and advice is based on personal experience. She talks to the reader as one with the same interests and problems so that, although some of the experiences she describes (such as working with gardeners) may be dated, the common sense remains untarnished by time.

But there is a further reason, perhaps the main one, as to why this book retains a lasting charm. Miss Jekyll experienced something that most of us envy her for: she had the time, money and taste to build her own home to her own design with the help of an architect of world stature (Sir Edwin Lutyens) and at the same time had the knowledge and skill to create a garden round it. In discussing with us her thoughts and ideas as well as her surprisingly objective assessments of the quality of workmanship we see a world which has almost disappeared.

At times the book assumes the form of a diary, at others there are reflections and experiences which she has enjoyed

and which come across to us over fifty years with a tran-
quillity and confidence which are at the very heart of
Edwardian England.

It is hard to imagine that anyone who dips into this
gentle book will not benefit from the slackening of pace,
and be fascinated by this journey to a warm sensible world.

HOME AND GARDEN

CHAPTER I

HOW THE HOUSE WAS BUILT

DOES it often happen to people who have been in a new house only a year and a half, to feel as if they had never lived anywhere else? How it may be with others I know not, but my own little new-built house is so restful, so satisfying, so kindly sympathetic, that so it seems to me.

In some ways it is not exactly a new house, although no building ever before stood upon its site. But I had been thinking about it for so many years, and the main block of it and the whole sentiment of it were so familiar to my mind's eye, that when it came to be a reality I felt as if I had already been living in it a good long time. And then, from the way it is built it does not stare with newness; it is not new in any way that is disquieting to the eye; it is neither raw nor callow. On the contrary, it almost gives the impression of a comfortable maturity of something like a couple of hundred years. And yet

13

there is nothing sham-old about it; it is not trumped-up with any specious or fashionable devices of spurious antiquity; there is no pretending to be anything that it is not—no affectation whatever.

But it is designed and built in the thorough and honest spirit of the good work of old days, and the body of it, so fashioned and reared, has, as it were, taken to itself the soul of a more ancient dwelling-place. The house is not in any way a copy of any old building, though it embodies the general characteristics of the older structures of its own district.

Everything about it is strong and serviceable, and looks and feels as if it would wear and endure for ever. All the lesser permanent fittings are so well thought out and so thoroughly made that there is hardly anything that can possibly get out of order; the house is therefore free from the petty worry and dislocation of comfort so commonly caused by the weakness or inefficiency of its lesser parts, and from the frequent disturbance occasioned by workmen coming to do repairs.

Internal fittings that are constantly seen and handled, such as window-fastenings, hinges, bolts and door-latches, are specially designed and specially made, so that they are in perfect proportion, for size, weight, and strength, to the wood and iron-work to which they are related. There are no random choosings from the ironmonger's pattern-book; no clashing of styles, no meretricious ornamentation, no impudence of cast-

iron substitute for honest hand-work, no moral slothfulness in the providing of all these lesser finishings.
It takes more time, more trouble; it may even take a
good deal of time and trouble, but then it is just right,
and to see and know that it is right is a daily reward
and a never-ending source of satisfaction.

Some heavy oak timber-work forms a structural
part of the inner main framing of the house.   Posts,
beams, braces, as well as doors and their frames,
window-frames and mullions, stairs and some floors,
are of good English oak, grown in the neighbourhood.
I suppose a great London builder could not produce
such work.   He does not go into the woods and buy
the standing timber, and season it slowly in a roomy
yard for so many years, and then go round with the
architect's drawing and choose the piece that exactly
suits the purpose.   The old country builder, when he
has to get out a cambered beam or a curved brace,
goes round his yard and looks out the log that grew
in the actual shape, and taking off two outer slabs by
handwork in the sawpit, chops it roughly to shape
with his side-axe and works it to the finished face
with the adze, so that the completed work shall for
ever bear the evidence of his skill in the use of these
grand old tools, and show a treatment absolutely in
sympathy with the nature and quality of the material.

Though the work of the London builder is more
technically perfect, it has none of the vigorous vitality
and individual interest of that of the old countryman,

and all ways of working according to local tradition
are necessarily lost. The Londoner has to take the
great baulks of foreign timber as they come from the
merchants' stacks, and shape them with the pitiless
steam-saw ; the timber then passes through several
hands, each working a different machine at every stage
of its conversion. The very atmosphere of the crowded
London yard, with its fussy puffings of steam, its
rumble, roar, and scream of machinery, the many subdivisions of processes of manipulation, all seem calcu-
lated to destroy any sentiment of life and character in
the thing made. And what have we in the end ? A
piece of work that, though it has the merit of mechanical precision, has lost all human interest ; it follows
the architect's drawing with absolute fidelity, but is
lifeless and inert and totally unsympathetic.

I am far from wishing to disparage accuracy or
technical perfection of workmanship, but in the case
of structural timber that forms part of a house of the
large cottage class such as mine, and in a district
that still possesses the precious heritage of a traditional
way of using and working it, such mechanical perfection is obviously out of place.

Then there is the actual living interest of knowing
where the trees one's house is built of really grew.
The three great beams, ten inches square, that stretch
across the ceiling of the sitting-room, and do other
work besides, and bear up a good part of the bedroom
space above (they are twenty-eight feet long), were

THE HOUSE FROM THE COPSE

growing fifteen years ago a mile and a half away, on the outer edge of a flr wood just above a hazel-fringed hollow lane, whose steep sandy sides, here and there level enough to bear a patch of vegetation, grew tall Bracken and great Foxgloves, and the finest wild Canterbury Bells I ever saw. At the top of the western bank, their bases hidden in cool beds of tall Fern in summer, and clothed in its half-fallen warmth of rusty comfort in winter, and in spring-time standing on their carpet of blue wild Hyacinth, were these tall oaks; one or two of their fellows still remain. Often driving up the lane from early childhood I used to see these great grey trees, in twilight looking almost ghostly against the darkly-mysterious background of the sombre firs. And I remember always thinking how straight and tall they looked, for these sandy hills do not readily grow such great oaks as are found in the clay weald a few miles to the south and at the foot of our warm-soiled hills. But I am glad to know that my beams are these same old friends, and that the pleasure that I had in watching them green and growing is not destroyed but only changed as I see them stretching above me as grand beams of solid English oak.

The memory of a curious incident of many years ago that I am quite unable to account for, and never can forget, belongs to this same lane; only a few yards further down and within sight of the lowest of the oaks.

"My house is approached by a footpath from a quiet, shady lane, entering by a close-paled hand-gate. There is no driving road to the front door. I like the approach to a house to be as quiet and modest as possible, and in this case I wanted it to tell its own story as the way in to a small dwelling standing in wooded ground." The watercolour of Munstead Wood and The Hut by Richard Sorrell, 1981, reconstructs a late summer garden as Gertrude Jekyll would have known it c.1900. Courtesy Mrs. Muriel Collins.

I was riding a big and rather nervous horse down the lane, which, though not exactly steep, has a fairly sharp fall. There had been a sudden and heavy storm of summer rain, and I had just ridden out from the shelter of a thickly-leafed oak, when I heard a two-wheeled country cart driving rather fast down the narrow lane behind me. As it came near, I judged by the sound that it was a heavy tax-cart such as a farmer would drive to market with two or three pigs behind him under a strong pig-net. I could hear the chink and rattle of the harness and of the loose ends of the tail-board chains. As the man driving was just about to pass me, he slapped the reins down on the horse's back, as a rough driver does who has no whip, and I noticed the sodden sound of the wet leather; at the same moment he gave a "dchk" to urge the horse. I was in the act of drawing my horse close to the near side of the lane, when, hearing the man, he made an impatient sort of bucking jump, followed by a moderate kick. The passing cart was so close that I thought his heels must touch the wheel, but they did not, and again I drew him as near as I could to the bank. As the cart did not pass I looked round, and as I turned the sound ceased, and nothing was to be seen but some hundred yards or so of the empty space of the hollow roadway.

My house is approached by a footpath from a quiet, shady lane, entering by a close-paled hand-gate. There is no driving road to the front door. I like the

PORCH AND TUB-HYDRANGEAS

approach to a house to be as quiet and modest as possible, and in this case I wanted it to tell its own story as the way in to a small dwelling standing in wooded ground. The path runs to an arch in the eastern wall of the house, leading into a kind of long porch, or rather a covered projection of lean-to shape. This serves as a dry approach to the main door, and also as a comfortable full-stop to the southern face of the house, returning forward square with that face. Its lower western side shows flat arches of heavy timber work which are tied and braced across to the higher eastern wall by more of the same. Any one entering looks through to the garden picture of lawn and trees and low broad steps, and dwarf dry wall crowned with the hedge of Scotch Briers. As the house is on ground that falls gently to the north, the lawn on this, the southern side, is on a higher level; and standing in front of the house and looking towards the porch, the illustration shows how it looks from the garden side in late summer when the tubs of Hydrangea are in flower(p.21). The main door leads into a roomy entrance and then to a short passage, passing the small dining-room on the left, to the sitting-room.

The sitting-room is low and fairly large, measuring twenty-seven by twenty-one feet, and eight feet from floor to ceiling. A long low range of window lights it from the south, and in the afternoon a flood of western light streams in down the stairs from another long

The Stairs

window on the middle landing. The stairs come straight
into the room, and with the wide, hooded, stone-built
fireplace take up the greater part of its western end.
The windows, after the manner of the best old buildings
of the country, are set with their oak mullions flush with
the outer face of the wall, so that as the wall is of a
good thickness, every window has a broad oak window-
board, eighteen inches wide. The walls are twenty-
two inches thick, and as the local stone is pervious to
water for some years after being freshly used, they are
built hollow, with an outer stone wall nearly fifteen
inches thick, then a three-inch air-space, and an inner
wall of brick firmly bound to the outer with iron ties.

The steps of the stairs are low and broad. There
are four short flights and three square landings; the
first landing giving access to a small book-room, which
has no door, but is entered by a curtained arch. It
is a pleasant little room; a room good to work and
read in. It always makes me think of St. Jerome's
Study in the National Gallery; not that it has the
least likeness in appearance, but because it has that
precious feeling of repose that disposes the mind to
study. The south wall is mostly window, the west
wall is all books; northward is the entrance arch and
an oak bureau, and on the fourth side is another book-
case and the fireplace.

The stairs feel pleasantly firm and solid; the main
posts at the angles go right down and rest on brick
masonry. The longest measures thirteen feet, and it

was a puzzle to the builder how to turn the finial out
of the solid, for no such work in this house is stuck on,
and no lathe that he had could turn so great a length;
but as there is no problem in woodwork that a clever
carpenter cannot solve, he just had it worked out by
hand.

The oak gallery to which the stairs lead is sixty
feet long and ten feet wide. One feels some hesitation
about praising one's own possessions, but it is a part of
the house that gives me so much pleasure, and it
meets with so much approval from those whose
knowledge and taste I most respect, that I venture to
describe it in terms of admiration. Thanks to my
good architect, who conceived the place in exactly such
a form as I had desired, but could not have described,
and to the fine old carpenter who worked to his
drawings in an entirely sympathetic manner, I may
say that it is a good example of how English oak
should be used in an honest building, whose only pre-
tension is to be of sound work done with the right
intention, of material used according to the capability
of its nature and the purpose designed, with due regard
to beauty of proportion and simplicity of effect. And
because the work has been planned and executed in
this spirit, this gallery, and indeed the whole house,
has that quality—the most valuable to my thinking
that a house or any part of it can possess—of con-
ducing to repose and serenity of mind. In some
mysterious way it is imbued with an expression of

cheerful, kindly welcome, of restfulness to mind and body, of abounding satisfaction to eye and brain.

It is just these desirable qualities that are most rarely to be found in a modern building, and that one so much appreciates in those examples that remain to us of the domestic architecture of our Tudor and Jacobean reigns, and still more frequently in foreign lands in the monastic buildings.   Indeed, one of the wishes I expressed to the architect was that I should like a little of the feeling of a convent, and, how I know not, unless it be by virtue of solid structure and honest simplicity, he has certainly given it me.

The gallery is amply lighted from the left by a long range of north window looking to the garden court.   On the right are deep cupboards with panelled oak doors, only broken by panelled recesses giving access to the doors of three bedrooms.   One space of eight feet is a shallower cupboard with a glazed front of sliding sashes, in which are arranged all the little treasures of some kind of prettiness or of personal interest, such as are almost unconsciously gathered together by a person of an accumulative proclivity. These are arranged with an attempt at pictorial effect, and the place serves the double purpose of having all my small miscellaneous goods easily within sight, and also of assuring me that they are safe from the destructive gambols of kittens and from the well-meant but occasionally fatal flicks of the household duster.

The Oak Gallery

Here are memories of many lands and of many
persons: of countries that I shall never see again,
for my travelling days are over; of kindly little gifts
from friends who are no longer among the living.
Some of the small objects are of absolutely no intrinsic
value but of a loveliness that is beyond all price, such
as beautiful shells and feathers.   Then there are tiny
ancient tear-bottles, both brilliant and dainty in irides-
cent colouring of their decaying surface-flakes; a little
silver Buddha; delicate pieces of Venetian glass; bronze
coins green with age; old Church embroideries of gold
and colours upon white silk now faded and discoloured;
ostrich eggs of ivory white and emu eggs of dim dusty
green; little objects innumerable—eight foot by four
of them as a carpenter would say—a life's history in
a hieroglyphic writing that is legible to one person
only, but that to all comers presents a somewhat pretty
show.

The deep panelled cupboards, too, are full of treasures, arranged in those handy dark-green boxes with
loose lids such as are used for ribbons and delicate
fabrics in drapers' shops.   Here are pieces of old
Venetian and Florentine stuffs; wall-hangings, Church
vestments, brocades, damasks, embroideries, fringes,
braids, and great silk tassels.   There are boxes of
Algerian and other embroidery silks, of crewels, of
chenilles, of coloured embroidery cottons; a box of old
English patchwork and another of the bright pretty
peasant handkerchiefs of France and Italy.   From

time to time many of the materials come into use, while the rest are for the pleasure of turning over myself and for showing to friends of like tastes. Then there are linen wrappers enclosing piles of silk, linen, and cotton fabrics, and about it all is the comfortable feeling that everything in the big cupboards is kept clean and safe and easily accessible.

One shorter length of cupboard holds a collection of objects mostly local, many of them now out of use. Here are a number of the brass "face-pieces" of waggon harness, the pride of the smart carter, and still in use; and the now obsolete ear-bells, dangling two on each side from a strap that passed over the horses' heads just behind the ears and buckled into the cheeks of the head-stall. The middle of the strap was further decorated by a brush-shaped three-tiered plume of coloured horse-hair rising from a smart brass socket. And there are the bright rosettes of coloured worsted braid also for dressing up the waggon-team on market days. Among the varied contents of this cupboard are trophies of brass snuffers and brass spoons and pepper-pots, wooden harvest bottles, tinder boxes and some of the earliest flat sulphur matches, and cocoa-nuts carved by sailors; a shepherd's crook of fine old pattern, and many forms of the old rush-light holders.

The space of the gallery is not encumbered with furniture, but has one long oak table of a fine simple type, oak linen chests (locally "hutches"), and a chair

or two. The large table is where needlework is cut out
and arranged. I chose a room for my own bedroom
near the further end of the gallery in order that I
might the oftener enjoy a walk down its length, and
every morning as I come out of my room, hungry for
breakfast and ready for the day's work, I feel thankful
that my home has on its upper floor so roomy and
pleasant a highway.

The building of the house was done in the happiest
way possible, a perfect understanding existing between
the architect, the builder, and the proprietor. Such
a concourse of salutary conditions is, I fear, rare in
house-building. It often happens that conflicting
interests are at war with one another; indeed it seems
to be usually supposed that the builder and the architect are in some degree antagonistic. Hence it arises
that in buildings of any importance the architect has
to post an expensive clerk of the works on the job, to
see that the builder does not cheat the proprietor.

But where all three are reasonable and honest
folk, at one in their desire of doing a piece of good
work, this extra source of expense is not needed, and
the whole thing, instead of being a cause of waste and
worry and anxiety during its making, and possibly a
disappointment when completed, is like an interesting
game of serious and absorbing interest, every move
having some distinct bearing on the one to follow;
every operation being performed in its due sequence to
the gradual building up of the completed structure.

NORTH SIDE OF THE HOUSE

PEWTER ON DINING-ROOM SIDEBOARD

From beginning to end there was no contract. The usual specifications were made out and were priced by a London firm, and as the total came out not greatly in excess of what the house might cost, the builder was set to work, with the understanding that certain reductions should be made where we could as the work went on, and it was arranged that he should send in all accounts for payment at the end of every month, and that he should receive in addition a sum of ten per cent. on the whole amount of the cost.

The architect has a thorough knowledge of the local ways of using the sandstone that grows in our hills, and that for many centuries has been the building material of the district, and of all the lesser incidental methods of adapting means to ends that mark the well-defined way of building of the country, so that what he builds seems to grow naturally out of the ground. I always think it a pity to use in any one place the distinctive methods of another. Every part of the country has its own traditional ways, and if these have in the course of many centuries become " crystallised " into any particular form we may be sure that there is some good reason for it, and it follows that the attempt to use the ways and methods of some distant place is sure to give an impression as of something uncomfortably exotic, of geographical confusion, of the perhaps right thing in the wrong place.

For I hold as a convincing canon in architecture

that every building should look like what it is. How
well that fine old architect George Dance understood
this when he designed the prison of Newgate! On
the other hand, does not every educated person feel
the shock of incongruity when a building presents a
huge front as of a Greek temple, and when, instead of
the leisurely advance of classically-robed worshipper
and of flower-garlanded procession of white-robed
priest and sacrificial beast, such as he has some right
to expect, he has to put up with a stream of hurrying
four-wheelers with piles of railway-passengers' luggage
and bicycles chained to their tops!

O! for a little simple truth and honesty in building, as in all else that is present to the eye and touches
daily life!

Many of my friends, knowing that I dabble in
construction and various handicrafts, have asked
whether I did not design my house myself. To which
question, though I know it is meant to be kind and
flattering, I have to give an emphatically negative
answer. An amateur who has some constructive perceptions may plan and build a house after a fashion;
and to him and his it may be, and quite rightly and
honestly, a source of supreme satisfaction. But it will
always lack the qualities that belong to the higher
knowledge, and to the firm grasp of the wider expression. There will be bungles and awkward places, and
above all a want of reposeful simplicity both in and
out. If an addition is made it will look like a shame-

faced patch boggled on to a garment; a patch that is
always conscious of its intrusive presence. Whereas an
addition planned by a good architect will be like one
of those noble patches such as were worked by some
Italian genius in needlework two hundred years ago.
The garment needed a patch, and a patch was put in,
but instead of a clumsy attempt being made to conceal
it, it was glorified and ornamented and turned into
some graceful arabesque of leaf and flower and tendril,
enriched by cunning needlework of thread or cord or
delicate golden purfling, so that what began by being
an unsightly rent, grew under the skilful fingers,
quickened by the ready wit of the fertile brain, into a
thing of enduring beauty and delight.

When it came to the actual planning of the house
I was to live in—I had made one false start a year
or two before—I agreed with the architect how and
where the house should stand, and more or less how
the rooms should lie together. And I said that I
wanted a small house with plenty of room in it—there
are seven bedrooms in all—and that I disliked small
narrow passages, and would have nothing poky or
screwy or ill-lighted.

So he drew a plan, and we soon came to an understanding, first about the main block and then about
the details. Every portion was carefully talked over,
and I feel bound to confess that in most cases out of
the few in which I put pressure on him to waive his
judgment in favour of my wishes, I should have done

better to have left matters alone.   My greatest error in
this way was in altering the placing of the casements
(hinged lights that open).   In every long range of
lights he had marked as a casement not the end lights
but the ones next to them.   I thought the end lights
would be more easily accessible, especially in bedrooms,
on account of the rather unusually large and long
dressing-tables, that I like : and the casements were
placed accordingly.   Afterwards I found this arrangement so inconvenient, on account of rain wetting curtains, and of the flying in and out of the thin linen
ones that act as blinds, that within a year I had them
altered so as to be as originally designed.

Naturally in the course of our discussions we had
many an amicable fight, but I can only remember one
when one might say that any " fur flew." I do not
now remember the details of the point in question,
only that it was about something that would have
added a good bit to the expense for the sake of
external appearance ; and I wound up my objections
by saying with some warmth : " My house is to be
built for me to live in and to love ; it is not to be
built as an exposition of architectonic inutility ! " I
am not in the habit of using long words, and as these
poured forth like a rushing torrent under the pressure
of fear of overdoing the cost, I learnt, from the architect's crushed and somewhat frightened demeanour,
that long words certainly have their use, if only as
engines of warfare of the nature of the battering-ram.

How I enjoyed seeing the whole operation of the building from its very beginning! I could watch any clever workman for hours. Even the shovelling and shaping of ground is pleasant to see, but when it comes to a craftsman of long experience using the tool that seems to have become a part of himself, the attraction is so great that I can hardly tear myself away. What a treat it was to see the foreman building a bit of wall! He was the head man on the job, a bricklayer by trade, but apparently the master of all tools. How good it was to see him at work, to observe the absolute precision, the perfect command of the tool and material; to see the ease of it, the smiling face, the rapid, almost dancing movements, the exuberant though wholly unaffected manifestation of ready activity; the little graceful ornaments of action in half-unconscious flourishes of the trowel, delicate *fiorituri* of consummate dexterity, and all looking so pleasantly easy that the movements seemed less like those of a man plying his trade than such as one sees in a strong young creature frisking for very pleasure of glad life.

I was living in a tiny cottage on the same ground, only eighty yards away from the work. How well I got to know all the sounds! The chop and rush of the trowel taking up its load of mortar from the board, the dull slither as the moist mass was laid as a bed for the next brick in the course; the ringing music of the soft-tempered blade cutting a well-burnt brick, the

muter tap of its shoulder settling it into its place,
aided by the down-bearing pressure of the finger-tips
of the left hand; the sliding scrape of the tool taking
up the overmuch mortar that squeezed out of the
joint, and the neat slapping of it into the cross-joint.
The sharp double tap on the mortar board, a signal
that more stuff was wanted. Then at the mortar-
mixing place the fat popping of the slaking lime
throwing off its clouds of steam; the working of the
mixing tool in the white sea enclosed by banks of sand
—a pleasant sound, strangely like the flopping of a
small boat on short harbour wavelets; the rhythmical
sound of the shovel in the sloppy mortar as it is
turned over and over to incorporate the lime and sand.

The sounds of the carpenter's work are equally
familiar though less musical. The noises of saw and
hammer are not pleasant in themselves, though satisfactory evidences that work is in progress, and a saw
being filed is no less than a torture to any tender
ear that may be near. On the other hand, I like to
hear the small melodious scream of the well-sharpened
plane as it shoots along the edge of the board and
gives out its long, fragrant ribbon of a shaving, and
the chop of the axe, and the blows of the mallet on
the chisel that is making the mortises; for the sound
of these blows, though of a dull quality, yet has a
muffled music that is pleasant to hear. And another
sound that is not displeasing is the beating of the
cow-hair that is mixed with the wall plaster, the

better to make it hold together ; for exactly the same
reason that in Egypt of old they made bricks with straw.
The hair, when shaken out of the bags, is in thick
lumps.　A man sits before a board, and with two
lissome sticks beats the hair till it separates.　The
air is thick with dust and particles of short hair;
and probably the work, though light, is none of the
pleasantest ; but it always looks, particularly if two are
at work near together, as if they were playing some
amusing game.

One picks up many varied scraps of useful knowledge on a building; indeed the whole thing is a
capital lesson for any reasonably observant person.
As one example out of many, one learns why bricks
should be used wet.　A soft cutting-brick has a dry,
sandy surface ; mortar laid on this scarcely takes hold,
it is inclined to fall off, carrying on its face the loose
red sand that prevented it from adhering, just as the
hod deposits its load of mortar surfaced with the dry
sand that the labourer has sprinkled over it in order
that the wet stuff should not cling to the wooden tool.
But when a brick is wet, the moisture of the mortar
at once fraternises with that of the brick, and the
mortar is actually sucked into the pores.　Dozens of
such examples might be noted in illustration of the
natures of building materials.　And then one learns
curious local terms, and from the older men many
odds and ends of lore and wisdom, and one hears
familiar words twisted in workmen's mouths into

unusual forms; thus I learn that "tempory" is the antithesis of "permerent." I also learn by inference that the maker of one useful material is deficient in the sense of smell, for when I came on a newly-unloaded stack of large rolls of something with an overpowering odour of creosote, and asked: "What is this very nasty-smelling stuff?" I was told it was the Patent Inodorous Felt!

So I would linger about the works, not exactly idle because always learning something new in the way of cause and effect, till the church clock of the distant town struck twelve and the foreman looked at his watch. Then came his cheery Yeo-ho, and at the welcome call the sounds on the building ceased and the men knocked off for dinner and the midday rest.

CHAPTER II

A WOOD RAMBLE IN APRIL

It is a windy day in early April, and I take my camp-stool and wander into the wood, where one is always fairly in shelter. Beyond the fir wood is a bit of wild forest-like land. The trees are mostly Oaks, but here and there a Scotch Fir seems to have straggled away from the mass of its fellows, and looks all the handsomer for its isolation among leafless trees of quite another character. The season is backward; it still seems like the middle of March, and the ground covering of dead leaves has the bleached look that one only sees during March and the early weeks of a late April. It is difficult to believe that the floor of the wood will, a month hence, be covered with a carpet whose ground is the greenery of tender grass and fern-like wild Parsley, and whose pattern is the bloom of Primrose and wild Hyacinth. As yet the only break in the leafy carpet is made by some handsome tufts of the wild Arum, just now at their best, and by some wide-spreading sheets of Dog's Mercury, one of the earliest of the wild plants. It is not exactly beautiful, except in some cases as sheets of bright green colour, but it is welcome as a forerunner of the cheerful spring flowers.

It is a poisonous plant, and one must beware of getting
it into a garden, so insidious and persistently invading
is its running root.

Where the undergrowth is not cut down at the
usual few years' interval, every now and then one
comes upon an old Hazel with a trunk six inches
thick, or perhaps with a sheaf of five or six thick
stems. It is only when one sees it like this that
one recognises that it is quite one of the most
graceful of small trees. The stems have a way of
spreading outward and arching from the very base,
forming a nearly true segment of a shallow circle.
The bark becomes rough after three years' growth,
but before that age, except for a thin scurf of
papery brown flakes, relics of an earlier skin, it is
smooth and half polished, the colour varying from
grey-green to a cool umber, with bands and clouds
of a silvery quality.

It is difficult to believe that we are well into
April, the season is so backward; with frosty nights
and winds that appear to blow equally cold from
all quarters. To-day the wind comes from the south,
though it feels more like north-east. How cold it
must be in northern France! Coming back through
the fir wood, the path is on the whole well sheltered,
yet the wind reaches me in thin thready little
chilly draughts, as if arrows of cold air were being
shot from among the trees. The wind-blown firs
in the mass have that pleasant sound that always

reminds me of a distant sea washing upon a shingly
beach.

The sun is away on my front and left, and the
sharp shadows of the trees are thrown diagonally
across the path, where the sunlight comes through a
half-open place. Farther along, for some fifty yards
or more, the path is in shade, with still more distant
stretches of stem-barred glints of sunny space. Here
the fir-trunks tell dark against the mist-coloured background. It is not mist, for the day is quite clear, but
I am on high ground, and the distance is of the tops
of firs where the hillside falls steeply away to the
north. Where the sun catches the edges of the nearer
trunks it lights them in a sharp line, leaving the rest
warmly dark; but where the trees stand in shade the
trunks are of a cool grey that is almost blue, borrow-
ing their colour, through the opening of the track behind me, from the hard blue cloudless sky. The trunks
seen quite against the sunlight look a pale greenish-
brown, lighter than the shadow they cast, and somewhat warmed by the sunlit dead bracken at their
feet. When I move onward into the shade the blue
look on the stems is gone, and I only see their true
colour of warm purplish-grey, clouded with paler grey
lichen. I wish I had with me some young student of
painting, the varying colourings of the trees in this
wood in to-day's light offer such valuable lessons in
training the eye to see the colour of objects as it
appears to be; the untrained eye only sees colour as

it is locally. I suppose any one who has never gone
through this kind of training could scarcely believe
the difference it makes in the degree of enjoyment of
all that is most worthy of admiration in our beautiful
world. But it enables one, even in a greater degree
than the other perceptions of form and proportion
that the artist must acquire or cultivate, to see pictures for oneself, not merely to see objects. And the
pictures so seized by the eye and brain are the best
pictures of all, for they are those of the great Artist,
revealed by Him direct to the seeing eye and the
receiving heart.

It is not so much that people are unobservant, but
that from the want of the necessary training they
cannot see or receive direct from nature what is seen
by the artist, and the only natural pictures that strike
them are those that present some unusual strength or
mass of positive colour, such as a brilliant sunset, or a
group of trees in yellow glory of autumn colouring,
or a field of poppies, or an orchard bearing its load
of bloom. To these untrained eyes the much more
numerous and delicate of Nature's pictorial moods or
incidents can only be enjoyed or understood when
presented in the form of a painted picture by the
artist who understands Nature's speech and can act
as her interpreter.

Now I come to the fringe of a plantation of
Spruce Fir some thirty years old. The trees meet
overhead above the narrow cart-track, and looking in

from outside in the late afternoon light it might be the mouth of a black-dark tunnel, so deep and heavy is the gruesome gloom. And indeed it is very dark, and in its depths strangely silent. It is like a place of the dead, and as if the birds and small wood beasts were forbidden to enter, for none are to be seen or heard. But about the middle of this sombre wood there is a slight clearing; a little more light comes from above, and I see by the side of the track on the hitherto unbroken carpet of dull dead-brown, some patches and even sheets of a vivid green, and quantities of delicate white bloom. And the sight of this sudden picture of daintiest loveliness, of a value all the greater for its gloomy environment, fills the heart with lively joy and abounding thankfulness.

It is the Wood-Sorrel, tenderest and loveliest of wood plants. The white flower in the mass has a slight lilac tinge; when I look close I see that this comes from a fine veining of reddish-purple colour on the white ground. White seems a vaguely-indefinite word when applied to the colouring of flowers; in the case of this tender little blossom the white is not very white, but about as white as the lightest part of a pearl. The downy stalk is flesh-coloured and half-transparent, and the delicately-formed calyx is painted with faint tints of dull green edged with transparent greenish buff, and is based and tipped with a reddish-purple that recalls the veining of the petals. Each of these has a touch of clear yellow on its inner base that sets off the bunch of tiny whitish stamens.

The brilliant yellow-green leaf is a trefoil of three broad little hearts, each joined at its point to the upright stalk by a tiny stalklet just long enough to keep the leaf-divisions well apart. In the young foliage the leaflets are pressed down to the stalk and folded together. The mature ones also fold and sleep at night. Each little heart does not fold upon itself, but each half is closely pressed against the half of its neighbour, so that the whole looks like a blunt three-winged arrow-head or bolt-head.

A few minutes more and I am out of the sombre Spruces, and again in the more open woodland, full of song of bird and movement of free air. The wood-path, following a nearly level contour of the steep hillside, dips across a sudden transverse gully. It is an old dead road or pack-horse track, one of many that scar the hillsides and indent the heathery wastes. A forgotten road of a day long since gone by; probably never made and certainly never mended. Centuries ago slightly hollowed, first by foot of man and laden or ridden beast, then grown more wide and deep by side-crumbling of sandy earth and sweeping wash of sudden storm-flood. In the steep descent of this old dead lane one can read the whole history of its making, down to the rich valley-bottom where the

washed-down soil lies nearly level in a wide flattened
drift, whose record is written in the richer growth of
tree and bush and the ranker depth of luscious grass
and weed.

I sit at the edge of the hillside path, and look
down the old lane. A steep sandy bank rises to the
left. Above it is a wood of Oak and Hazel enriched
with groups of mighty Hollies. To the right, also
steeply rising, is rather open woodland. In the hollow
is a thick mass of dead leaves, and below them a rich
leaf-mould, for the old lane holds not only the leaves
that fall into it, but the many more that are blown in
from all sides. Twenty yards ahead and nearly in the
bottom is a large Beech, showing by its evident age
that for a hundred and fifty years, and who knows how
long before, the road has been out of use. Still nearer
and a little to the side is a great Holly. Its smooth
pale grey stem fifteen inches thick rises unbranched for
twelve feet; then the lower branches sweep boldly
down and the outer boughs meet the steep banks.
The great Beech-tree arches overhead, and the old
hollow way goes steeply down till its further progress
is hidden by a bend and by the projection of the
right-hand bank. Dog's Mercury here grows thickly,
and the sunlight from beyond makes it show as a
mass of brilliant green colour.

As I sit quite quiet I hear in the wood high up on
my left some small animal hunting among the dead
leaves. By the smallness of the sound it should be a

field-mouse; the movement is not heavy enough for
a weasel, still less for a stoat; it is the sound of an
animal of less than three ounces weight. Now I move
on to a place where some underwood has lately been
cut, and then to where the ground is naturally open,
a half-acre of wild turf on the sunny hillside, of the
fine grasses native to the sandy soil, with occasional
tufts of the pretty Wood-Sage that will flower in the
full summer. The little Cinquefoil, with a flower like
a small wild Strawberry, is in bloom, and Dog-Violets
and Stitchwort, and here and there is a fine clump of
Burdock, whose grandly-formed leaves with their boldly-
waved edges I always think worthy of a place in a
garden.

Just above this open space is a low hedgerow of
Hazels, with still rising wooded ground above. What
a pretty and pleasant place that wise rabbit has chosen
for his " bury," as the country folk call it; at the foot
of the low sandy bank, and where it is kept quite dry
by the roots of the old Hazels. Just above is a carpet
of wild Hyacinth backed by Hollies, and a little garden
of the same comes right up to his front-door, where a
tuft or two is partly buried by some of his more recent
works of excavation. Here also are more Burdocks.
Their leaves have almost the grandeur of those of the
Gourd tribe, but without their luscious weakness, and
the vigour of the Rhubarb without its coarseness. I
never cease to admire their grand wave of edge and
the strength of line in the "drawing" from root to

leaf-point. It is a plant that for leaf effect in the
early year should be in every garden; it would hold
its place as worthily as Veratrum or Artichoke. Later
in the year there are other plants of bold leaf-beauty,
but in April and May they are so few that none should
be overlooked.

In several woods in my neighbourhood there are
old groups of common Laurel that have never been
cut or pruned. They all look to be about the same
age, and must have been planted early in the century,
for they were already old trees when I was a child.
There are large groups of them on four adjoining
properties, in one wood or coppice of each. It looks
as if four neighbouring squires had agreed to try a
good patch of them as experimental undergrowth. I
have a rather strong dislike to the clipped Laurel of
the ordinary shrubbery, but growing at will in the
woods they are handsome small trees with a good deal
of pictorial value. Their smooth grey stems are something like elephants' trunks or some kind of grey serpent, the more so that they curl about and seem almost
to writhe, often turning downward and lying along the
ground, and then rising and twisting again. A shrub
showing such a habit of growth sends one's mind
wandering away to some of the old Greek myths that
dealt with the transformation of man or beast into
some form of plant or tree life; and though the shrub
of this family we know best is a native of the

Caucasus, and the Russian and Turkish provinces adjoining, I think I have heard of it in Greece, where such thoughts may have arisen in the minds of those pastoral poets of ancient days, whose wanderings would have led them among the snake-like trunks of the wild-grown mountain Laurels.

CHAPTER III

A GARDEN OF WALL-FLOWERS

I AM never tired of watching and observing how plants will manage not only to exist but even to thrive in difficult circumstances. For this sort of observation my very poor sandy soil affords me only too many opportunities. Now, on a rather cold afternoon in April, I go to a sheltered part of the garden, and almost at random place my seat opposite a sloping bank thinly covered with Periwinkles. The bank is the northern flank of a mound of sand, thinly surfaced when it was made with some poor earth from a hedge-bank that was being removed. This place was purposely chosen for the Periwinkles, in order to check their growth and restrain them from running together into a tight mat of runners, as they do so quickly if they are planted in better soil. This poverty of soil and the summer dryness of their place keeps them very much at home, and they make stout, well-flowered tufts, with only a few weak runners. There is something among them on the ground looking like bright crimson flower-buds, about an inch long. I look nearer and see that they are acorns, fallen last autumn from a tree that overhangs this end of the bank. The acorns have thrown off their outer shells, and the inner skin, of a pale greenish-yellow colour when first uncased, has turned, first to pale pink and then to a strong crimson. The first root has been thrown out and has found its way firmly into the ground, though the acorn still lies upon the surface.

The Periwinkles are the common *Vinca major* and its variegated variety; *Vinca minor*, the kind most frequent in gardens, blue, white, and often parti-coloured; the half–double one with dull red-purple flowers; the double blue, and a wild white one from North Italy, with an abundance of small flowers, and a close, tufty habit of growth that give it a distinct appearance, and make it a very desirable garden plant. The double blue is with me much more shy in growth than the others; I suspect it would be happier on a stronger soil. I have heard rumours of a double white, which ought to be a pretty plant, and have even had it promised, but it has never reached my garden. One of this family that I much admire and grow in rather large quantity is *Vinca acutiflora* from Southern Europe. Unlike its more northern relatives it likes a sunny bank, so I have it on the south side of the mound near the clumps of Acanthus, where in late autumn it displays to the best advantage its handsome polished foliage and largish blooms of tenderest, palest blue.

Between and among the lesser Periwinkles on the northern bank are spaces where neighbouring Wall-flowers have shed their seed, and seedlings have sprung up. Some of these, evidently on the poorest ground, have branched all round without throwing up a stem, and look like stiff green rosettes pressed close to the earth. Others, a little more well-to-do, have stout stocky stems and dense heads of short, almost horny, dark-green foliage, with promise of compact but abundant bloom. Like the inhabitants of some half-barren place who have never been in touch with abundance or ease of life or any sort of luxury, they are all the more sturdy and thrifty and self-reliant, and I would venture to affirm that their lives will be as long again as those of any sister plants from the same seedpod that have enjoyed more careful nurture and a more abundant dietary. No planted-out Wall-flower can ever compare, in my light soil, with one sown where it is to remain; it always retains the planted-out look to the end of its days, and never has the tree-like sturdiness about the lower portions of its half-woody stem that one notices about the one sown and grown in its place. Moreover, from many years' observation, I notice that such plants only, show the many variations in habit that one comes to recognise as a kind of individual or personal characteristic, so that the plant acquires a much greater and almost human kind of interest. I have one such charming seedling that gives me great pleasure. The flower is of a full, clear, orange colour, more deeply tinged to the outer margins of the petals with faint thin lines of rich mahogany, that increase in width of line and depth of colour as they reach the petal's outer

THE PEONY GARDEN

edge, till, joining together, the whole edge is of this
strong, rich colour. The back of the petal is entirely
of this deep tint, and though the flower is of some
substance, I always think the richness of colouring of
the back has something to do with the strong quality
of the deep yellow of the face. The calyx, which forms
the covering of the unopened bud, is of a full purple-
brown. The leaves are of a dark dull green, tinged
with brown-bronze, much like the colour of the brown
water-cress. The habit of the plant is close and
stocky, but does not look dwarfed.

If I had plenty of suitable spaces and could spend
more on my garden I would have special regions for
many a good plant. As it is, I have to content myself
with special gardens for Primroses and for Pæonies
and for Michaelmas Daisies. And indeed I am truly
thankful to be able to have these; but we garden-
lovers are greedy folk, and always want to have more
and more and more! I want to have a Rose-garden,
and a Tulip-garden, and a Carnation-garden, and a
Columbine-garden, and a Fern-garden, and several
other kinds of special garden, but if I were able, the
first I should make would be a Wall-flower garden.

It should be contrived either in connection with
some old walls, or, failing these, with some walls or
wall-like structures built on purpose. These walls
would shock a builder, but would delight a good
gardener, for they would present just those conditions
most esteemed by wall-loving plants, of crumbling

masonry built of half-formed or half-rotting stone, and
of loose joints made to receive rather than to repel
every drop of welcome rain.   Wall-flowers are lime-
loving plants, so the stones would be set in a loose bed
of pounded mortar-rubbish, and there would be sloping
banks, half wall half bank.   I should, of course, take
care that the lines of the garden should be in suitable
relation to other near portions, a matter that could
only be determined on the precise spot that might be
available.

But for the planting, or rather the sowing of the
main spaces, there would be little difficulty.   I should
first sow a packet of a good strain of blood-red single
Wall-flower, spreading it over a large stretch of the
space.   Then a packet of a good yellow, either the
Belvoir or the Bedfont, then the purple, and then one of
the newer pale ones that have flowers of a colour between
ivory-white and pale buff-yellow.   I would keep the
sowings in separate but informal drifts, each kind
having its share, though not an equal share, of wall
and bank and level.   Some spaces nearest the eye
should be filled with the small spreading Alpine Wall-
flowers and their hybrids, but these are best secured
from cuttings.   The only ones I know of this class are
Cheiranthus alpinus, whose colour is a beautiful clear
lemon-yellow; *Cheiranthus mutabilis*, purple, changing
to orange; and *Cheiranthus Marshalli*, the deep orange-
coloured hybrid of *C. alpinus*.   Seed of *C. alpinus*
ought to be obtainable, though I have not tried to

keep it. *C. Marshalli* never forms seed, and I have not seen it on *C. mutabilis*. A few other plants would be admitted to the Wall-flower garden, such as yellow Alyssum on sunny banks and Tiarella in cool or half-shady places, and in the wall-joints I would have in fair quantity the beautiful *Corydalis capnoides*, most delicate and lovely of the Fumitories. Leading to the Wall-flower garden I should like to have a way between narrow rock borders or dry walls. These should be planted with Aubrietias, varieties of *A. græca*, of full and light purple colour, double Cuckoo-flower in the two shades of colour, and a good quantity of the grey foliage and tender white bloom of *Cerastium tomentosum*, so common in gardens and yet so seldom well used; I would also have, but more sparingly, the all-pervading *Arabis albida*.

These plants, with the exception of the Cuckoo-flower, are among those most often found in gardens, but it is very rarely that they are used thoughtfully or intelligently, or in such a way as to produce the simple pictorial effect to which they so readily lend themselves. This planting of white and purple colouring I would back with plants or shrubs of dark foliage, and the path should be so directed into the Wall-flower garden, by passing through a turn or a tunnelled arch of Yew or some other dusky growth, that the one is not seen from the other; but so that the eye, attuned to the cold, fresh colouring of the white and purple, should be in the very best state to receive and enjoy the sumptuous splendour of the region beyond. I am not sure that the return journey would not present the more brilliant picture of the two, for I have often observed in passing from warm colouring to cold, that the eye receives a kind of delightful shock of surprise that colour can be so strong and so pure and so altogether satisfying. And in these ways one gets to know how to use colour to the best garden effects. It is a kind of optical gastronomy; this preparation and presentation of food for the eye in arrangements that are both wholesome and agreeable, and in which each course is so designed that it is the best possible preparation for the one next to come.

I think I would also allow some bold patches of tall Tulips in the Wall-flower garden; orange and yellow and brown and purple, for one distinct departure from the form and habit of the main occupants of the garden would give value to both.

YOUNG ASH AND YOUNG BEECH IN CRUMBLING BANK

CHAPTER IV

TREES AND LANES

WITHIN half a mile of my home is a deep hollow lane whose steep sides are barred with strata of ragged sandstone, with layers of yellow sand between. In summer it is shaded by the wide-spreading branches of the trees, mostly Beeches, that grow above. Some of these come forward to the actual edge of the scarp, and as there is no stone quite near the surface, the gradual crumbling away of the sandy earth where they first took root, threatens to leave the trees without support. Now the Beech is evidently a tree with a strong instinct of self-preservation and no small degree of constructive ability, for I see that wherever this has happened the tree has thrown down a great stem-like root, a reversed counterpart of the stem above the ground level, that not only carries the weight with absolutely security, but so well satisfies the eye of the critical observer that the tree looks as if it had support and to spare, and bears itself gracefully upon its admirably designed pillar. The root-stem seems to become a piece of true trunk, and is covered with exactly the same kind of smooth bark as above ground. Several fair-sized Beeches with trunks about from two and a half to three feet in diameter, have done the same thing, and in each case the sense of balance and adequate support could not have been better expressed.

One small Beech with a trunk only as yet eight inches in diameter has one large backward root firmly clutching the bank, but it now depends on one of these under-stems where two main roots have joined and grown together, and are actually thicker than the trunk above. The little tree seems to have a perfect feeling for balance and construction, and its gracefully poised trunk shoots upward with a staunch consciousness of structural stability.

Some eight yards farther down the lane one sees how an Oak gets over the same difficulty. Here there is no main supporting column, but it has thrown down a number of roots—about twenty of from three to six inches diameter, and many lesser ones. They fork and lace and intertwine in a kind of complicated web —where they touch they become welded together, greatly to the increase of strength and bearing power. The actual weight of the tree stands over space, so much has the sandy bank crumbled away under the butt. The whole arrangement is evidently effectual, for there the tree stands, a well-grown Oak with a two-foot-thick trunk, and by no means young, for I can remember it looking nearly the same all my life. But the method of the Oak is much less satisfactory and convincing to the eye and also less graceful than that of the Beech, just as the tree itself has a more rugged

"An unmade woodland track is the nearest thing to a road-poem that anything of the kind can show. It is full of a sympathetic mystery that inclines the mind to open wide in readiness to receive any impression that may be presented. The trees meet overhead; the light coming through the thick leafage is dim and green; the drowsy hum of many little winged creatures comes faintly from far overhead; the track winds, and one cannot see far onward. What will the next reach disclose? ... Most mysterious of all are the tracks that pass through the woods of tall pines, for these woods are so solemn and so silent."

character. For the Beech always seems to me to be the true aristocrat among trees, and in all circumstances to bear himself with the graceful dignity that befits his high estate.

The Oak in question has not troubled himself about appearances. His tangle of supporting root answers his purpose and he cares no more about it, but he lays himself open to criticism in that his method does not give one's eye the same comforting conviction of sound construction. I always think that if some weight suddenly settled in the branches, such as a flight of rooks, or a wood-nymph or two, that the supporting mass of root would "sit down" a little like a spring cushion when sat upon, and that it would rise again when released from the weight; whereas all the gods of Olympus might alight in one of the neighbouring Beeches without giving one the least feeling of apprehension for their safety.

Lower down the same lane a little deeply-bending Ash is making a brave fight for life and root-hold, but a fight in which I fear it will be conquered. It makes a kind of frantic clutch at the bank both above and below; indeed, the appearance of strenuous action is so vehement that it looks as if it had been suddenly arrested while in the act of making a despairing grasp for safety. I much fear how this little tree may fare. Every year, as its over-balancing trunk grows heavier, it bends down lower. Just below the drooping swan-necked base of the trunk, and now only a few inches

Oak Roots

from it, is a nose of rock jutting out of the bank.
When it comes down those few inches and rests upon
the stone what will happen ?   Will the stone give it so
much rest and support that the roots, instead of ex-
pending all their strength in merely clutching for dear
life, will be able to grow into supporting strength ?
Or will it act as a fulcrum and hasten the tree's destruction by giving a resisting point whereby the weight of
the head, by the force of leverage, will prise the roots
upward out of the ground ?   Or will the stone itself,
after giving delusive support for a time, fall out of the
bank ?   In this case I do not see what could possibly
save the tree.   I often pass that way, and always look
with sympathetic interest to see how it goes with my
brave little friend.

Its next neighbour, a Beech, only a few yards away,
is firmly seated on a strong ledge of rock, and looks as
if its support had been built up from below with well-
planned masonry.   But as it has no tap-root, I think
nothing could save it if these rocks gave way.

In the same lane, a few hundred yards away, are
some larger Beeches.   Among these, one presents a
kind of wall of root to the side of the lane.   I never
fail to notice how well and beautifully that tree
has managed its means of support.   The bank is of
hard yellow sand, with strata of spongy half-formed
rock.   The main roots have turned back under the
butt, and wind forward and back like a closely down-
pressed S, running horizontally along one inhospitable

*"So frequent are some wild plants in hedge-banks, and so comparatively scarce in
other places, that one might almost think the hedges had a flora of their own...
Is it only an instance of patriotic prejudice, or is it really, as I believe, a fact, that
no country roads and lanes in the temperate world are so full of sweet and homely
pictorial incident as those of our dear England?"*

shelf and turning under and back at some vulnerable spot, always searching for firm support. The ends of the roots have travelled away, right and left, more than thirty yards from the base of the tree, and their feeding points are still more distant, rambling just under the surface of the bank in search of the rather sparse nutriment.

A few miles away, where a road cuts through the foot of a steep hill thickly clothed with Scotch Fir, the same decay of the sandy soil is going on, and the Firs at its extreme edge, evidently aware of their danger, are providing against it in much the same manner, by throwing down a thick columnar root. To the Scotch Fir this constructive method seems to come even more naturally than to the Beech, because it has a strong taproot, which easily adapts itself to the transformation into true stem ; indeed, in one example it is difficult to believe that the tree was not originally rooted at the lower level ; the true roots that hold to the top of the bank look almost out of place, and as if by some capricious freak some branches had rooted into the edge of the scarp. The transformation is all the more complete in that the converted root is clothed with a true bark in all respects like that of the upper trunk, separating when mature into the same upright scale-like plates.

The hollow sandy lanes in my near neighbourhood seem exactly fitted to demonstrate the ways and wants and manner of rooting of all the different trees, and the bright yellow sand makes one all the more enjoy

BEECH BUTT AND ROOT

the delicate beauty of colour of silvery bark of Birch
and Beech and Holly, and that of the bases of great
Oaks, more rugged of texture, but just as tender in
colourings of grey and silver-green lichens. And it is
fine to see a giant Holly with smooth white stem more
than two feet thick—one hedgerow Holly that I know
girths seven feet three inches—the white stem shoot-
ing up into its own forest of dark-green prickly
leafage.

Dense cushions of Polypody Fern grow about the
bases of many of the hedge trees, especially where the
road or lane passes through woodland. The Poly-
podies seem to like best the roots of Oaks and Hazels,
and then of Beeches, and to grow at the extreme edge
or side of the bank; for though the ferny mass may
spread to be a yard wide on the top of the bank, it is
much less usual to find it on any level ground away
from the edge.

I have more than once observed that the northern
Hard Fern (*Blechnum boreale*) seems to have some
liking for growing near Hollies. I do not know if it is
the same elsewhere, but I think of three damp hedge-
banks with wet ditches at the foot, where there are
both Hollies and Blechnums; in most cases where a
Holly occurs there is a Blechnum just under it. Two of
these hedges are three miles apart, and the third is six
miles away from the nearest of the other two.

So frequent are some wild plants in hedge-banks,
and so comparatively scarce in other places, that one

Root of Scotch Fir

might almost think the hedges had a flora of their
own.   The Cuckoo-pint (*Arum maculatum*) is one of
our most constant hedge-plants, for though one may
come on a fine clump here and there in copses and
cool woodland slopes, it is only on the sides of hedges
and at their foot that one sees it by the square yard.

Is it only an instance of patriotic prejudice, or is it
really, as I believe, a fact, that no country roads and
lanes in the temperate world are so full of sweet and
homely pictorial incident as those of our dear England ?
For apart from the living pictures of tree and bush,
fern and flower, rampant tangle and garland of wild
Rose and Honeysuckle, Hop and Briony, and of all
these combined with rocky bank and mossy slope,
there are the many incidents of human interest.   The
lowly cottage dwellings of the labouring folk; the
comfortable farmstead, almost a village in itself, with
its farmhouse and one or two cottages, its barns,
stables, cowhouses and piggeries, waggon sheds and
granaries.   The cottages are of the older type, built
before the times of easy communication, when what
are now well-kept bye-roads were only sandy tracks.
They are precious examples of the true buildings of
the country, for they must have been made of the
material available from within a few miles only, and
they were built by the men who knew no other ways
of working than those of their fathers before them.
This is why these farms and cottages seem to grow
out of the ground, and are the true and living ex-

Mary Huntingford

pression of the needs and means of fulfilling them proper to the country.

Many are the defects of the old buildings, for when they were reared no provision was made for preventing the damp from the earth from rising into the walls, and the brick flooring was laid straight on the earth or sand, without any under layer of damp-proof concrete. One has to admit that modern-built cottages are warmer, drier, and more healthy; but, to those who feel as I do, it is a matter of never-ending regret that those who build them have so little care for local tradition, and for the import-ance, from some of the higher points of view, of using local material in the same spirit of simple truth that animated the builders of old days. The ease of modern communication, and the pressure of trade competition, together with the sordid striving for cheapness, are the regrettable causes of the building of the wretched mongrel cottages, roofed with slates from Wales, or machine-pressed tiles from Stafford-shire, that are hung on rafters of cheap white fir from Norway; no wonder the poor things look hideous and ashamed, and as if aware that they have no right to exist. It is just as easy, though a little more costly both of money and thought, to build the perfectly sound and wholesome cottage of the right local material. In several cases it is being done in my neighbourhood by owners who make it a matter of conscience to build well and rightly. In my own

ENTRANCE DOWN TO FARMHOUSE FROM ROAD

small way I have done what I could, and three good
cottages will survive me.

In the old country dwellings by the roadsides, not
only is the main fabric of near-at-hand material, but,
if the cottage stands a few feet above the road, there
will be a bit of dry wall and rough steps made of the
wide slab-shaped stones that occur in some of the
upper strata of the stone-pits. When they come out
of the quarry they are rough and rugged of surface,
but they are soon worn smooth. Often there are a
few square yards of paving at a cottage entrance, and
most commonly some of the same sandstone slabs are
laid flat, and the rest of the pavement is a " pitching "
of the black stones that are found in and near the
heathlands just below the surface. They are water-
washed stones containing a large proportion of iron;
a large number of them have one flattened edge that
makes an admirable paving surface; they are so hard
that their wearing power is almost indefinite. Smaller
pieces of the sandstone are also used in the same way.
The picture shows a paved path just within the roadside wicket that gives access to a row of three vine-
clad cottages. It is a mixed pavement of sandstone
slab, sandstone and ironstone pitching, and brick.
The Pinks and Wall-flowers, Pansies and Sweet-Williams
of the cottage flower-borders never look so well as
when hanging over the edges of these paved paths;
in the case of the present illustration the two-flowered
Everlasting Pea (*Lathyrus grandiflorus*) under the dove's

Paved Cottage Entrance-path

cage, a favourite cottage plant, grows thrivingly in the already crowded border, barely a foot wide, between the building and the pavement.

It is in the old cottages that we find the true old country people, some of whose womenkind have hardly ever been more than ten miles from home ; people who still retain the speech and ways of thought and plain simple dress of the early part of the century. All my life I can remember my old friend with the donkey-cart, in intimate association with the lanes near my home. He worked under the road-surveyor, trimming overgrowing hedges and road edges, and removing incidental obstructions, as of the many Hazels pulled down and left hanging into the road by nut-hunting boys in September, and boughs blown down by winter storms, and drifts of dead leaves in November. The white donkey, who carried tools and worker, waited all day on some handy wayside patch of grass where he found food and rest. Man and beast grew old together in many a long year's companionship of toil, until at length neither could work any longer. A farmer who was a kind neighbour to the old man told me a pathetic story of how he had come to ask him to shoot the old donkey, who could no longer feed and was evidently very near his end. " The old man he sobbed and cried something turrible," said my friend the farmer. Afterwards, when I asked how old the donkey was, and how long the two had worked together, the old road-man said : " I know his age

JAMES FURLONGER

exactly; he is the same age as my youngest son, and
that's twenty-seven." When he had made an end of the
poor old beast, the farmer observing what a thick long
coat the donkey had, took off the skin and had it
cured at the tannery. Some months later, seeing
what a handsome pelt it made, I bought it of him,
and now my friends take it for the skin of a polar
bear, for it is almost white, and the mass of soft hair
is nearly three inches deep.

Full of interest as are the hedges, with their trees
and bushes and flowery growths, the roads and lanes
that pass unfenced through wood or waste are more
beautiful still, indeed an unmade woodland track is
the nearest thing to a road-poem that anything of the
kind can show. It is full of a sympathetic mystery
that inclines the mind to open wide in readiness to
receive any impression that may be presented. The
trees meet overhead; the light coming through the
thick leafage is dim and green; the drowsy hum of
many little winged creatures comes faintly from far overhead; the track winds, and one cannot see far onward.
What will the next reach disclose? Some living wild
thing, scarcely fearful because the way is so seldom used
—squirrel, rabbit, red-deer, wild-boar? charcoal-burners,
coming from the yet wilder wooded heights beyond? a
knight in shining armour? a ring of fairies dancing under
an oak? all equally possible in the dim green forest light.

And most mysterious of all are the tracks that
pass through the woods of tall pines, for these woods

A Woodland Lane

are so solemn and so silent. Sometimes one may
hear the harsh scream of the jay or the noisy flight of
the wood-pigeon, but for the most part in windless
weather they are almost without sound, for here there
are none of the small song-birds that love the summer-
leafing trees.   Winter and summer these woods wear
nearly the same aspect, except that the Bracken that
grows where the Firs are thinnest, is green in summer
and rusty-brown in winter.   But where the trees stand
thickly nothing grows upon the ground.   Even moss
is absent.   The peaty earth shows purplish-grey
through the dull brown of the carpet of fir-needle;
the same colouring being exactly repeated in the
trunks of the trees.   The whole scene is painted in a
monotone of purple-grey—solemn, quiet, by no means
unbeautiful.   And in harmony with the subdued
colouring is the endless repetition of upright tree-
stem, adding, as such an arrangement of line always
does, to the impression of solemn dignity.

Why this is so I know not, though it is plain to
feel.   For whether it be in our own home woods or in
the great Fir forests of Alpine regions, or in the masts
of shipping in the crowded port, or the succession of
columns in some great building, or in the upright
shafts of the soldiers' lances in the "Surrender of Breda"
of Velasquez, there can be no doubt that a distinct
impression of dignity and solemnity is aroused by the
presentment of some such close grouping of aspiring line.

A simply-built bridge is always a pleasant thing to

One of the Old Bridges

see, and I am happy in having within easy driving
reach six good old bridges, built of the rough sandstone quarried in the neighbouring hilly ground, span-
ning the same small river at different points. I amuse
myself by conjecturing how the arches were built,
because their ragged outline points to some ruder
method of support than the usual wooden " centering "
of modern work.   I suppose that there was some
rough construction of tree trunks and faggoting and
earth put up to build upon, just as the vaulted rooms
are built to this day in Southern Italy, where wood is
not to be had, by building up faggots of brushwood
and earth into the form of a filling of vault or dome
or waggon head.   The wooden railing and way of
supporting the posts is the old way of the country,
though doubtless the original railing was of oak roughly
split, not sawn.   In some cases a wall about two feet
high is carried up, but this takes away some of the
space of the none-too-wide roadway ; in one case, I
regret to say, in place of the older parapet of wood or
stone, the fine old bridge has been hopelessly disfigured
by a cast-iron railing, painted white.

It is interesting to see that by the side of each one
of these old bridges there is the plain evidence of a
still older ford ; where the river had been widened and
shallowed, and where the water, there only a few inches
deep, still flows over the artificial stony bed, and the
hollow track of the old road still shows, through some
centuries' overgrowth of grass and weed.

CHAPTER V

WILD HONEYSUCKLE

MANY and various are the ways of the wild Honeysuckle. In woody places it will trail about the ground and weave a loose copse-carpet from ankle to mid-leg deep, making many a snare for the unwary walker. One must step high and clear the foot each time, or one is likely to be thrown down by the tangled web of vegetable cordage. In this state it does not flower, but where there is a clearing and more light it takes advantage of any suitable support, and then seems to go up with a rush, and tumbles out in swags and garlands that in the long summer days are lovely and fragrant with the wealth of sweetly-scented bloom. During my wood walk I come upon a young Oak with a trunk about a foot thick. I should judge that it is sixty feet high, and the top is full of Honeysuckle. In this case the Honeysuckle throws up three main stems from the ground. At a foot from the root two of these have twined together and make a fairly even two-stranded rope. A little higher they are joined by the third, and at six feet from the ground the three twine tightly and look like a badly-spun rope nearly two inches thick. So they advance up the tree, sometimes leaping away from each other, and then again coming together and twining rope-fashion. The lowest branch of the Oak must be twelve feet from the ground, and I do not know how the climber may have reached it, for it has only twined upon itself, not upon the tree, but there may have been smaller branches, since dead and fallen, that helped it to rise.

The Honeysuckle does not seem to be willing to twine round anything of large diameter; I never see it about trunks whose thickness is more than ten inches or thereabouts, and when it does coil about an Oak of that size, the tree, then coated with its strong rough bark, has enough rending power as it expands to burst its bonds and be free.

But smaller trees often suffer a good deal from the close constriction of the woody creeper. For the Honeysuckle is a true tree, and its long stems are of true wood, of a quality both hard and tough, and all the tougher because the fibres of the individual stems are twisted like a rope. In the copse part of my own ground there are many examples—young trees badly hurt and scarred for life. One young Beech, whose stem is only four inches through, has thrown out thick swellings that look like a couple of close coils of a great python, and that more than double its diameter at the point of injury. The living Honeysuckle is no longer there, but I suspect that some of its hard wood is enclosed within the swollen twists, and that throughout its lifetime the tree will bear the mark of the early injury.

Beech stem distorted by Honeysuckle

Within a few paces a young Oak, with a trunk five inches thick, is tightly girthed with close coils of Honeysuckle. Some of the coils are deeply imbedded in the bark. This tree has also thrown out python-like swellings, which seem to close over and compress and strive to choke the invading climber. In some cases the grip is deadly to the Honeysuckle; in others it still lives, buried in the substance of the Oak. But if here and there it is gripped to death it matters little to the Woodbine, whose assault is in force of numbers, for besides nine distinct coils round this young tree, there are eighteen ropes and cords leaping into it from below; some of them direct from the ground, and some from a young Spanish Chestnut whose root is only three feet from that of the Oak. I see that the original stem of the Chestnut stops short about four feet from the ground, above which is eighteen inches of dead and rotting snag. It looks as if the fight between tree and climber had here ended in the tree's defeat, and as if its top had died and fallen, bringing down the Honeysuckle to share and endure the ruin it had planned and brought about.

But the Chestnut is evidently a clever and even crafty little tree, for not only has it repaired its disaster by throwing out a lusty young upward growth to take the place of its fallen top, but at the point where this springs from the short original trunk it has placed a small lateral branch which leads away the Honeysuckle right into the neighbouring Oak.

I do not know what ethical standard may prevail among vegetation, but it looks like a mean action on the part of the Chestnut: to decoy the enemy away from himself, and to deliver his near neighbour into the same enemy's hands. Or is it an example of heroic self-sacrifice on the part of the Oak? Perhaps the Oak said, "Neighbour, throw out a little branch and send me the enemy. I am doomed already; a little more can only bring the end somewhat sooner. You have made one brave fight already, and though scarred for life, will live and do well. When I die and fall, as I must within a very few years, our enemy, now held up by me to the sunlight and gaily flowering, will lie in a mangled heap on the floor of the wood, where, over-shadowed by your spreading branches, he will never bloom again, but must remain content with a lowlier way of life." The little Oak seems to be vainly striving for its life; it was gripped while still young, and the greater part of it is killed already—slowly but surely throttled by the deadly coils; indeed it is now no longer an Oak tree but a Honeysuckle tree.

Not far off is another young Oak, but this has a thicker trunk, quite seven inches through, and strong enough to burst any ropes of Honeysuckle that may be round it, while some of rather less diameter, also strong enough to get free at last, show by diagonal swollen ridges, with a hollow channel in the middle, the place where the serpent-like coil encircled them for perhaps a

year or two. Where these evidences of former constriction are not very deep or thick, they will in time dis-
appear, but if the swelling has grown over the hard
rope and entirely shut it in, the python-like shape will
probably last for life.

On some Spanish Chestnuts, with trunks about nine
inches through, some young shoots of Honeysuckle are
trying to establish themselves.   But they are only the
size of round leather boot-laces, and I see by dark
marks on the Chestnut's smooth, deep olive-green-grey
bark, sometimes above and sometimes below the present placing of the laces, that their position has been
shifted by the growth of the tree, which, at its age and
strength, has no longer anything to fear.

The strength of the Woodbine band and its hard-
ness are quite surprising, and many a young stem of
Oak and Beech, of Birch and Chestnut, gripped by its
iron coil, remains maimed and distorted for life.

In my own copse, within a space of less than half
an acre, all these examples occur, and others of young
Beeches, some of them good examples of the python
coils thrown out by the constricted tree.   It would, of
course, be easy to relieve the trees of the damaging
climber, but it is so interesting to watch the struggle,
and to see what comes of it, that in this part of the
wood I leave it to do as it will.

For a long time, seven or eight years as nearly as
I can remember, there was one out of the many young
Scotch Firs in the upper part of the wood whose then

THE LANE OF THE GHOST-CART *(See page 20)*

four-inch-thick trunk showed that it had had a fairly strong twist of Honeysuckle round it. About shoulder-high for some eighteen inches it was of a mild cork-screw shape, and as it stood close to a path on the way to church, it became our habit always to look at it, and to observe whether Crinkum, as we called it, would always retain the twist. But as the years passed, and the tree grew on in its vigorous young strength, it became quite clear that the twist was being surely drawn out, and now Crinkum, though he still answers to his name, is as straight of stem as any of his fellows. In another part of my woody ground is a spreading Holly with many stems ; three of them fairly large and seven smaller. Here the Honeysuckle runs up in the usual ropes, but having reached the top, it tumbles down by the side of the shaded path nearly to the ground in a straight cataract some eleven feet high. It does not seem to harm the Hollies, but in a general way when it rushes up them, and throws out its crowns and garlands of sweetest scent, they seem to be only on the best and friendliest of terms.

It is in our wild hilly lands that the lovely Wood-bine is seen at its best : where it climbs up some bush or small tree, Thorn or Juniper for preference, and flings out its fragrant wreaths of lovely bloom, a very embodiment of sun-loving gladness.

And if I have perhaps dwelt overmuch on the way it has of sometimes injuring its forest neighbours, it is only because it has always seemed to me a thing so strange and interesting to see how the lesser growth can attack and overcome the greater, and because from childhood those spirally twisted and swollen stems, so often met with in the woodlands, have always had for me an almost mysterious attractiveness.

But none the less do I feel and know that it is one of the most delight-giving of our native plants. No other flowering thing that I know leaps and laughs as does the fragrant Woodbine. It is as if it sang aloud : Let all who have eyes to see and hearts to feel, be glad with me in the long sweet days of mid-most summer.

Through the commonest hedgerow it will feel its way, and lightly twine a crown of glory on the head of the humblest vegetation ; and when in our hills a moss-grown Thorn or Juniper dies of old age, the Woodbine will give it glorious burial, covering the hoary branches with a freshness of young life and a generous and gladly-given wreathing of sweetest bloom.

CHAPTER VI

BRIER ROSES

I AM always dreaming of having delightful gardens
for special seasons where one good flower should
predominate; but for June with its wealth of flowers
there would have to be several special gardens. And,
though I have not the means wherewith to do it as
fully as I should wish, however strong may be my
desire, I can at least show an attempt on a small
scale, and also put down what ideas I may have,
so that others, more bountifully endowed, may read
and profit if they will. For June demands an Iris
garden, and a Pæony garden, and an early Rose
garden, and a garden for Poppies, besides half wood-
like gardens for Azaleas and for Rhododendrons.
But in early June the garden-wish that lies nearest
to my heart is to have a beautiful planting of Brier
Roses.

I have already a sunny bank of Briers some twenty-
five yards long and six feet wide, and many will no
doubt ask, " Is not that enough ? " I can only answer,
" No, it is not enough." If one has a picture to paint,
whose subject and method of treatment demand a
large canvas, one cannot be contented with a small

BRIER ROSES

one. I am truly thankful that I have my bank of
Briers, but satisfied I am not. Because now, seeing
how they may be worthily treated, largely, broadly,
beautifully, I desire to do it, and to do it carefully on
my own ground where I can watch and wait and
correct, and at last get it to such a state that it grows
into a picture that I am not ashamed to show. And
as the blooming time of the Brier Roses is a short
one, I should group with them another family of
plants whose flowering season would immediately
follow. Such a family is at hand in the *Cistineæ*. And
I would carpet the whole with the common English
Heaths, always allowing the wild *Calluna* to be in
chief abundance, with here and there a wide-spreading
patch of the white *Menziesia*. Such a garden or half-
wild planting would by no means preclude the use of
the Briers in other ways, for if I had to deal with a
perfectly formal garden, full of architectural detail,
the dainty little laughing Briers would be called in
to show how well they would also grace the well-
ordered refinements of garden-building. For everywhere, and in all sorts of gardens, they are equally at
home; looking as well and as rightly placed by the
wrought-stone balustrade that bounds the terrace of
the palace, as in the narrow spaces given to flowers
that border the path from the high-road to the
peasant's cottage.

My Brier Rose garden should have grass paths;
whether wide or narrow, straight or winding, could

only be determined on the spot and in relation to all
that was near about it. It is one of the few kinds
of gardening that could be easily done on such poor
sandy soil as mine, because its hungry dryness suits
the companion Cistuses and also the setting of wild
Heaths which should be mingled with the fine grasses
natural to the heathy soil, while the path and planting
should join by a gentle and gradual passing of the one
into the other rather than by any hard or abrupt
transition. The Briers themselves will want a more
careful preparation of the ground ; trenching without
any manuring will do for the Heath and grass and
Cistuses, but though the wild English parent of the
garden Briers is at home in sandy heaths, and though
it will just exist if planted in the poor ground, it takes
so long to grow that it is well to moderately enrich
its place with some good leaf mould and spent manure.
Then the Briers will grow apace, and though they make
but little growth the first year, they are all the time
working underground ; by the second year they will
make good promise, and by the third there should be
a fair show.

The Briers are mainly the garden varieties, single
and double, of the Burnet Rose (*R. spinosissima*).
They are old garden plants, and though I have been
always collecting them, I daresay that in many a good
old English garden there may be more and better
variants than just those I have been able to get together. My first to bloom, within the earliest days of

June, and even in the latest of May, is a single one of
pale pink colour. It is a plant of weak half-trailing
habit, often scarcely rising from the ground; but the
crowded bloom has a tender loveliness that is full of
charm. Then follows the Burnet Rose, standing up in
bold bushy masses and covered with its crowds of
lemon-white single flowers. The next in order of
blooming is the half-double rose-coloured. I have had
several forms of this, differing a little in shape of
flower, and a good deal in colour. One or two have
been discarded as less good in colour, only the one I
thought best being kept. This has lively flowers of a
bright rose-crimson; the colour brightest in the half-
opened bloom, in which state also it looks more double
than it really is, for it has only three rows of petals.
As the flower expands and shows the full yellow
bunch of stamens and the white base of the petals, it
becomes paler in colour, passing at last into a pale
pinkish-white.

The next Brier to bloom is the double pink, with
the strong sweet luscious scent; the perfect Rose-
scent; the true attar. Perhaps it is this perfect Rose-
sweetness that makes this Brier my prime favourite, or
it may be the combination of this delightful quality
with the merit of its perfect form. But however it
may be, this little flower seems to carry me back
through the lifetime of past generations, and to put me
in friendliest fashion in touch with the flower-lovers of
them all; for to me it bears in its tender half-opened

blossoms, with their dainty rosy depths and sweetest perfume, the whole sentiment of the deeply-rooted English love of flower-beauty and purest enjoyment of garden-delight.

The Rose of this class that seems to be the most vigorous of all, and that comes next in time of blooming, is the double white. In habit of growth it is the one most like the common ancestor, the wild Burnet Rose, making dense bushy masses and bearing a profusion of neatly-shaped flowers. Then comes the double yellow, the slowest and weakest of growth, but with large loosely-shaped flowers of a very tender and beautiful pale yellow colour. I suppose it to be a hybrid, and to derive the tint from the yellow Austrian. This Austrian Brier in the single and double forms is also on the same bank, with its splendidly coloured variety the Austrian Copper; but they are of Oriental origin and do better against a warm wall. In the Austrian Copper, the vivid scarlet of the inside of the petal is laid on in a thin film over a ground of yellow. To get the same powerful quality of red colouring a painter has to use exactly the same artifice. I notice that Nasturtiums are painted in the same manner, but here the film of colour is laid on still more delicately, for whereas in the Brier petal one can peel off the red surface and show the yellow ground, one cannot do it in the Nasturtium. Here the texture of the petal is not so tough, and the most delicate touch with a fine needle breaks up the fragile skin, leaving

a wet discoloured wound. The surface colour seems
to be lightly dusted on, and by taking a flower of a
middle orange colour, not too deep, one may see on the
lower petals, where the colour lightens towards the
little fringe of pointed slashings, how the brilliant
powdering gradually ceases, and here and there how
the yellow ground is laid bare, where the surface of the
flower has received some gentle abrasion, more delicate
than can be done by hand, as of wind-rubbing of one
petal upon another.

With the Scotch Briers I have a bush of *Rosa
altaica,* hardly distinguishable from the Burnet Rose,
except that the pale lemon-white flowers are a size
larger, the leaves a shade bluer, and the whole growth
rather more vigorous.

The hybrid Brier, Stanwell Perpetual, is also on
the bank. It deserves the term "Perpetual" better
than any Rose I know, for besides its fairly full
bloom in early June, it bears a straggling succession
of its fragrant pale pink flowers throughout the
summer.

There is a look about the leafage of the varieties
of *Rosa rugosa* that seems to fit them for association
with the Briers. The colour of the type *rugosa* is unpleasant to me, so I have only the paler pink one and
the white. But these are on the top of the bank, and
with them, now a large bush seven feet high, is the
good and long-blooming hybrid, Madame Georges
Bruant. A lovely thing is the newer double white

Blanche de Coubert. It is quite the purest and coldest white of any Rose I know, and one is so un-accustomed to seeing a Rose with distinctly blue shading, that the first sight of it in bloom out of doors gave me a sort of pleasing shock, and an impression as of a Rose doing something quite new.

The common Sweet-brier and the beautiful Penzance hybrids would have their place in the large Brier garden that I like to imagine; there would be whole brakes of them in the background, some growing at will without support and some ramping through Thorns and Hollies.

The Scotch Briers have the great merit as garden plants—a merit that scarcely any other family of Roses can claim—of being in some kind of beauty throughout the year; for in autumn the Burnet Rose and some of the varieties bear large black fruits that are distinctly handsome, and the foliage assumes a rich duskiness of smoky red-bronze; while in winter there is a pleasant warmth of colour about the dense bushy masses

When I advised the planting of the common Heath (*Calluna*) as a groundwork of the Briers, it was with no thought of its flowering, for that is not till August, but for the sake of its quiet leaf-colouring; grey-green when the Briers bloom, and later of a sober rustiness; its own change of colouring keeping pace with that of the small Rose bushes. In neither case do the companion plants imitate or match each other in colour, but both advance in the progress of the year's transformation by such a sequence of quiet harmonies, that at every season each is the better for the nearness of the other.

CHAPTER VII

MIDSUMMER

" THOU sentest a gracious rain upon thine inheritance;
and refreshedst it when it was weary."

The whole garden is singing this hymn of praise
and thankfulness. It is the middle of June; no rain
had fallen for nearly a month, and our dry soil had
become a hot dust above, a hard cake below. A
burning wind from the east that had prevailed for
some time, had brought quantities of noisome blight,
and had left all vegetation, already parched with
drought, a helpless prey to the devouring pest.
Bushes of garden Roses had their buds swarming
with green-fly, and all green things, their leaves first
coated and their pores clogged with viscous stickiness,
and then covered with adhering wind-blown dust, were
in a pitiable state of dirt and suffocation. But last
evening there was a gathering of grey cloud, and this
ground of grey was traversed by those fast-travelling
wisps of fleecy blackness that are the surest promise
of near rain the sky can show. By bedtime rain was
falling steadily, and in the night it came down on the
roof in a small thunder of steady downpour. It was
pleasant to wake from time to time and hear the wel-

come sound, and to know that the clogged leaves were being washed clean, and that their pores were once more drawing in the breath of life, and that the thirsty roots were drinking their fill. And now, in the morning, how good it is to see the brilliant light of the blessed summer day, always brightest just after rain, and to see how every tree and plant is full of new life and abounding gladness; and to feel one's own thankfulness of heart, and that it is good to live, and all the more good to live in a garden.

The rain-drops still lodge in the grateful foliage. I like to see how the different forms and surfaces hold the little glistening globes. Of the plants close at hand the way of the Tree-Lupin is the most noticeable. Every one of the upright-standing leaves, like a little hand of eight or ten fingers, holds in its palm a drop more than a quarter of an inch in diameter. Each leaflet is edged with a line of light; the ball of water holds together by the attraction of its own particles, although there is a good space between the leaflets, offering ten conduits by which one expects it to drain away. Quite different is the way the wet hangs on the woolly leaves of *Verbascum phlomoides.* Here it is in long straggles of differently sized and shaped drops, the woolly surface preventing free flow. In this plant the water does not always seem to penetrate to the actual leaf-surface; occasionally it does and wets the whole leaf, but more usually, when the drops remain after rain at night, they are held up by the hairy coating.

Many of these downy leaves seem to repel water altogether, such as those of Yellow Alyssum and the other tall Mullein (*V. olympicum*), in whose case the water rolls right off, only lodging where there is a hollow or obstruction. The drops always look brightest on these un-wetting surfaces, and while rolling look like quicksilver.

Before the rain came it was a puzzle to know what to do with the half-hardy annuals. Although carefully pricked out and well spaced in the pans and boxes, they were growing fast and crowding one another, and we knew that if put out, the planting would have to be followed up by a daily watering. In a normal season they would have been out a fortnight ago, for it is unusual to have so long a drought so early in the year.

Any one who is in close sympathy with flower and tree and shrub, and has a general acquaintance with Nature's moods, could tell the time of year to within a few days without any reference to a calendar; but of all dates it seems to me that Midsummer Day is the one most clearly labelled, by the full and perfect flowering of the Elder. It may be different in more northern latitudes, but in mine, which is about half way between London and the south coast, the Festival of St. John and the flowering of the Elder always come together; and though other plants, blooming at other seasons, are subject to considerable variation in their

time of flowering, scarcely any is noticeable in the
Elder. So that one may say that however changeable
in their characters may be the other days most prominent in the almanac from their connection with
Feasts of the Church or matters of custom, yet
Midsummer Day always falls on the 24th of June.
Indeed I have often noticed that however abnormal
may have been the preceding seasons, things seem
to right themselves about the middle of this month.

The country people say that the roots of Elder
must never be allowed to come near a well, still less
to grow into it, or the water will be spoilt. The
young shoots are full of a very thick pith; we used
to dry it in my young days, and make it into little
round balls for use in electrical experiments. The
scent of the flowers, especially wind-wafted, I think
very agreeable, though they smell too strong to bring
indoors. If I were not already overdone with home
industries, I should distil fragrant Elder-flower water;
but I let the berries ripen and make them into Elder-
wine, a pleasant, comforting, and wholesome drink for
winter evenings.

It is always convenient to have names for the
different parts of a garden. I made this remark to
a friend as we were passing a solid wooden seat under
one of the tall Birches that give rather a distinct
character to the lawn and garden space just north of
the house, and I added that a name for that seat was

MULLEIN *(Verbascum phlomoides)* *(See page 256)*

much wanted.   As if inspired, he at once said: " Call
it the Cenotaph of Sigismunda."   The name was so
undoubtedly suitable to the monumental mass of Elm,
and to its somewhat funereal environment of weeping
Birch and spire-like Mullein, that it took hold at once,
and the Cenotaph of Sigismunda it will always be as
long as I am alive to sit on it.   It is a favourite resort
of the pussies, sheltered, and receiving the alternate
benefits of full afternoon sun and its milder filtration
through the still taller Birches opposite.   Pinkieboy's
portrait, on page 325, was done there while he was
enjoying his after-dinner *siesta*.

How endlessly beautiful are the various kinds of
Iris, of which so many bloom in June.   In fact they are
plants for nine months of the year, for *stylosa* begins
to flower in November, and before its long blooming
season, extending to April, is over, there comes the
glorious purple *Iris reticulata* and its varieties, and in
a snug sunny place at the foot of a south wall *Iris
persica*, whose delicate petals of palest greenish-blue
are boldly painted with stronger colours; and the
curious *Iris tuberosa* of Italy, made of black velvet
and green satin.   Then come the wonderful Irises of
the Oncocyclus group, not plants for every garden,
because some arrangement has to be made for keeping
the bulbs dry to ripen after flowering, without removing
them from the ground.   But those who will take the
trouble of giving them the needful treatment have the
reward of seeing some of the most wonderful and yet

THE CENOTAPH OF SIGISMUNDA

beautiful flowers that can be grown, and, moreover,
flowers that are surprisingly large for the size of
the plant.   The dwarf Irises, types and varieties of
pumila, olbiensis, and *Chamœiris*, and some other dwarf
broad-leaved species, begin to flower in the end of
May with the lovely pale blue Crimean variety of
pumila, the only Iris I have seen except *persica* that
may truly be called blue; for though the common
blue Flag, or so-called German Iris, is of a fine bluish-
purple, it is very far from being blue.   The best one
I am acquainted with of this class of colouring and
the nearest to blue is the beautiful and free-flowering
I. Cengialti, a little taller than the dwarf Flags, but
shorter than the mass of those that bloom in June.

The varieties of flag Iris have a large geographical
distribution through the warmer latitudes of Southern
and Eastern Europe and Asia Minor; the many others
that grace our gardens coming from all parts of the
Northern temperate zone.   For garden purposes the
flag-leaved Irises are put under certain heads which
may be briefly described thus :—

Iris albicans, pure white ; a beautiful plant in the
type, but the variety Princess of Wales is still better.

Iris florentina.   The grey-white Iris so common
about Florence.   The dried root is orris, a word which is
only a corruption of iris.   The Florentine Iris is one of
the earliest of its class to bloom, and at the same time
one of the most free ; a grand garden plant.

Iris pallida.   This and the splendid *I. pallida*

dalmatica are the next to bloom; the flowers are of two shades of clear pale-bluish lavender-lilac.

Iris flavescens. The type, whose flowers are all of a clear pale yellow, I think a better plant than any of the varieties, though many of these are desirable.

Iris variegata. This family also has a yellow ground colour, stronger than in *flavescens;* a deeper coloured, all-yellow variety called *I. variegata aurea* is a grand garden plant, and others, veined and clouded with crimson-brown on the broad lower petals, are highly desirable.

Iris amœna has the upright petals always white, while the lower ones are veined or largely blotched with purple of various shades.

Iris neglecta. In this section the upright petals are lavender-coloured or grey-lavender, and the falling ones purple, or some shade of purple with white veining.

Iris aphylla. These have all a white or nearly white ground throughout; the upright petals are strongly waved at the edge; both these and the lower ones are beautifully pencilled with delicate colourings of tender bluish-lilac.

Iris squalens. The children of this family may be known by either clearly-defined colouring of smoky bronze in the upright part of the flower, or some suspicion of the same, while the lower petals are usually heavily veined and blotched with purple or brownish-red. Though some of the best growers have of late years weeded their stocks of the varieties of lesser merit, there are still too many kinds, but among the best are Arnols, Bronze Beauty, La Prestigieuse, Rachel, Salar Jung, Van Gheertii, and Walneriana.

The position of my garden, on a dry hill in the poorest soil, makes it impossible for me to grow the beautiful Japanese water-loving Irises (*I. lœvigata*). Others that would prefer a damp place if they might have it, such as the related kinds *I. sibirica* and *I. orientalis*, do fairly well, but do not attain more than half their proper height. An Iris that likes damp may be known, like many another water-loving plant, by a hollow reed-like stem.

Many of these beautiful plants I cannot grow well for want of a stronger soil. Such are the fine varieties of the English and Spanish bulbous-rooted Irises; I specially regret being unable to grow with any degree of success the splendid Thunderbolt, a garden development of *Iris lusitanica*. It grows four feet high in rich strong soil; its garden name fitly describes its lurid thunder-cloud-like colouring.

Our two native Irises are both worthy of a place in the garden. *Iris Pseud-acorus*, the Yellow Flag of our river banks, is a conspicuously beautiful plant, not only because of its bold growth and bright flower, but also because of the harmony of colouring between the full yellow of the bloom and the yellow-green of the foliage. The summer value of *Iris fœtidissima* consists chiefly in the handsome tufts of dark-green half-

St. Bruno's Lily and London Pride

polished leaves, but its time of beauty is from late
autumn till mid-winter, when the large pods show the
brilliant scarlet seeds.   But as the heavy heads bend
down and get splashed with earth, I cut them as soon
as they burst open, for indoor winter decoration, first
hanging them up stalk upwards in bunches, for the
stems to dry and stiffen.   The flowers, which are out
in June, are small, and though curiously veined and
coloured, and interesting to examine in the hand, are
of no garden value.

One of the happiest mixtures of plants it has ever
been my good fortune to hit on is that of St. Bruno's
Lily and London Pride, both at their best about the
second week of June.   The lovely little Mountain Lily
—fit emblem of a pure-souled saint—stands upright
with a royal grace of dignity, and bears with an air of
modest pride its lovely milk-white bloom and abundant
sheaves of narrow blue-green leaves.   It is not a real
Lily but an *Anthericum ;* no plant, however, better
deserves the Lily-name, that, when used in its broader
significance, denotes some plant that bears bloom of
Lily shape, and bears them so worthily that the name
is in no danger of dishonour.

The well-grown clumps of this beautiful plant (it
is the large kind and nearly two feet high) are on a
narrow westward-facing bank that slopes down to the
lawn.   The place would be in the full blaze of the late
afternoon sun, but that it is kept shaded and cool by a
large Spanish Chestnut whose bole is some ten yards

"I am always dreaming of having delightful gardens for special seasons where one good flower should predominate . . . [among others] June demands an Iris garden . . . How endlessly beautiful are the various kinds of Iris, of which so many bloom in June." The water-loving Japanese Iris Kaempferi Laevigata which Gertrude Jekyll regretted she could not grow in her garden "on a dry hill in the poorest soil."

away.　Between and among the little Lilies is a wide
planting of London Pride, the best for beauty of bloom
of its own branch of the large family of Saxifrage.
Its healthy-looking rosettes of bright pale leaves and
delicate clouds of faint pink bloom seem to me to set
off the quite different way of growth of the Anthericum
so as to display the very best that both can do, making
me think of any two people whose minds are in such
a happy state of mutual intelligence, that when talking
together bright sparks of wit or wisdom flash from
both, to the delight of the appreciative listener.　The
only other flower that bears its part in this pretty show
is a cloudy mass of Venus's Navelwort (*Omphalodes
linifolia*), showing near the right side of the plate.
The picture (p. 111) is the better in that no other flowers
are in sight.　There is a near backing of small shrubs,
Daphne and dwarf Rhododendrons, then a woody space
in shadow, and sunlit copse beyond ; nothing to distract
the eye from the easy grouping and charming tenderness of colour of the simple little summer flowers.

LILIES AND CANNAS IN THE TANK-GARDEN

"There is no spot of ground, however arid, bare, or ugly, that cannot be tamed into such a state as may give an impression of beauty and delight. It cannot always be done easily; many things worth doing are not done easily; but there is no place under natural conditions that cannot be graced with an adornment of suitable vegetation." Agapanthus mingles with Artemisia (Silver Queen); Michaelmas Daisies behind.

CHAPTER VIII

ROSES AND LILIES

APART from their high place of standing in our gardens and in our hearts, the Rose and the Lily are, of all familiar flowers, the two that for many centuries have been given a special degree of prominent distinction in matters altogether outside the domain of horticulture. For throughout the history of the civilised world within the last thousand years, the Rose and the Lily occur again and again, in closest bond with the most vital of human interests, and always in association with something worthy of fame or glory, whether in religion, in politics, or as devices of honour carried on the shields of those found worthy to bear them.

In our own history, the Rose of England and the Lilies of France, how often have they played their part, whether in the crimson field of blood or in the golden field of peaceful amity! And though the Rose of England was not actually blazoned upon the shield of her kings, yet it has occurred so frequently among their badges that it is of distinct heraldic significance, and has stood for centuries as our national emblem. These two flowers may well be the badges of two noble nations, for, putting aside all lesser considerations as of use as a mere party emblem, the Lily stands for purity, for uprightness, for singleness of purpose. And the Rose, what does it typify ? Is not its beauty and sweetness, its bright wholesome gladness, a type of strength, of righteous purpose, and of bountiful beneficence ? Is it not a badge proper to the good knight, whose nature is strong and brave and tender, cheerful and courteous; who goes forth to battle for the weak, to establish good rule in place of oppression; whose work is to " cleanse the land," to " clear the dark places and let in the law " ?

And so throughout our gardens there are many plants which are not botanically either Roses or Lilies, but because they are beautiful, and have a form that somewhat recalls that of these two kinds of flowers, the words Rose and Lily, with some other, either descriptive or qualifying, make up their popular name. So we have Christmas Rose and Lenten Rose for the flowers of the Hellebore family that are so welcome from mid-winter to April; Rock-Rose and Sun-Rose for *Cistus* and *Helianthemum*, Guelder Rose for the white ball-flowers of the garden form of the Water-Elder, so good a shrub for many uses, not the least among these being as a wall-covering. For though it is absolutely hardy, it is right and reasonable to clothe our garden walls with whatever will make them look best, whether thoroughly hardy or not; and beautiful as the Guelder Rose is as a flowering bush, I think it

GUELDER ROSE AND GARDEN DOOR

better still on a wall; moreover, for wall spaces with windy or cold exposures there can be nothing more suitable. The accompanying illustration shows how well it graces wall and doorway(p.119).

Rose of Sharon is the popular name of the autumn-blooming shrubs of Syrian origin allied to Mallow and Hollyhock, botanically known as *Hibiscus syriacus* or *Althœa Frutex;* the names are synonymous. They are slightly tender, and do best against or near a wall, or in any case in a warm, sheltered place. All are pretty things, but among the later grown kinds there are two especially good, one a double white, the other of quite a good blue colour; the type colour is a rather wild-mallow-like pink.

The word Lily is still oftener used as a component of honour in the names of beautiful flowers both within and beyond the large botanical order of *Liliaceœ.* And when I am asked whether such a plant is really a Lily or not I cannot say, or how far beyond the actual genus Lilium our botanists would allow the name to be used. Nor indeed does the popular name concern them as botanists, for scientifically the botanical name only is wanted, though I am glad to know, having the good fortune to be on friendly terms with more than one learned botanist, that in the garden they seem to be more lovers of beautiful plants than scientists only, and talk about Primroses and Daffodils, Roses and Lilies, just as I do myself.

The Cape Lily (*Crinum*, GARDEN VARIETIES)

So among our popular Lily names we have Lily-of-the-Valley (*Convallaria*), St. Bruno's Lily (*Anthericum*), Arum Lily (*Calla*), African Lily (*Agapanthus*, one of the grandest of tub plants); Cape Lily (*Crinum*), splendid in its later developments; Amazon Lily (*Eucharis*). Then there is the beautiful Belladonna Lily (*Amaryllis*), one of the noblest of pink-flowered plants and very sweet of scent. This lovely Lily is not often seen in gardens, but there is no difficulty if it is planted close to the outside of the south wall of a plant-house where it may have the benefit of some of the warmth of the pipes within. There is hardly a garden I go round that does not neglect the opportunity of growing this grand thing. Scarborough Lily is the common name of the beautiful *Vallota*. Why this good plant is not so often grown as formerly I am unable to understand, for in my young days there was hardly a garden that had not some well-established pots of it, whereas now, though one sees a plant here and there, it is certainly much less frequent.

The Lilies of France and the Lily of Florence are, of course, Irises, and indeed the beauty of this wonderful family entitles them to a place within the most exclusive aristocracy of flowers.

How well the Lily name of honour is deserved by the white Water-Lily (*Nymphœa alba*), and its near relations the coloured Water-Lilies of other countries, and the beautiful garden kinds that have been raised by

the eminent French horticulturist, M. Latour-Marliac.
To this gentleman's labours we owe a whole new
range of lovely varieties of the highest garden value.
Throughout the country our best amateurs are making
ponds and tanks on purpose for their culture, and
some day I shall endeavour to point out how their
use might be adapted to some of the most highly
refined developments of formal or architectural
gardening.

And the true Lilies, the many lovely flowers com-
prised within the botanical family of *Lilium*; what
would our gardens be without them ? Ever first and
best comes the White Lily, emblem of spotless purity,
and noblest and loveliest of garden flowers.

To my great regret this grand Lily is almost impossible to grow in my poor, hot soil, even in well-
prepared beds. It thrives in chalk and nearly all rich
loams, and I am full of a pardonable gardener's envy
when I drive down into the clay lands of the neighbouring weald and see how it thrives in every cottage
garden.

It is not generally known that there are two distinct forms of the White Lily; one a far finer garden
plant than the other. The better one has altogether
larger flowers, with wide overlapping petals that are
strongly ribbed and curled back. In the other the
petals are narrower, and the whole flower, seen from
the front, is thinner and flatter, and more star-shaped.
Though the distinction seems of late to have been

almost lost sight of, it was well known in the days of Queen Elizabeth, when Gerarde plainly describes and figures the two kinds, calling the star-shaped one the " White Lily of Constantinople."

The only Lilies that do well in my poor soil are *croceum*, *auratum*, and *tigrinum*. *Croceum* is the early blooming Orange Lily that grows so well in London. It is the Herring-Lily of the Dutch, blooming at the time when the great catches of herrings take place. I have got into the way of thinking of it and talking of it as the Herring-Lily, and there are so many other Lilies of an orange colour that for the sake of distinctness the name seems worthy of general adoption. Like other Lilies long in cultivation, there are better and worse forms of it. The best one is a magnificent garden plant; in my borders, when full-grown, the third year after planting, it is seven feet high; a sumptuous mass of the deepest orange colour. When the bloom is over, it is cut away, and there are still left the stems of handsome foliage in regular whorls. But as I have it in the flower-border in rather large patches, and as by the late summer the mass of foliage, though wholesome and handsome, is a little too large and deep in colour, I grow behind it the white Everlasting Pea, training the long flowering shoots over and among the Lily stems, with what seems to me the very happiest effect.

In "Wood and Garden,"* I explained rather at length the way I thought best of arranging the se-

* Reprinted by the Antique Collectors' Club, 1981.

THE TWO KINDS OF WHITE LILY

quence of colour in a large border of hardy flowers,
namely, in a gradual progression of colour-harmony in
the case of the red and yellow flowers, whose numbers
preponderate among those we have to choose from;
but saying that as far as my own understanding of
the colour-requirements of flowers went, it was better
to treat blues with contrasts rather than with harmonies. And I had observed, when at one point,
from a little distance, I could see in company the
pure deep orange of the Herring-Lilies (*Lilium croceum*)
with the brilliant blue of some full-blue Delphiniums,
how splendid, although audacious, the mixture was,
and immediately noted it, so as to take full advantage of the observation when planting-time came.
In the autumn, two of the large patches of Lilies
were therefore taken up and grouped in front of, and
partly among, the Delphiniums; and even though
neither had come to anything like full strength in
the past summer (the first year after removal), yet
I could see already how grandly they went together,
and how well worth doing and recommending such
a mixture was. The Delphiniums should be of a
full deep-blue colour, not perhaps the very darkest,
and not any with a purple shade.

Tiger-Lilies also do well in well-prepared beds in
my garden, the large variety "splendens" being the
best and the tallest. Here they should be replanted
at least every three years. By a poorer and smaller
growth and an earlier yellowing of leaf, they show

A Jar of China Roses

when they have exhausted the goodness of their bed and want it renewed. They bear numbers of bulbils in the axils of the leaves that can be grown on, and come to flowering size in about five years. It is a valuable Lily, not only from its own beauty of free flower, black-spotted on salmon orange, of bold turn-cap shape, but because it is a true flower of autumn, blooming well into the third week of September. I always grow them in front of a yew hedge, the dark background of full, deep, low-toned green showing up their shape and colour to the fullest advantage.

The only other Lily that I can depend on is *Lilium auratum*. I cannot afford to buy the home-grown bulbs that are so much the most trustworthy and satisfactory, but from time to time buy a case of imported ones, when they are to be had at about a pound a hundred, and take my chance. If I am lucky with bulbs and season they do fairly well.

They are among Rhododendrons in beds of peat and old hot-bed stuff. If the bulbs do not rot and die outright, or if the young shoots are not eaten off by mice in the spring, they make a fair growth the first year, and increase in strength for some four or five years; after that they deteriorate. But by buying a case every two years, and picking out some of the best for pots and planting out the rest, I manage to keep up somewhat of an outdoor show. For some reason that those who know better than myself can perhaps explain, they flower over a very long period. The earliest will bloom in the end of June, and the latest in October.

One of the prettiest ways I have them is planted among groups of *Bambusa Metake*; in this way they scarcely want staking, and I always think look their very best. I was advised to do it by a friend who had seen them so grown in Japan, and I always feel grateful for the good advice when I see how delightfully they go together.

This fine Lily, like some others, makes additional roots a little way up the stem. The roots thrown out by the bulb get to work first and prepare it for the effort of throwing up the flower stem. When this is a little way advanced, large hungry roots are thrown out from the stem itself, quite two inches above the bulb This points to the need of deep planting, or better still, of planting first in a deep depression, and filling up later with a rich compost to such a depth as may leave these stem-roots well underground, for these are the roots that feed the flowers.

The same way of having two storeys of roots is seen in some other plants of rapid and large growth, such as the great annual grasses of the Maize and Millet tribe.

Roses are with us for six months out of the twelve; as bushes large and small, as trim standards, as arbour and pergola coverings, as wall plants, as great natural fountains, and as far-reaching rambling growths rushing through thickets and up trees and tossing out their flower-laden sprays from quite unexpected heights. But of all the Roses of the year I think there are none more truly welcome than those of autumn.

The long-branching Teas, that one can cut of lavish length, and especially the Noisettes, are always faithful in the quantity and persistence of their autumn bloom. From the end of August to the end of September, sometimes even later, one can enjoy these lovely things in quantity. Most trusty of all is Climbing Aimée Vibert, with its wide-spread terminal clusters of charming warm-white flower and rose-edged bud. The flowers of Madame Alfred Carrière, another white Rose, are also in plenty; large and loose and of a warm-white colour impossible to describe, but that may sometimes be seen in some shell of delicate structure. No Rose of all the year is lovelier in water in a loose long-stalked bunch; the pale polished leaves being also of much beauty.

I have found it well to plant a number of such Roses for cutting, training them down to a slight fence-like support of post and rail; bending them over all one way, so that the head of one comes far beyond the root of another.

This kind of low training, like pegging down Roses over beds, has also the advantage of inciting them to bloom more freely, as they then form flowering shoots along a greater length of the stem.

It should not be forgotten that some Roses are in fact evergreens; retaining all or part of their foliage

Autumn Roses

throughout the winter.　One would expect this in the rambling cluster Roses that have their origin in *Rosa sempervirens*, but I do not know what parentage accounts for the splendid winter leafage of that grand rambling Reine Olga de Wurtemburg, whose half-double flowers of a fine crimson colour, of great beauty in the half-opened bud state, gladden us throughout the summer, and whose large and healthy deep-green leaves, on yearling shoots fifteen feet long, remain in perfection till long after Christmas

CHAPTER IX

LARGE ROCK-GARDENS

THOUGH I have to be contented with an Alpine garden on a very small scale, I like to plan a large rock-garden in imagination. It is in the lower part of a steep hillside, a little gorge or dell with its own stream and natural rock cropping out. At the desired spot I would build a pond-head across the dell, and following the indication of local stratification, I would arrange large masses of the natural stone so as to form a rocky heading, with deep rifts well packed with soil for Ferns. The water would be led over this rocky head, which should be about twenty feet high, in various ways; in one place by a clear fall into a deep pool, in others by shorter cascades and cunningly-contrived long slides of differing angles. How well I remember such places in the Alps, and how delightful it was to watch the different ways of the water.

In one place there should be a splash on to a rock for the benefit of *Ramondia* and *Soldanella* and *Saxifraga aizoides*, that delight in nearness to water and a bath of spray. Excepting just these plants, I think I should let this region be devoted to Ferns, so as to give a simple picture of one thing at a time, and not

even too many different kinds of Ferns, but in some
long rocky rifts an abundance of Hart's-tongue, and in
some half-dusky region at the foot of the rocky wall,
so placed as to be reflected in a quiet backwater of the
main pool, a goodly planting of the Lady Fern, and then
some handsome tufts of Royal Fern.   And in the
margin of the pool I would only have, besides the
Ferns, one or two native water-plants; and of these
the chosen ones would be the Water Plantain (*Alisma*)
and the Flowering Rush (*Butomus*), bearing in mind
that the Ferns are to have the mastery.   I am not
even sure that it would not be better to have those
spray-loving Alpines in some lower reach of the dell, if
just the right place could be contrived for them, and
to have Wall-Pennywort in their place in the greater
rocky wall, in order to keep the place of rock and pool
and Fern as quiet as possible, and to present one
simple picture of rock and water, and restful delight of
cool and beautiful foliage.   And such a picture would
also serve to show what could be done with our native
plants and these alone.   Some stretches of native
Heaths, the pink Bell-Heather (*Erica Tetralix*) and the
white Irish Menziesia would not be out of place; and
in mossy beds such dainty things as *Pyrola, Linnæa,* and
Trientalis would do well, for while serving as delightful
surprises of tender plant-beauty in detail, they would
not be so conspicuous as to mar the unity of plan of
the main picture as a whole.

The path downward would lead out of this upper

place through a planting of some kind of bushy growth hiding the pool, of which the best I can think of would be Sea-Buckthorn, the native Bog-Myrtle, and the broad-leafed American kind—all again carpeted with native Heaths. This rather low-toned mass of bushes of dull colour and dry texture would be a good preparation for arrival at the Fern and water picture, and the sound of the water, more important here than in the trickling of the lower rills, would arouse a feeling of interest, and an anticipation of something pleasant and beautiful hidden beyond the bushy screen.

I should wish that the ground above the glen on both sides should be wooded; not with the largest forest trees, such as Beeches, but mainly with Birch and a good deal of Mountain Ash and Holly, Thorn and Juniper; and some of these would be allowed to seed and spring up in the rocky banks, always watching how they came, and retaining or removing the seedlings so as best to suit the grouping of such a picture as may be intended. As the dell descends it should widen out until it dies away into nearly level ground, and as it flattens, the trees might fall into thinner groups, or be altogether absent if the ground were of Heath or pasture.

But such a little planted valley might also well come down into the rougher part of the garden or shrub plantation or garden-orchard. Given the dell and the stream, an endless variety of simple pictures

could be made. By using native plants at the upper
end, and then by degrees coming to plantings of
foreign things best suited to wild ground, such as the
white Wood Lily (*Trillium*) of Canada and the
northern States of America, the wilder ground would
pleasantly and imperceptibly join hands with the
garden, and would be without any of the painful
shocks and sudden jolts that so often afflict the soul
of the garden-artist on his journey round even well-
ordered rockeries of the usual type. I venture to
repeat my own firm conviction that this kind of
gardening can only be done well and beautifully by a
somewhat severe restraint in numbers of kinds. The
eye and brain can only take in and enjoy two or three
things at a time in any one garden picture. The
lessons taught by nature all point to this; indeed
one thing at a time is best of all; but as all natural
or wild gardening is a compromise, the nature-
lessons must be taken mainly as the setting forth of
principles. If these principles are well taken in, and
digested and assimilated, we shall find no difficulty
in rightly using that part of their teaching which
bears upon gardening, and we shall see how to treat
wild nature, not by slavish imitation, not by driving or
forcibly shaping, but by methods that can hardly be
described in detail, of coaxing and persuading into
pictorial effect.

The upper end of my little dell I suppose to be
to the south, so that the rocky wall-head is always

in shade, and as one comes downward the right hand slope gets a good deal of sun from noon to the middle of the afternoon. The one on the left is nearly all in shadow, so that for such plants as do best entirely screened from the sun, a suitable place can easily be chosen or arranged. It would be important, in order to preserve a certain unity of effect throughout the whole valley, that there should be a general ground-work of certain plants from end to end. If it were a place of sand and peat, these plants should be the three common wild Heaths, Whortleberry, *Gaultheria Shallon*, and the Bog-Myrtles. Between and under these should be long stretches of common Mosses and Mossy Saxifrages.

I would have everything planted in longish drifts, and above all things it should be planted *geologically;* the length of the drift going with the natural stratification. In all free or half-wild garden planting, good and distinct effect (though apparent and enjoyable to every beholder, even though he may not perceive why it is right and good) is seldom planned or planted except by the garden artist who understands what is technically known as " drawing." But by planting with the natural lines of stratification we have only to follow the splendid drawing of Nature herself, and the picture cannot fail to come right.

In the planting of my little valley I should be inclined to leave out some of the best-known mountain plants such as Arabis, Aubrietia, Alyssum, and

Cerastium.   These are so closely associated in our
minds with garden use that they have in a way lost
their suitability for places where we want to foster the
illusion of being among pictures of wild nature.

As the dell becomes shallower, the less sloping
sides will want more careful planting.   Here I would
have on the cool side the bushy Andromedas and
Vacciniums, remembering that some of the latter have
an autumn leaf-colouring of splendid scarlet, and that
therefore other bushes of like colouring would fittingly
accompany them ;   so that here might come the hardy
Azaleas, thankful for a place where they have cool
peat at the root, and passing shade as of not far distant
Birches.

The opposite side in full sun would be a happy
home for the Cistuses ;   the larger pictorial effects
being made with bold plantings of *C. ladaniferus* and
C. laurifolius, and nearer the path *C. florentinus*, and
the yellow-flowered *Cistus formosus*, which, though commonly called a Cistus, is botanically a *Helianthemum*.
Then the smaller yellow-flowered and more prostrate
H. halimifolium and the lesser Rock-Roses.   In the
most sun-baked spot I would have, on a rocky shelf
and hanging over it, a wide planting of Barbary Rag-
wort (*Othonnopsis cheirifolia*), Lavender and Rosemary,
and big bushes of Jerusalem Sage (*Phlomis fruticosa*)
and yellow Tree-Lupin, and the great Asphodel.   It
would suit the character of most of these plants to
show between them some small stretches of bare sandy

soil and bare rock, varied with an undergrowth of the sun-loving Heaths, Lavender-Cotton, and the aromatic Artemisias, in wide plantings and long drifts, always faithfully following the run of the rocks.

These plants and shrubs, among a good many others that might be employed in the same way, came first to mind because of a general likeness or harmony of leaf-colour ; for I should think it desirable, had it ever been my happiness to be able to plant such a large wild rock-garden, to avoid too great a mixture of quality of leaf-colour in the main masses.   And just as it seemed the better plan in the shaded region of the upper pool to have a preponderance of the cool, fresh yellowish-green of Fern and Moss, so on the sun-baked rocky banks below I should try for a distinct picture of the greyish and low-toned blue-greens so prevalent among those herbs and bushy growths of the Mediter-ranean region, that are good enough to make them-selves at home in more northern latitudes.

Though such a large half-wild rock-garden as I have attempted to sketch may only be possible to a very few among the great number of those who love rock-plants, such a more extensive view of its possi-bilities does not in the least degree put one out of sympathy with the small rock-gardens now so abun-dant, and that give their owners so much pleasure. My own covers but a few square yards, but many are even smaller, and perhaps a little worse built and disfigured by labels, and yet I can heartily sympathise with all, for I consider that in dealing with these matters one must never forget, or be afraid to repeat by word or in writing, the plain fact that a pleasure garden is for the purpose of giving pleasure, and that though my own delight in a garden may be worked out in one way, yet other people may take their pleasure quite rightly in ways altogether different.

It has always seemed to me that when there is a very small space to be dealt with, as in the gardens of hundreds of small villas in the suburbs of London and other large towns, that to lay it out as a rock-garden would be the best way of making the most of it. No doubt many clever owners of such houses have done it already, but others may not have thought of it, and though in a restricted area one cannot have large effects, yet there is no reason why one should not have well-designed ones, such as would be in perfect proportion and suitability of scale to the space at command; while such a little garden would admit of a much greater variety of forms of plant beauty than could be appropriately used in any other way.

"Though I have to be contented with an Alpine garden on a very small scale, I like to plan a large rock-garden in imagination. It is in the lower part of a steep hill-side ... with its own stream and natural rock cropping out. At the desired spot I would build a pond-head across ... I would arrange large masses of the natural stone so as to form a rocky heading, with deep rifts well packed with soil for Ferns. The water would be led over this rocky head, ... in one place by a clear fall into a deep pool, in others by shorter cascades and cunningly-contrived long slides of differing angles ... and it seemed the better plan ... to have a preponderance of the cool, fresh yellowing-green of Fern and Moss."

CHAPTER X

SMALL ROCK-GARDENS

An artificial rockery is usually a bit of frankly simple make-believe. Nine times out of ten there is something about it half funny, half pathetic, so innocent, so childish is its absolute failure to look like real rocky ground. And even if for a moment one succeeds in cheating oneself into thinking that it is something like a bit of rocky nature, there is pretty sure to be the zinc label, with its stark figure and ghastly colouring, looking as if it were put there of cruel purpose for the more effectual shattering of the vain illusion. I suppose that of all metallic surfaces there is none so unlovely as that of zinc, and yet we stick upright strips of it among, and even in front of, some of the daintiest of our tiny plants. We spend thought and money, and still more money's-worth in time and labour, on making our little rocky terraces, and perhaps succeed in getting them into nice lines and planted with the choicest things, and then we peg it all over with zinc labels! I am quite in sympathy with those who do not know their plants well enough to do without the labels; I have passed through that stage myself, and there are many cases

where the label must be there.   But I considered that
in dressed ground or pure pleasure ground, where
the object is some scheme of garden beauty, the
label, even if it must be there, should never be
seen.   I felt this so keenly myself when I first had
a piece of rock-garden that I hit upon a plan that
can be confidently recommended: that of driving
the ugly thing into the earth, leaving only just enough
above ground to lay hold of.   In this case also the
zinc strip can be much shorter; only enough length is
wanted to write the name; the writing with metallic
ink also remains fresh longer in the damp ground,
and shows clear when the peg is pulled up to be
looked at.   And then one finds out how seldom one
really wants the label.   In my own later practice,
where the number of different plants has been reduced
to just those I like best and think most worthy of a
place, they are so well known to me that their names
are as familiar as those of my best friends; and when
I admit a new plant, if I cannot at once learn its
name, it is purposely given a big ugly label, as a self-
inflicted penance that shall continue until such time
as I can expiate by remembrance.

I have two small rock-gardens, differently treated.
The upper one leads from lawn to copse, and is made
with a few simple parallel ridges of stone, clothed for
the most part with small shrubs, such as Gaultheria
and Alpine Rhododendron, with hardy Ferns, and
groups of two or three plants of conspicuously hand-

some foliage, such as *Saxifraga peltata* and *Rodgersia podophylla*. The object of this one is to lead unobtrusively from lawn to copse, and at the same time to accommodate certain small shrubs and handsome plants with a place where they would do well, and where I should wish to see them. The other little rock-garden, between the lower end of the lawn and a group of Oaks, has another purpose. It is absolutely artificial, and only pretends to be a suitable home for certain small plants that I love. A rock-garden takes a great deal of skilled labour, and I can only afford it my own, so that its size is limited to little more than I can work with my own hands and see with extremely short-sighted eyes. Four broad and shallow steps lead down to the path-level; there is a long-shaped island in the middle, and sloping banks to right and left, all raised from the path by dry-walling from one to two feet high. The joints of the dry-walling are planted with small Ferns on the cool sides, and with Stonecrops and other dwarf sun-loving plants on the sides facing south. The walling as it rises changes to rocky bank, with again a course or two of walling in the cooler face to suit some plantings of *Ramondia* and the rarer *Haberlea rhodopensis*. The cool, sloping flats between are covered with *Dryas octopetala*, and neat Alpines such as *Hutchinsia* and *Cardamine trifoliata*, and little meadows of *Linnœa borealis*, *Campanula pulla*, *Veronica prostrata*, and *V. satureioides*, *Linaria pallida* and *L. hepaticæfolia*; while in the joints of the stones and

just below them are little Ferns, and in all vacant
places tufts and sheets of mossy Saxifrage, coolest and
freshest-looking of alpine herbage.   These various
members of the mossy branch of the great Saxifrage
family are some of the most valuable of rock-garden
plants, and in a small place like mine can be well
employed to give some sort of feeling of unity to what
would otherwise be only a piece of floral patchwork,
especially if the plants and their mossy setting are
placed as much as possible in long drifts rather than
in compact patches.   I think this principle is of so
much importance that I shall not refrain from
repeating it, for I have found it to be of value in all
kinds of planting, whether of small or large plants in
rockery or border, of Daffodils in copse or meadow, or
of tree and shrub in larger spaces.

For the effectual destruction of any pictorial
effect in a rock-garden, no method of arrangement can
be so successful as the one so very frequently seen, of
little square or round enclosures of stones placed on
end, with the plant inside conspicuously labelled.   It
always makes me think of cattle-pens in a market,
and that the surrounding stones are placed prison-
wise, less for the plant's comfort than for its forcible
detention.   And it leads to the stiffest and least interesting way of planting.   If there are three plants
they go in a triangle; if four, in a square; if five, in a
square with one in the middle, and so on.   For even
if a little rockery be avowedly artificial, as in many

cases it must be, it is better that its details should be all easy and pretty, rather than stiff and awkward and unsightly.

The sunny side of my small rock-garden has long groups of *Othonnopsis*, and the woolly-leaved *Hieracium villosum* and Prophet-flower (*Arnebia*), and good stretches of *Achillea umbellata* and of *Iris cristata*, without doubt one of the loveliest among the smaller members of its beautiful family, and of the flowers that bloom in May. This little Iris is only five inches high, and the flowers are two and a half inches across, so that they look large for the whole size of the plant. When placed as it likes best, on a sunny rock-shelf in nearly pure leaf-mould, it shows its appreciation of kind treatment by free growth and abundance of bloom. The leaves, at blooming time only four inches high, though much taller afterwards, are in neat flat little sheaves of from three to five, one leaf always taking a prominent lead. The clear lilac-blue of the flower has a daintily-clean look that is very charming, and taken in the hand I always delight in the delicate beauty of the raised and painted ornament of the lower petals. In the middle of the broadest part is a white pool with a strong purple edging; the white turns to yellow, and runs in a lane an eighth of an inch wide down into the throat, between two little whitish rocky ridges. The yellow stripe is also decorated with a tiny raised serpent wriggling down its middle line, and with a few fine short strokes of reddish-brown.

Another great favourite, equally at home in sun or shade in the rock-walls, is *Corydalis capnoides ;* masses of feathery daintiness of warm white bloom and fern-like foliage. The flower is of the labiate form, characteristic of the Fumitory group. Its upper member rises from the pouch-like spur in an admirable line of simple strength, and ends above in a narrow turned-back hood, whose outer edge is waved and bluntly toothed in a way that gives an impression of the most delicate decorative finish. The leaves are of the tenderest yellow-green, and the aspect of the whole plant is so refined that it makes all the surrounding growths look coarsely built.

In one corner of the rock-garden are two kinds of Violet, both good and worthy of their place, though both without scent. One is a white Dog-Violet, the white strikingly pure and bright. The leaves are of a very dark green, sometimes with a tinge of blackish-bronze; two rather narrow upright petals stand up in a way that always reminds me of a frightened rabbit. The other is the splendid North American *Viola cucullata.* Its large round flowers, of a strong pure purple colour, nearly an inch and a half across, are on purplish stems from nine inches to a foot long. Where the lower petal leaves the small white eye there is a sharply-distinct veining of still darker purple. The size of the flower is all the more remarkable because it is a true Violet; there is nothing of the Pansy about it. Pansy and Violet are, of course, closely related, but their characters are quite distinct; and though, as a rough rule, Pansy is large and Violet small, yet there are many small true Pansies, and in this case there is one very large Violet.

No rock-garden should be without *Achillea um-bellata* in fair plenty. Even out of flower it is one of the neatest of plants, with its silvery foliage so deeply cut that the leaves are almost like double combs, and its bountiful heads of milk-white flowers, whose centres, dusky at first, change to a dull nankeen colour as the bloom becomes perfect. There is no better plant for an informal edging, or for any alpine carpeting, in long pools or straight drifts; it delights in a hot place, and, like many silvery-leaved plants, will bear a good deal of drought.

I am very fond of the double Cuckoo-flower. It has such a clean, fresh look, and the doubling makes such a pretty round rose-shaped flower of each little bloom. The single wild one of the meadows is a pretty plant too, and sometimes grows so thickly that one understands how it came by its old English name of Lady's-smock; for its close masses of whitish bloom might well remind one of linen wear laid out to bleach. Many years ago a dear old friend among our neighbours bought a plant of the double kind. Her meadow was already well stocked with the wild one, and she had the happy idea of planting the double one with it. In course of time it increased and spread over a large space, and was so pretty and pleasant to see that nearly

CUCKOO-FLOWER AND SANDWORT IN THE ROCK GARDEN

every spring I used to go on purpose to visit it. And one day, to my great delight, I found among it one plant of a much deeper colour, quite a pretty and desirable variety from the type, that has proved a good garden plant. My friend Mr. George Paul, after growing it for a season, thought so well of it that he took it to a meeting of the Royal Horticultural Society, where he received for it a notice of commendation; this, with kindly courtesy, he was good enough to pass on to me, having given my name to the variety. The Cuckoo-flower has a curious way of increasing by dropping its leaflets; they root at the base, and it is easy to make a panful of cuttings in this way, dibbling in the leaflets, and pretty to see the spruce little plants that soon grow from them. It also makes little plants, with roots and all complete, in the axils of the leaves on the lower part of the flower-stems after the bloom is over. These will drop off when mature, but as a good many perish under the natural conditions of my dry garden, I look out for them as soon as the roots are formed and grow them on in boxes till some wet day in July or August, when they can be safely planted out.

There is a good group of this pretty plant at the cooler end of my small rock-garden, where a bit of dwarf dry-walling supports the raised sides. The walling is here only a foot high, and is clothed with the little creeping Sandwort (*Arenaria balearica*). The two plants together make a pretty picture; the Sandwort

Of her own rock-garden Gertrude Jekyll wrote: "In the joints of stones . . . are little Ferns, and in all vacant places tufts and sheets of mossy Saxifrage, coolest and freshest-looking of alpine herbage. These various members . . . of the great Saxifrage family are some of the most valuable of rock-garden plants, and in a small place like mine can be well employed to give some sort of feeling of unity to what would otherwise be only a piece of floral patchwork." Water Saxifrage and Tiarella Cordifolia (Foam Flower).

is rather the later of the two, but is already fairly well in flower before the bloom of the Cuckoo-flower is over. Nothing can be better than this little *Arenaria* for any cool place against stonework. A tuft or two planted at the foot in autumn will creep up and cover a good space of stony face in a short time. One has only to see that it does not cling on to plants as well as stones, for I have had it growing all over the surface of *Ramondia* leaves, only catching it just in time to prevent the *Ramondia* from being smothered. I am watching with some interest a little patch that has found a lodging in the middle of a spreading sheet of *Linaria hepaticæfolia*, another of the small irrepressibles. I want to see which of the two will have the mastery, as it is the habit of both to completely cover any space of ground or stonework they may be on.

Any one who wishes to see silvery-green satin of the highest quality should look at the back of the leaves of *Alchemilla alpina*. Indeed the whole plant, though anything but showy, is full of what one may call interesting incident. I remember finding this out one hot afternoon, when after a hard morning's work I sat down, a good bit tired, on the lowest of the steps leading into the little rock-garden. Just under my hand was a tuft of this Lady's-Mantle, and half-lazily, and yet with a faint prick of the moral spur that urges me against complete idleness, I picked a leaf to have a good look at it, and then found how much, besides the well-known beauty of its satin back, there was to

admire in it. The satin lining, as is plain to see,
comes up and over the front edge of the leaf with
a brightness that looks like polished silver against
the dull green surface. The edge of each of the
seven leaflets is plain for two-thirds of its length, and
then breaks into saw-teeth, which increase in size,
always silver-edged, till they reach the end and nearly
meet. And at this point a surprise awaits one, for
instead of the endmost jag, in the base of whose body
the mid-rib dies away, being as one would expect the
stoutest and largest, it is smaller than the two next
on each side, so that the tip of the leaflet has a blunt
and even depressed shape; indeed the tips of the last
five saw-teeth are nearly on a line and at a right angle
to the mid-rib, and the middle one is always a little
the lowest. Then there is another curious thing to
notice, that, though not invariable, is so frequent as
to seem to be a law in the plant's structure. The
normal number of divisions in a full-sized leaf is seven,
and they all join together with the exception of the
first and last, at a distance of a quarter of an inch
from their common insertion into the stalk. But in
most cases either the first or the seventh leaflet has a
sub-leaflet of its own, usually smaller, but sometimes
nearly as large as itself, joined to it much further
up, but with its own mid-rib and distinct system of
veining. The heads of small green flowers, set on
lesser stalks that leave the main stem by springing
out of a frilled collar half leaf half bract, are not

"*It always seems to me that one of the things most worth doing about a garden is to try to make every part of it beautiful ... And to get into the habit of considering and composing ... arrangements, and to worry out the way of doing them, is by no means one of the least of the pleasures of a garden.*"

exactly beautiful, but have a curious squareness of plan, still further accentuated by the four stamens also squarely planted at the inner angles of the petals. Close to the Lady's-Mantle, and also within hand-reach, is a frequent weed, but a weed so lovely that I let it be—the common Speedwell. I remember how delighted I was as a child when I found out for myself how the two lines of fur that run up the stalks between each pair of leaves, changed sides with the next pair of leaves, and ran up the other sides, and how I used to think the little blue flower itself had something the look of a tiny Pansy. I suppose this impression arose from the veins gathering to the middle to a firmer depth of blue, and then giving place to a white eye.

My little rock-garden is never without some stretches of the common Thrift, which I consider quite an indispensable plant. Its usefulness is not confined to the flowering season, for both before and after, the cushion-like growths of sober greenery are helpful in the way of giving an element of repose and quietude to a garden-space whose danger is always an inclination towards unrest and general fussiness. And it should be cautiously placed with regard to the colour of the neighbouring flowers, for its own pink is of so low-toned a quality that pinks brighter and purer spoil it completely. I should say its best companions would be some of the plants of woolly foliage and whitish flower such as Cerastium or the mountain Cud-weeds.

The flowering plants on this small rockery only extend as far as the hand can reach, for convenience of weeding and all requirements of easy access. Beyond this point is a permanent planting of small shrubs, mostly of the Alpine Rhododendrons. These were chosen as the main background for the little flowering plants, because they seemed just to have the desired qualities of a small, neat habit of growth, on a scale not unsuitable to that of the Alpines, a steady moderation of yearly increase, and a richness of deep colouring, highly becoming to the small bright things below them. Beyond them are Gaultherias which will grow a little higher, and then Hollies, so that the whole background of the dainty Alpine jewels will show as a richly-dark and somewhat sombre setting. But besides these dwarf Rhododendrons and the sweet-leaved *R. myrtifolium*, only a little larger in growth, there is also in the upper part of the rock-work a planting of the smaller Andromedas, with Gaultheria and Skimmia, and groups of *Daphne pontica*, whose abundant yellow-green bloom fills the garden with fragrance in the early days of May. And planted with these, and running down among the flowers, is the white Menziesia, taking an equal place among flower and small shrub, and always delightful with its large white blooms of long ball-shape—just right for fairies' footballs—and its wholesome-looking foliage of a deep rich green.

CHAPTER XI

THE WORKSHOP

FROM childhood I have always felt at home in a workshop, and wherever I have lived there has always been
some such delightful place. When my father gave
up his London house, and for the sake of his young
family made a home in the country, his always busy
mind and well-developed mechanical genius found
occupation in many branches of constructional ingenuity. His ability did not so much consist in
working at a bench himself, as in planning and
directing the handiwork of others. One of the
ground-floor rooms he turned into a workshop, and
for fourteen years a clever young engineer was a
member of the household, and worked under his
direction. During these years a number of working
models were made, illustrating the principal types
of steam motive power of the day. But the ones
that gave us children the greatest pleasure were the
marine engines of the little steam-ships that were
also built in the workshop. We had two ponds,
one of about four acres, and great was our delight
to see the little steamers careering about in large

circles in its middle waters, and puffing away merrily just like real live ships.

In the village near us was a large smithy, and attached to it a small iron foundry. Here were made the castings for the various portions of the little engines, the wooden patterns being made at home; then the castings, coming rough from the foundry, were worked up ready for fitting. Often some of us would go and watch the tapping of the molten metal, and well do I remember the feeling of mixed fear and delight when the white-hot stream came rushing out into the two-handled cauldron, that was quickly carried away by two men, who poured the terrible fluid into the black sand moulds. This was for the heavier castings wanted in the smith's business; those for my father were of course very small, and mostly of brass and gun-metal.

I remember one day at the foundry, when I was old enough to understand a joke—some of my father's were worth remembering—Smith (his name was Smith as well as his trade) had been telling him with some pride about a rather complicated set of castings he had lately turned out. My father, with the jolly twinkle that I used to like to see in his face, said : "Do you think you could cast a horoscope ? " Smith evidently did not know what a horoscope was, but being unwilling to make any confession of incompetence, he gave the guarded answer : " I think I could, sir, if you would provide me with a proper pattern." My father thought that in this encounter the honours of war remained with Smith.

One of three streams that flowed through the property had a good fall, and this was soon made use of to work a waterwheel and pump, to force up water for the house-supply; indeed, I do not know which my father liked best, playing with water in every shape— he was also a good practical sailor—or experimenting with electricity. The days I am thinking of were five-and-forty years ago, when the science was then comparatively in its babyhood, and I have often thought how unbounded would have been his interest in its immense later growth, for his eager mind and strong intelligence were always on the bright lookout for every new development of practical science.

However, such as electrical knowledge was in those days, he followed it closely, making fresh sets of apparatus as improved methods came into use. I remember how the earlier electrical generators were large glass barrel-shaped things, mounted horizontally, and scraped, as they were turned by a handle at the end, by a flap of black silk coated with a mercurial amalgam. Then there came a better machine in the form of a thick glass disc, but how the friction was obtained I now forget. My small fingers were often called in for the preparing of some of the humbler appliances; for pasting zigzags of tinfoil upon sheets of glass, and painting sundry portions with the non-conducting sealing-wax varnish. Indeed, had I been

asked at the age of ten, " What is electricity ? " I think
I should have answered, " It is glass things and tinfoil,
and red paint and little sparks."

Electricity was a winter game, and others were
magic lantern and fireworks, all from the home workshop. I suppose the element of uncertainty always
enters into the results of amateur pyrotechny; but
then the audience is not critical, and if in a shower
of rockets some are eagerly restive, and others show
a dilatory sulkiness that hinders the intended simul-
taneity of the display, why nobody much minds, and
there were positive shrieks of applause when a patriotic
set-piece, reserved for the end, unfortunately placed
wrong side before, but lighted at what should have
been the right end, read " neeuQ eht evas doG " !

Then there was the little model theatre, an exact
copy of Drury Lane in its old days. The opening of
the proscenium was about two feet long by eighteen
inches high. The proscenium and boxes adjoining it
were exactly to scale, and decorated as in the theatre.
It was originally used by Clarkson Stanfield to test
the effect of scenery; I have some of his little scenes
now. The stage must have been nearly six feet deep,
and the mechanical arrangements both above and
below were all complete. It was worked from the two
sides, which were open, and when we had a perform-
ance a screen on each side hid the operators. My
father got up little processions; the Duke of Wel-
lington's funeral was one of them, and later there

were moving panoramas, of which the most successful was a journey in the Arctic regions, of which subject the chief artist was a friend who had lately taken part in one of the Franklin search expeditions.

So it was that the workshop was a kind of heaven of varied delights after the fixed restraints of the schoolroom hours, and indeed its many lessons were by no means an unworthy part of a child's education, for an early acquaintance with tools and materials and mechanism is a valuable possession in any one's life, making clear and therefore interesting so many matters that would otherwise be passed by unknown and unnoticed. And there is a distinct comfort in having a certain familiarity with the parts of an engine and their names and uses, so that one thinks with as little confusion and ambiguity of furnace and boiler, of cylinder, crank, and piston, as of the head, arms, and legs that belong to a body.

And so in later years none of the lessons of the workshop have been lost; indeed everything there learnt has been helpful both to direct practice and as a stepping-stone to further experience. The mere fact of having got over the early awkwardness of using a tool is a considerable gain; an awkwardness whose degree a right-handed worker can hardly appreciate till he takes the tool in the left hand; or let any handy needlewoman try how it feels to work with needle and thimble in the left. And as I think that a shred of my father's mantle may have fallen upon his daughter, in that I have always taken much pleasure in working and seeing things grow under my hand, so I feel that the mechanical part has come much easier because of the ever-busy workshop of the old home. And though I have never had occasion to make an engine, or fireworks, or scientific apparatus, yet the same teaching applies to the manual part of every handicraft, and of some of the fine arts. And as I have had to do with the fitting-up and decorating of houses and the arrangement of gardens, so I have thought it a needful part of the business to have some practical understanding of all the means and methods, and I have never missed an opportunity of learning from good workmen, especially when I have passed a winter or some months in any one foreign place. The most consecutive of these slight apprenticeships was to a carver and gilder in Rome. An Italian who has " carver and gilder " over his shop really does carve and gild. The kindly *padrone* put me through a piece of work from beginning to end. First, the carving of the frame, then the successive coats of size and whitening, and the use of certain steel tools that complete the shaping of the forms and give the delicate finish. Then the coats of clear-size and bole of two kinds, and the floating on of the gold-leaf. For the work was water-gilding, a method far more complete and elaborate than oil-gilding, in that it admits of the valuable distinction of the bright and dull surfaces, each having its distinctive preparation.

My master was an artist in his way, and of
necessity; for the drawing of the designs, sometimes
special to suit some picture or set of room decorations,
and the free modelling of form in the plaster preparation, had need be the work of an artist-craftsman.
And he taught me to know which are the parts to be
burnished, for there are regular rules and reasons for
this, pointing it out on several frames and then
bidding me show him on others, to see that the lesson
was rightly learnt. And now, when in French or
English or other work I see these rules ignored, and
the wrong portions burnished, it always gives a false
look to the work, for all such well-founded traditions
should be carefully preserved. The one in question
runs through all the best Italian decorative work, and
surely no school of ornament ever attained to a height
so satisfying to the beauty-loving eye as did that of
those Italian decorators whose work was so closely
bound up with that of the noble painters of the school
of Venice.

I would always rather have an Italian as an in-
structor in a handicraft. He is so kindly and humanly
helpful. English workmen in general (though I have
met with some delightful exceptions) seem to have an
idea that the amateur's practice may come into competition with their trade. Those who show this spirit
can hardly know how hugely the compliment—evident
though not intended—flatters the vanity of the amateur. But though, for instance, I can use many tools

"All the hardy Heaths are happy in poor, sandy soil ... There are so many
beautiful kinds that it is hard to resist getting a larger number of varieties than
look well together. Our own heathy wastes show a good example of how two, or
at most three, suit each other's company ... I should always plant them in the
long drifts that seems to me by far the most natural and pictorial way of placing
most plants."

in a rudimentary sort of way, if I have any piece of
plain carpenter's work to do, other than the roughest
trifle, I take it to a carpenter, because, though it is
worth my while to have a general knowledge of how a
thing is done, it is not the least worth my while, indeed
it would be an absurd waste of time, to put it myself
into practice. But the same class of operation that
the skilled workman performs in doing any job of
plain work may be applied to some piece of decoration
that I wish to design and carry out, and that the carpenter cannot possibly do ; because, though every detail
of manipulation he could do better than I, yet I, having
a certain degree of training in the fine arts and he
having none, he cannot, as it were, make the tool
speak the same language.

In many cases the result required of the trained
workman is absolutely destructive of good effect. As
one example, I think of the finishing of the large mass
of silversmith's work, such as in all but the very best
houses, is the only thing presented to the public. In
nearly every case the brilliant polish of the burnisher,
and the white frosting given by the acid bath, are so
much overdone, that no portion of the piece shows the
true quality of a pure silver surface.

But the cause that is most certainly destructive to
artistic value is the passing of the piece through many
hands, so that the finished article is not any one man's
work, but only the lifeless product of the many depart-
ments of a factory. This, in addition to a low standard

of design, is no doubt the chief cause of the poor quality of decorative value in the mass of jewellery and plate and the many so-called ornamental objects that are seen in shop windows. On the other hand, the work of the simplest Oriental jeweller has that precious quality of rightness of purpose and distinct human interest. It bears on its face the evidence of the one man's clear intention; it tells its story as the work of a man's hand and not that of a machine, for he has beaten somewhat of his own soul and brain into the simply-wrought object of gold or silver. For none of those mighty agencies of modern times, of steam machinery, of business calculation, of backing by money, can possibly stand in the place of that divine combination of artist and craftsman that alone can as surely bring forth the good work, as the union of soul and body must go to the making of the most perfect living being.

Then there is a lovable quality about the actual tools. One feels so kindly to the thing that enables the hand to obey the brain. Moreover, one feels a good deal of respect for it; without it brain and hand would be helpless. When the knife that has been in one's hand or one's pocket for years has its blade so much worn by constant sharpening that it can no longer be used, with what true regret does one put it aside, and how long it is before one can really make friends with the new one! I do not think any work-man really likes a new tool. There is always some

feeling about it as if something strange and unfamiliar
and uncongenial, somewhat of the feeling that David
had about Saul's armour.   What an awkward thing a
new spade is, how long and heavy and rough of handle!
And then how amiable it becomes when it is half
worn, when the square corners that made the thrust
so hard are ground away, when the whole blade has
grown shorter, when the handle has gained that polish,
the best polish of all, that comes of long hand-friction.
No carpenter likes a new plane; no house-painter likes
a new brush.   It is the same with tools as with clothes;
the familiar ease can only come of use and better
acquaintance.   I suppose no horse likes a new collar;
1 am quite sure I do not like new boots!

Some years ago I knew a young carpenter who was
dying of consumption.   I can never forget how he
spoke of his tools.   He had wife and children and a
happy home, but when he spoke of what he knew was
before him, it was the inanimate companions of his
working hours that seemed most to bind him to his
waning life.   I remember his actual words: "It's not
that I am afraid to die, but it's when I think of my
tools I feel as if I couldn't bear to go."   And it was
only when he came to the word "tools" that his voice
broke and his eyes filled with tears.

Some of the tools that are the most precious are
those that one has to make oneself.   Chasing tools, for
instance.   For though some chasing tools may be bought,
yet in working out delicate ornaments in gold and silver

there is sure to arise some need for a special tool, and unless one has the luck to buy some good workman's old tools there is nothing for it but to make them. The more important tool shops sell blank lengths of good steel. The chaser buys these, and first shapes the tool and then hardens and tempers it. Tempering requires a good deal of practice. Chisels, gouges, and all tools for wood except saws are hard, and those for working metal necessarily soft, except files, which are very hard. But files are made of good steel, and when they are worn out are useful to " let down " and make into soft tools such as cold chisels. Some of the most delicate tools of the file tribe that are used in getting up small castings in gold and silver are only to be had in Paris; their tiny teeth are hardly to be seen with the naked eye.

The workshop has a large range of drawers occupying the greater space of one wall. Here are stores of materials; woods for inlay: box, ebony, lignum-vitæ, satinwood, and others; sheets of horn, ivory, bone, and tortoiseshell, slips of mother-o'-pearl and haliotus shell, and all the many materials and appliances wanted for various kinds of decorative work; modelling wax and tools, hard wax mixtures of various colours for rubbing into subjects engraved on wood, bone, and ivory; collections of ornamental hinges, keys, handles, and various small fittings, both ancient and modern, frequently coming into use; drawings, patterns, and stencils; patterns and small pieces of various fabrics for reference in work of house decoration; several

drawers full of patterns for colour, and odds and ends
of material too many to enumerate. Then there is a
carpenter's bench with the usual wood screw, and at
one end an engineer's vice, a tool chest, nests of drawers
for nails, screws, and such small tackle, and a tall cupboard with many shelves holding handy long-shaped
boxes like long drawers, one for bradawls, one for
files, one for soldering gear, and many others for suchlike subdivisions. A shelf runs all round the workshop walls about eighteen inches below the ceiling,
except where windows come, or where tall cupboards
run up the whole height. On it is arranged a collection of pottery, gathered out of many lands; thick-
handled jugs and pitchers of southern France, large
and bold and one may almost say luscious of form,
and of rich though not gaudy colouring of green
or orange glaze. Then there are several pieces of
black ware from Spain, and from Spain also jugs
and large dishes of a dull blue on dull white, a quiet
colouring of excellent harmony. Swiss earthenware
buff-glazed; short upright jugs striped and spotted
in many colourings; soup-tureens and dishes decorated
with the heraldic bears of Berne. Turkish and Arab
pottery, mostly unglazed, and some pieces of Khabyle
ware, curious because they are not formed on a wheel,
but are laboriously built up by hand. One large
piece is shaped much like a Roman amphora; all are
painted with buff and dull red and stripings of dull
black. Then there are Italian wine-jugs inscribed

with "*Bevi molto*," or some such encouraging legend;
tall hand-lamps of ancient pattern with double handles,
and on the top the little pool for oil, with one or more
lips for wicks.   Here and there an old majolica drug-
pot; some decorated with a free arabesque only, but
most with the addition of the arms of the family
to whose private pharmacy they once belonged, also
the name of the drug or preparation; all painted with
the most delightful freedom and the truest decorative
feeling both for form and colour.

The illustrations show a few pieces of embossed
and chased work in silver, inlay, and embroidery.   A
necklace of blue Egyptian mummy-beads is shown in
the upper picture, because the stringing of the beads
was quite one of the most fidgety and difficult pieces
of work I ever undertook; the only thing about it
the workshop actually made was the heavy little gold
beads that show three together at the upper angles
of the squares.   The black stand holding a silver bowl
is also one of the usual Oriental ones, not made at
home.

The small black figure in the same picture is
PIGOT, the tutelary divinity of the workshop.   "By
the eyes of Pigot" is the most solemn and binding
asseveration that can be uttered within its walls.
Indeed it was from hearing this form of words used
frequently by a friend that the idea of the personality
of Pigot arose in my mind, and that his form took
shape.   His eyes, bland, passionless, mildly benevolent,

SOME PRODUCTS OF THE WORKSHOP

but capable of flashes of scornful indignation when
bad work is done or the glue-pot boils over, are of
mother-o'-pearl; his spotless waistcoat (he has a scut
to match) is of ermine. His necklace is of coral beads
and little pink cowries; its middle ornament of silver,
suggesting the form of a hand. All the joys and
sorrows of the workshop are known to him; his mild
eyes beam in glad sympathy with the elation of success,
and smile a kindly encouragement to weariness or the
dejection of failure. All my best friends know Pigot,
and never fail, on entering the workshop, to offer him
a respectful salutation.

CHAPTER XII

THE KINSHIP OF COMMON TOOLS

WHAT a history they have—our common every-day
tools! The oldest and simplest I always think of as
Anglo-Saxon tools—axe, adze, wedge, hammer, anvil.
their names barely changed for a thousand years. No
doubt many an old English house before the Conquest
was built with axe and wedge alone, or perhaps with
the addition of some simple kind of auger to make
the holes for the pins. For the axe will fell the tree,
and with the wedge will rend it into quarters, and
then into rough planks; and smaller trees, roughly
squared, will serve for the framing and for rafters.
The axe will also make the pins that hold the framing
together, and the back of it will drive them.

Saws and chisels must have come to us from
France, with those fine old building monks, for their
names are French; and planes too, or some of the
ways of using them, for the French for plane, *rabot*,
remains with us in the term "rabbeting," just as our
clout nail is their *clou* and our vice their *visse* (a screw).

Any one who has been accustomed to the use of
many sorts of tools can hardly fail to notice a kind
of relationship between them; what one may call the

comparative anatomy of implements, the most important of them being distinct evolutions from primary
types. I suppose that the earliest tool is the hammer,
and that next would come the axe. The axe grows
naturally out of the hammer; it is a hammer with
a cutting blade, and the two of them are evidently
the ancestors of the whole range of implements of
the pick and mattock class. Nearly related is the
hoe, and from the hoe comes the spade. Intermediate
between these is the powerful cultivating tool that
takes the place of the spade in many foreign countries,
and I believe round the whole of the Mediterranean
region. It is the short-handled hoe with the large,
slightly curved, spade-like blade, used like a mattock.
The only tool that in England is at all its equivalent
is the "beck," or Canterbury hoe, but this, instead of
having the undivided blade, has three flat prongs.
The foreign tool is easier to use in the hard, dry earth
of southern Europe, as it comes down and cleaves the
ground with a heavy mattock stroke, whereas the
spade goes in with a less powerful thrust, by the
worker throwing his weight on it by his foot on its
shoulder. It is interesting to note that the French
shape of tool in our country should take its name
from Canterbury, a place that has always had a large
French population.

Another tool-link with France is the Cornish
shovel, the *pelle* of France and Italy, a long-handled
shovel with ace-of-spades-shaped blade, only used in

England, as far as I am aware, in the extreme south-west; the implement lingering as if in company with the racial relationship. We have the same word in the baker's peel, the long-handled wooden shovel used for taking the hot loaves from the oven. As this word is still in general use, it points to a wider use in former days of the foreign-shaped tool that, except in the one remote county, has given way to the short-handled shovel with wider blade.

Then the hammer-axe family branches into all the smaller tools of the chopper class: hatchet, hand-bill, and butcher's cleaver, and from these come the reaping-hook or fag-hook, and the scythe. But the stroke of these harvesting tools is much lighter, for whereas the choppers are used with a hammer stroke, that of the fag-hook, and still more that of the scythe, have a light swing in it that seems to be allied to that of the axe, and perhaps has some relation to light strokes of sword and cutlass; but as I am unacquainted with the use of these weapons, in their case I can only surmise. My impression is that the sword is used with a rather tighter grasp, whereas in many tools the tight grasp makes the stroke in-effective. I sometimes see a woman with a hammer held tight and short, making stiff and feeble dabs at a tin-tack; but then, of course, the right knack can only come by practice. What a joy it is, after much trying, to catch the trick of a tool! When it is known, its exercise becomes quite unconscious, and could scarcely be described; just as in riding, for instance, any one not accustomed to teach, could hardly say how the horse is made to do certain things. I could not say myself; I could only say I wish him to do it and he does it.

The stroke of axe and scythe have much in common; in both the tool is swung far back to give it the chance of gathering the greatest amount of momentum; in both the tall man with long arms has the advantage; in both he throws his strength at exactly the right point into the tool, relaxing his hold to a slight guidance at precisely the right moment. In both the whole man is in strenuous action, man and tool one living thing. The English scythe is much longer than the continental tool, and has a slower, longer, lighter stroke; the foreign one has a quick, short cut. In some foreign countries the scythe is not whetted with a stone, but the blade is drawn out to a keen cutting edge by being lightly hammered on a rounded stone, just as the blacksmith at home draws out the blunted points and edges of pick and mattock.

A sight worth seeing is the felling of a tree by a man who is a thorough master of his axe; full of instruction in the use of a noble tool, of interesting incident, and of pictorial value; the movements, though of full action, having a certain deliberation that stops short of violence. And it is good to see how he will make the tree fall exactly where he wishes. But

a mower at work is a still better picture, for not only
are the movements of the labourer full of vigorous
grace and beauty, but so are also the subtly-curving
lines of the scythe and sneathe; while the splendid
skill of the strong young man, often at work throughout the long daylight of middle June, makes light the
lengthy hours of arduous toil.

The action in another department of farm work,
even though it be a digression in a chapter on tools,
cannot be overlooked. It is that of the sower. His
work is of still more ancient origin, and is even more
rhythmical, and carries with it in a yet higher degree
the sentiment of poetry of action. For all tool he has
the seedlip of bent wood, the vessel that holds the seed.
In older days, and as it seems to me more conveniently,
the seed was held in a rough apron. Any one who has
sown a field of grain, and has some feeling for the
power of ordered motion, cannot fail to be struck by a
kind of lulling sense caused by the repeated movement.
The round sweep of the arm comes with the advance
and planting of the left foot, the right going forward
while the handful of grain is being gathered and the
arm thrown out ready for the new cast. And though
it is no light work to tramp over many acres of the
new-turned furrows, yet the power of rhythm carries
one along, and it is only at the end, when the task is
done, that the tired body calls for rest.

To come to indoor tools, the chisel may be considered as the sub-head of a family whose ancestor

was the axe.   Its function is to pare, to chop, driven by the mallet, and to rend.   Its rending action is akin to that of the coarser wedge driven by the heavy two-handed mallet called the bittle.   A plane is merely a chisel so set in a wooden block as to take a thin slice of wood, whose thickness can be regulated at will. A bradawl, is a small chisel used without mallet with a wriggling motion; gimlets, augers, and centre-bits are revolving chisels, the two former having screw action.

Saw, rasp, and file are nearly the same thing.   A thin file, with teeth on its edge only, becomes a saw, while a saw with teeth on the flat as well as the edge is a rasp.

CHAPTER XIII

CUT FLOWERS

WHEN cut flowers are to be sent a journey, it is a mistake to collect them in the early morning, and pack and send them off at once. This way is often recommended, but no one would follow it and do it on a large scale if the better way were known. The only flowers for which such treatment is suitable are Roses and Violets, and even those should be put in water for an hour or two before their journey. The better plan is to collect the flowers the afternoon or even the morning before they are to go; to take them to a handy bench in a cool shed, look them carefully over, bunch them in sorts, and then stand them deep in pails of water. I use the common galvanised pails, and the small baths of the same kind for flowers with shorter stalks. As the smaller bunches would tumble about in the baths if they were not full, I stand in them three garden pots, which make a convenient support. In a dozen pails and a dozen baths a large quantity of bunched flowers can be closely placed, to drink their fill till packing time arrives. Next morning, when they are packed, they are fresh and stiff and in the best possible state for travelling. I make an exception in the case of Roses

179

and Violets whenever it is possible, because, excepting
Tea Roses, they last in a good state a shorter time than
most flowers. That is why in a London shop a good
bunch of Roses is never cheap, and it is also why un-
scrupulous dealers have been known to doctor stale
Violets with an artificial essence when their natural
sweetness is gone, and would soon be followed by the
very unpleasant evidence of the earlier stages of decay.
I should say that the very best way of packing Roses
and Violets is to stand them in water for two
hours after being cut and bunched, and to pack
them in tins lined with any fresh leaves—Rhubarb,
Cabbage, Lettuce, Spinach, Dock, or any leaves that
are large and cool and succulent. There is a
handsome Dock that I grow for this and other
like purposes as well as for its merit as a plant of
fine foliage; the Monks' Rhubarb (*Rumex alpinus*).
The leaves are large and tough and pliable; they
may be rolled up into a ball in the hand without
being crushed; they will tuck and fold most kindly
into spaces and crevices in one's flower package, and
no leaf is so useful for wrapping round a bundle of
seedlings. I grow it in plenty near the packing-shed,
so that a handy leaf is always at hand.

Cut flowers, whether for home use or for preparing
to go away, should never lie about before being put
into water. Any one will see at once when it is
pointed out, though many do not happen to think of
it, that as the flower in water draws in the moisture

chiefly at the cut end of the stalk, it is most important to keep that cut end in the clearest touch with the water. If it is left lying about for some time the cut dries up, and the water, if it reaches the flower at all by this end, reaches it only in such a way as liquid matter passes through a drain that is much clogged and nearly stopped. The surface of the stalk of most plants has a certain degree of feeble drinking power, but if the flower is to be given the best chance of enduring, the cut end must be a free inlet.

Therefore, on receiving flowers after a journey, every stalk should be cut afresh, and cut only the instant before being placed in the water. When flowers arrive from the South of France or from any far distance, the stalks should be prepared with a long slanting cut, or be slit up in order to expose a larger surface to the water, and they should be plunged deep in the water, right up to the flower itself, and left all night. If the water is warm, so much the better. Even for an ordinary journey, many things must have such a deep bath, or even total immersion. Leaves of Artichoke, so grand in large decorations with long-stalked Oriental Poppy, or the taller of the Flag-leaved Irises, such as *Pallida dalmatica*, are plunged over-night in the garden tank.

Flowers that have milky juice, such as Oriental and other Poppies, Stephanotis, and Physianthus, want special care. I have often been told that you cannot make these live in water, and unless treated with

simple common-sense you certainly can not. These
flowers and some others have a fast-flowing milky juice
that dries quickly and hardens over the cut as if it had
been purposely sealed with a waterproof coating of
india-rubber.   Therefore, when I bunch up Oriental
Poppies, the moment before the bunch is put into its
deep pail, the ends are cut afresh, and the stalks are
also slit up two or three inches, and as the juice flows
out they are plunged into the water, which washes it
away.

Lent Hellebores, whose white and dusky red flowers
are so precious in March and early April, live excel-
lently in water if their stalks are freshly cut and slit
up rather high.   If this is not done they fade at once.
I had two letters one day in the end of March by the
same post—one from a flower customer in London
asking me not to send any more Lent Hellebores, as
they would not live ; the other from a friend to whom
I had sent some ten days before with instructions how
to keep them.   This letter said that they were still
perfectly fresh, and that she saw no reason why they
should not go on for a fortnight.   And yet I always
send a memorandum with the London flowers if anything goes that needs special care ; but I suppose that
the many distractions of my always honoured but now
rather carefully avoided birthplace stand in the way
of the giving of attention to such small matters.   Still
it may be that such a flower as this, which, by the
need of special care, shows its unwillingness to be

parted from its parent plant, may be more impatient than some others of the artificial heating and general atmospheric conditions of a London drawing-room.

Flowers of trees and shrubs and everything hard-wooded, such as Lilacs, Guelder-Roses, Spiræas, and Cluster-Roses, should always have the cut end so treated as to enable it to take up the water more readily. This is best done by slitting up the stem for some distance, or by the easier though rather less effective means of slicing one side, or tearing up a ribbon of the bark for an inch or two, but not removing it. I have done the same thing by crushing and opening the fibres of a woody stalk by hammering the last two inches on an anvil. I do not venture to suggest this method of treatment for general adoption, because I know that a smith's anvil is not a usual item in the equipment of a London house, but mention it because it is a further illustration of the principle.

When it comes to the actual packing, it should be remembered that it must be done as tightly as possible—the firmer the better, only just short of actual crushing. If flowers are at all loose, the joggling and vibration rub and abrade and distress and fatigue the flowers far more than would a well-packed journey of twice the length. "Pack tight and keep out the air" is the safest rule. Tin boxes are the best of all, and such boxes fitted with trays are much used in private places for sending flowers to London, but their costliness unfits them for business purposes. Here we use the usual florist's wooden boxes with loose lids. A sheet of newspaper is spread on the bottom; two sheets of thin paper laid out at the ends protect the flowers from contact with the rough surface of the inside of the box, and fold over the top of the flowers, or if the box is smaller, one sheet does the same work. These papers also help to keep out the air. The loose top is placed on, and the box is tied with one girth of Manilla cord which is fastened to it.

Many are the handy ways of packing and sending single flowers by post for comparison or reference or other purpose. I find nothing more convenient than corrugated paper, and though I have quantities of all sorts of little boxes in store I much oftener use the ribbed paper, it is so easy to cut a piece to exactly fit the small parcel; a little damp moss at the stalk end and a leaf of Monk's Rhubarb to envelop the whole, a little dry moss or crumpled paper near the flower to make the package the same thickness at both ends, then the ribbed paper rolled round and a wrapping of paper outside. A flower can be packed in this way with dry and damp moss and leaf and outside wrapper, even without the corrugated paper, though the contents are much safer with it. The one thing I always avoid in packing flowers is the use of cotton-wool; nothing absorbs moisture so quickly. Gardeners have it at hand for packing peaches, and

they also use it mercilessly in packing Orchids and
Gardenias, Stephanotis and Camellias. It is much
better in the case of these flowers to have some of the
tin trays perforated with ranges of holes, and with
twine and a packing-needle to sew down the flowers
firmly to the bottom of the tray so that they cannot
move.

When garden flowers are scarce it is often desirable to bring home a bunch of wild flowers, but
many seem unwilling to live in water. I have found
that if the whole plant is pulled up by the root and
a part of the root-stalk retained, it will live perfectly.
The brilliant field Poppies do well like this, and
some of the delicate umbelliferous plants that are
so charming in bouquets of field flowers. Primroses
are no trouble; indeed I think the delicious wild
Primrose must have some special quality of kindly
sympathy with humanity, and particularly with children, and that it really likes to be gathered and
brought into our houses; for not only does it live
well after being picked and carried home, but even
bunches, long held tight in hot little hands, will
flourish when released and put in water. But Wood
Anemones protest against being picked, and come
home limp and closed and looking very unhappy;
all the same they will recover if they have a complete
bath for an hour or two, and all the quicker if they
are pulled up with a bit of root. The most difficult
to keep alive are some of the water plants, Horse-tail

(*Equisetum*) and the tall Reed (*Arundo Phragmites*), but here again a bit of the base is a help as well as the slitting of the stems. In the case of Bamboos, after years of regret that I could not use them in decoration I have found out a way of making them live in water. It is by having some tall jar deep enough to immerse at least three joints, and by cutting notches in the upper part of each internode that will be under water so that the water flows in and fills each length. During the long and harmful drought of the late season, one of my clumps of Bamboo on a raised bank was showing signs of great distress for want of water. This seemed to be a good time for testing this process, so before watering the whole clump I cut a few of its tall sprays, notched them, and put them in water. Looking at them an hour later I had the satisfaction of seeing that the drooping leaves, that were brought in looking withered, pale, and shrivelled, had risen and flattened out and regained their healthy colour. The tall water Reeds do well in the same way, and such treatment may be generally advised as suitable for the Eulalias or any of the giant grasses or other plants that have jointed, hollow stems.

In room decoration with flowers, the old tight pudding-like arrangement of many flowers crammed together is happily no longer seen, and it is only in exceptional cases that the mistress of a house or her grown-up daughters have not cultivated their taste

in some measure in the better ways of arranging them
freely, with long stalks and plenty of foliage.

One can hardly go wrong if a bunch of any one
kind of flower is cut with long stalks and plenty of its
own leafage, and especially if it is cut without carrying
a basket. I cannot explain why it is, but have always
observed that no intentional arrangement of flowers in
the ordinary way gives an effect so good as that of a
bunch held easily in the hand as flower by flower is
cut, and put in water without fresh arrangement. The
only glimmer of a reason I can see for it is that they
are cut of uneven lengths, and that the natural way of
carrying them in the hand is with the stalks fairly
even, and that this gives just that freedom of top outline that is so much to be desired. In the case of
small flowers, such as Lily-of-the-Valley and Violets,
that are picked into a basket and afterwards tied in
bunches, I find the uneven lengths of the stalks the
greatest help in preventing unsightly stiffness. One
has only to compare a bunch of long-stalked Czar
Violets, with the ends of the differently-lengthed stems
kept even, and a few leaves included in the bulk of the
flowers, with a shop bunch of the usual pattern, the
flowers tight and level, surrounded by a stiff collar
of leaves, to see the merit of the free arrangement.
When I do them for my own use, I take both flowers
and leaves in the hand in this free way, and put them
lightly, without tying, in one of those deep and heavy
old cut-glass finger-bowls, such as were used on their

grandly-polished mahogany dinner-tables by our great-grandfathers : first standing inside the glass a smaller one, rather taller, to raise the middle blooms a little higher.

In using bowls or anything that is broad, or in any way shallow in comparison with its width, it is well to make use of some of the many devices for helping to support the flowers. In a wide bowl one can arrange a smaller bowl inside, or any of the many articles of the jug tribe, gallipot or stoneware salt jar. Salt jars are capital, because they are heavy and rather tall. The folded strip of sheet-lead at the bottom, whose use is now generally understood, and of which a number should be kept handy, will make it all the heavier ; the better to counteract the inclination of a tallish spray to topple, and also to serve its intended purpose of catching and holding the end of the stalk. I have sometimes done a large china bowl of Roses by putting common flower-pots one inside the other, raising the inner and smaller ones by means of clean crocks of broken pots ; but the best way of all for a porcelain bowl that is in frequent use, is to have a slight wire frame made to fit loosely inside, with two floors of galvanised wire netting, the lower one half an inch from the bottom of the bowl, and the upper half an inch below the top. This one should be shaped highest in the centre like an inverted saucer. Any ironmonger or tinsmith, or country blacksmith, would make such a " liner," and also prepare the sheet lead strips 1½ or

1¼ inch wide, and of different lengths according to the
sizes of the jars they are to be used in. They are
folded together S-wise and rather closely so as to leave
continuous pairs of loops. Another handy device is
to have pieces of galvanised wire netting of about a
¾-inch mesh, loosely crumpled into a vague ball-shape,
such as will fill the lower half of the receptacle. The
same kind of support may be given by twigs of Holly
or Box, or of any close and stiffly-twigged shrub
such as White-thorn or Black-thorn. Where nothing
else was at hand I have used the dissected remnants
of a worn-out birch broom.

It is obvious that these ways of compelling the
flowers to stand up can only be used in non-transparent
vessels; none of them, except perhaps the green twigs,
can be used in glass. But though glass things are in
many ways the pleasantest and prettiest and cleanest to
put our home flowers in, and though there is a certain
satisfaction in seeing the stalks, and knowing that we
can all the more readily come to the rescue by seeing
the water becoming foul or low, yet in almost every
house there are cherished flower-holders of other
material than glass. Among those I have in constant
use are bowls and jars of the ever-beautiful porcelains
of China and Japan, English makes of Worcester and
of the delicate cream-white earthenware of Wedgwood,
old Italian majolica, glazed pottery from all Europe
and some of Asia and Africa, Indian brass lotahs and
large Dutch and Venetian pails and jugs and wine-

coolers of beaten copper. Some of the latter are more generally used for pot-plants, but when flowers are large and in plenty, as at the times of Tulip and Rhododendron and Peony, the most roomy things one has are none too large.

As in all matters of decoration, so also it should be borne in mind in the use of flowers indoors that one of the first and wholesomest laws is that of restraint and moderation. So great is the love of flowers nowadays, and so mischievous is the teaching of that hackneyed saying which holds that "you cannot have too much of a good thing," that people often fall into the error of having much too much of flowers and foliage in their rooms. There comes a point where the room becomes overloaded with flowers and greenery. During the last few years I have seen many a drawing-room where it appeared to be less a room than a thicket. Where a good mass of greenery is wanted in a house, it is best kept in the hall or some place near the entrance, and even in quite a large room, one very large arrangement of foliage and flower will probably be enough, though of pot-plants in suitable receptacles and of smaller things of carefully arranged and disposed cut flowers it may take a large number. But it must be borne in mind that it can be easily overdone. And a watchful eye must be kept on greenhouse and stove, and the gardener must come into friendly consultation as to the pot-plants that are brought in. Ferns

are always safe; the fresh green of well-grown pots
of Maidenhair is delightful in any room, and they
have a look of modest and well-dressed refinement
that is always charming. A good supply should be
at hand, so that each individual may only be kept
for a few days in a heated room, and may be returned
to the moister heat of the stove before the tender
fronds are damaged by the warm, dry air of the
room. *Pteris tremula* is one of the very best and
handsomest of indoor Ferns and rather less impatient
of dry air.

To come back to the cut flowers, it is important
to observe the way of growth of the flower in relation to the thing that is to hold it. The illustration
shows an attempt to carry out a simple arrangement
of boughs of Lilac in an old Italian jug of bluish-
white glazed earthenware. I tried to arrange the
stiff branches not only in good proportion to the
size and height of the jug, but also so that they
should shoot upwards in the way suggested by the
shallow flutings of its upper part; jug and flower being
also chosen to go together because of the tender
colour-harmony of the bluish glaze with the white
of the Lilac-bloom.

In the case of the spray of Rose-Bramble (*Rubus
rosæfolius*) shown on page 183, the far-leaning spray,
showing the natural grace of growth, needed some
weight to satisfy the eye in the matter of balance,
and the round black-glazed pot, of a black that

WHITE LILAC

is sometimes grey-green and sometimes brown-red, seemed not only to fulfil the physical need, but to be the exact colour-complement demanded by the delicate milk-white flower and pale soft leaves.

This kind of study and practice may seem to some to be an unnecessary complication of what many people may hold to be the very simple matter of putting flowers in water; it will come naturally to those who have had some training in the fine arts, and have therefore acquired some critical power. It may moreover in itself be reckoned as valuable training in a domain that closely borders upon their infinitely greater one. For it demands that close ob-servation, and cultivation of the power of comparison, followed by exercise of judgment, that, even though at first unconscious, becomes ripened by constant repetition. The trained eye accepts the grouping of certain forms; probably in its earlier stages of training some chance arrangements came well and were retained; they were seen to be good, though the operator could scarcely say why; but later, the grouping is formed with deliberate intention, and the result can be lucidly demonstrated.

The elaborate system of flower arrangement prac-tised by the Japanese shows firstly, and throughout, a recognition of beauty of line as the supreme law. It may be of one main line only, or of a grouping of several, but it is always there. It has become a fashion to attempt to imitate this system; and among

some successes at the hands of those who cannot be
content with anything short of "good drawing" there
are the many absurd failures of those to whom it
is nothing but sticking flowers and branches upright
in shallow vessels, and whose only reason for doing
it is because it is the fashion. Delightful and desirable as are the results of this kind of arrangement
in the best hands, I cannot think that it will ever
supersede, or even seriously compete with, the loose
and free ways of using our familiar garden flowers.
For one thing, to do it well, ample leisure and a quiet
mind are needed, as well as mechanical dexterity
and highly-trained eye, for it is like seriously composing a picture; and in our case one whole group
of motives that is absorbingly present to the mind
of the Japanese decorator is absent, namely, those
that have to do with traditional law and symbolism.
For, happily, we can pick a bunch of Primroses in
the wood and put it in water without having to consider whether we have done it in such a way as to
suggest a ship coming home or a matrimonial en-
gagement in contemplation. I do not say this in
any spirit of derision, for I gladly acknowledge how
much we may learn from the Japanese in the way
they insist on beauty of line; but, at the same time,
I cannot but rejoice that we are not hampered by
other considerations than those that lead us to combine and place our flowers so as to be beautiful in
themselves and fitting for our rooms.

The room itself must be considered; and though in most forms of decoration, both indoors and out, my own liking and what knowledge I may have gained lead me to prefer using colour in harmonies rather than in contrasts, in the case of cut flowers I find in practice that I use as many of the one as of the other.

If I may suggest a general rule, I should say, use warm colours (reds and yellows) in harmonies, and cold ones (blues and their allies) in contrasts. But one must be content to be able to suggest in the vaguest way only when writing about colour, except in the case of a flower or substance whose colour is constant, for except by such reference no tint can be accurately described. It is very easy to say pink, but pink covers a wide range, from warm ash-colour to pale salmon-red, and from the tint of a new-born mushroom to that of an ancient brick. One might prepare a range of at least thirty tints—and this number could easily be multiplied—all of which might be called pink; yet with regard to some room, or object, or flower of any one kind of red, only a few of these will be in friendly accordance, a good number will be in deadly discord, and the remainder more or less out of relation.

To give a few illustrations: if the walls and main furnishings of a room are blue, all pale yellow and warm-white and creamy-coloured flowers will do well, such as sulphur Hollyhocks and Iris flavescens, Evening

Of arranging flowers Gertrude Jekyll wrote: "It is important to observe the way of growth of the flower in relation to the thing that is to hold it ... This kind of study and practice may seem to some to be an unnecessary complication of what many people may hold to be the very simple matter of putting flowers in water ... The trained eye accepts the grouping of certain forms; probably in its earlier stages of training some chance arrangements came well and were retained; they were seen to be good, though the operator could scarcely say why; but later, the grouping is formed with deliberate intention, and the result can be lucidly demonstrated."

Primrose and shrubby Spiræas such as *S. ariæfolia*,
S. lindleyana and double Meadowsweet, and all pale
yellowish-green foliage, as that of Maize and *Funkia*.
If the room has walls of pale yellow or ivory-white,
the colour of the flowers would be reversed, and
one would use Delphiniums, pale and dark, avoiding
those of purplish colour; *Clematis Flammula*, and bowls
of Forget-me-not. In a room with warm-white walls
any colour of flowers does well, so long as they
are kept to one range of colouring at a time. I
do not say that colours may not be mixed, but it
is best and easiest to begin with restriction in their
number. In a white or neutral-coloured room, if a
mixture is desired, the colours would be best in the
simple mixtures as proposed in the case of flower
and room colour, as blue and pale yellow flowers, or
blue and warm-white with pale green foliage.

In a red room, other than a rosy red, scarlet and
yellow flowers have a fine effect—*Gladiolus*, *Tritoma*,
perennial Sunflowers, scarlet and yellow Dahlias; these
are also fine in a white-walled room. My house has
the walls of all rooms plainly lime-whited, giving a
white of delicately warm colour, and though at first
I thought I should feel quite free to use all kinds of
coloured flower-schemes in it, yet I find that the different
rooms have their distinct preferences. For instance,
the sitting-room, whose window curtains are of madder-
dyed cloth, and whose other furniture is mostly covered
with stuff of a dull orange colour, likes to have the

furniture colour repeated in its flowers, and is never so happily beflowered as with double orange Day-Lily or orange Herring-lilies (*Lilium croceum*), and with this it often insists on some bowls of purple flowers. This is where they show on the warm-white wall, away from the madder-dyed curtains, in combination with the cool grey-brown of the large oak beams and braces.

The aspect of a room will also have much to do with the colours of the flowers that look well in it; the same flower even, seen in a sun-lighted room of south aspect and in a northern one, the quality of whose lighting is largely affected by a blue sky, will appear to be of quite a different tone.

It should also be remembered how the colour of flowers is affected by artificial light. There are some forms of electric light of the colder qualities that show colours almost as in daylight, but under all other forms of artificial light it is safest to use white, red, and yellow flowers mainly. Flowers of full blues and violets become dull and colourless; in pale blues the purity is lost, while some reddish-purples show as a dull red. In all colourings of mauve and lilac the warm quality is increased, so that though purple flowers are best avoided for evening decoration, many kinds, such as the lighter and warmer-coloured of the Michaelmas Daisies, are very pretty and useful. Bright fresh greenery, such as the leaves of *Funkia grandiflora* and of forced Lily-of-the-Valley, are all the brighter under the

yellow light, and all reds and yellows are much
intensified.

As the summer advances, and larger things are
to be had, the flower arrangements grow bolder.
Tea-Roses and many of the free-growing kinds are
cut three to four feet long. The Eryngiums are
fine in a cut state, the bluish *E. oliverianum* grouping delightfully with long branches of the white
Everlasting Pea, while the still bolder and more
silvery *E. giganteum* not only lives long in water,
but is a handsome object if kept dry, lasting well
for several months, and losing but little of its form
and lustre.

In the earlier part of the year, unless there is
an old-established shrubbery to cut from, it is sometimes difficult to find good greenery to go with
flowers. In March I make a good deal of use of
the leaves of the wild Arum, so abundant in hedges,
pulling up the whole sheaf of leaves and preparing
it by standing it deep in water. It goes capitally
with Trumpet Daffodils. The later Daffodils look
well with leafy twigs of Birch, which comes just in
time to accompany them; and later still, in the end
of April and beginning of May, Poet's Narcissus and
Sweet-brier branches go happily together.

Many of the flowers of May and June—Lilac,
Guelder-Rose, Rhododendron, and Pæony — are well
furnished with their own greenery, and from then
onwards there is plenty to choose from. Still for

Eryngium and White Everlasting Pea

autumn I find it useful to have a line or patch of one of the maize-like Sorghums or Millets; the one I use is the *Sorgho à balais* of the French. If when half grown the main stem is cut out, it branches into a number of side shoots, good to group with Gladiolus, or to wreathe about with the white clusters of the late-blooming *Clematis flammula* of September and the still finer *C. paniculata* of October.

And with late autumn what a wealth of beautifully-coloured foliage there is to choose from, both in the garden and in the wood; of Vine and Virginia Creeper and Scarlet Oak; of yellowing Beech and ruddy Bramble and Guelder-Rose; the single Guelder-Rose grand with berry also. *Rosa lucida,* always one of the best of Roses for clumps and bushes in any shrubbery spaces, is brilliant in late autumn with the red and yellow of its foliage and the abundant clusters of its ripe scarlet fruit.

Even in middle winter one can make green foliage groups without flowers that are worthy room-ornaments, for there are always sprays of green Ivy to be found and fronds of Hart's-tongue and Polypody Ferns, and in woodland places where scrub Oak was cut down last winter the yearling shoots bear their large green leaves far into the next, giving us a handsome type of deciduous leafage otherwise not to be had. Sprays of Oak are of value also early in the year, for some bear small strongly waved leaves of a golden green in May and June, while for bowls of Tea-Roses

MIDWINTER—POLYPODY AND IVY

MIDSUMMER—CHINESE PEONIES

in late summer no leaf-accompaniment that I can think
of is better than the young summer shoots of Oak,
richly beautiful in their "subdued splendour" of
crimson and red and russet-bronze.

Some years ago, seeing that there was a want of
flower-glasses of simple shape that would hold plenty
of water and would be moderate in price, I made
some designs which were taken up by a large firm
in the glass and china trade, Messrs. James Green &
Nephew, 107 Queen Victoria Street. Their "Munstead" glasses made from these designs are already
widely known, but I am still so often asked for the
address that I give it here. They have a pattern
sheet that gives all particulars; the most useful shapes
are shown in the illustration opposite on page 255.

CHAPTER XIV

CONSERVATORIES

THE gardeners in private places often spoil their plants by overdoing the size. It is no doubt tempting to a man who is a good cultivator to push the cultivation on to its utmost possibility, but it is easy to go beyond the bounds of beauty, and to get a coarse look. The plants are in perfect health, but are fed up so that they have that over-fat look of prize beasts at a show. Besides Chrysanthemums, the plants that gardeners favour most in this way are Calceolarias of the show sorts, Cinerarias, and Begonias. Often, in conservatories and drawing-rooms, I think how pretty that plant would be if the flowers were only a little smaller; not that I ever think these Calceolarias and Cinerarias are good room plants; they have no natural grace or refinement, and except in the case of the clear blue and the white, the range of colouring of the Cinerarias is of a coarse and unpleasant character. *Begonia metallica* is one of my favourites among room plants. It makes a plant of fine size, and is full of the truest beauty and refinement, both of flower and leaf.

How seldom does one see a conservatory arranged

with good taste.   The usual thing is a crowded mass
of incongruous flowering plants; just anything that
happens to be in bloom in the plant-houses; and
they are arranged so as to bring the bloom all to
one even surface, sloping up from front to back.   It
looks as if the largest amount of material was used
in order to produce the least effect, for the quantity
of ill-assorted flowers brought together without design
is sure to prevent the full enjoyment of the beauty
of any.

   This is already generally understood in the case
of cut flowers for room decoration, where we no longer
see the old mixture of all sorts of flowers tightly
crammed together, but, on the contrary, simple
arrangements in good taste of fewer flowers; or more
often of one sort only at a time, with a suitable
quantity of good foliage.   One may often see this in
the drawing-room, while the old kind of muddle is
in full force in the adjoining conservatory; whereas
if the better system were also practised here, the
beauty of the place would be increased tenfold, while
the number of flowering plants required would be
reduced to at most a quarter.

   The first thing in a well-arranged conservatory
is to have plenty of handsome foliage.   Nothing can
surpass the utility of *Aspidistra*, and for massing, the
green is better than the variegated.   Aralias of different sizes should be fairly plentiful, and Arums
whether in flower or not.   *Funkia grandiflora*, potted

in early autumn, will be in grand foliage by February,
and no plant gives better green in the conservatory.
These and a few Ferns, of which *Pteris tremula* should
be one, should be in quantities large enough to make
some bold effects of good greenery, among which the
flowering plants should be introduced in groups of
a few pots of the same, or single pots, according to
the nature of the plant. No one who has ever seen
a conservatory arranged in this way, with due regard
to good colouring, will ever wish to go back to the
old muddled mixture.

I often think, when I go round the gardens of
some great place, and see evidence of the money
that is expended in structures and labour, in cultivation and maintenance, how all the best service
that the indoor plants might render is absolutely
wasted. It is like keeping sixty horses in a stable
with all the needful staff and equipment, and never
having them out for riding or driving. For though
there is a certain pleasure in going round greenhouse
and stove and Orchid and Fern houses, and seeing the
individual plants, it is after all only like going round
and seeing the horses in the stable; and though this
also is very pleasant, one expects something more
of the horses. So also I expect more of the plants;
and though a certain number are saddled and brought
round for dining-room table and drawing-room ornament, yet by far the larger number remain in their
stalls " eating their heads off," unless they are driven

into the conservatory to bite and kick each other in the usual huddled crowd.

I do not venture to say that a better use of indoor plants is never made; indeed I know that in the case of places where the owners are people of taste a much better state of things exists. But these bright exceptions are lamentably rare, and I do not think I am exaggerating when I estimate that out of every hundred collections of stove and green-house plants there are scarcely three in which any serious attempt is made to use them for the enjoyment of well-arranged beauty. And it is not fair to expect the ordinary gardener to be able to do it. The guiding motives of such arrangements (unless he be a man of exceptional gifts) are beyond his reach of apprehension, and he cannot be expected to have received the refined education of the highest order, which can alone form the foundation on which such motives are built.

I take pleasure in picturing to myself various forms of pleasant winter gardens; of places where there shall be no discordant note of obtrusive staging or gaudy tile or blue-white paint, or any ostentatious or unseemly elaboration; but where beautiful flowers and foliage should hold their own in undisputed possession. What groupings I would have of tropical Ferns and Orchids, overshadowed by great groups of Bananas, and how much better to give the needed shade by means of Bananas or tall Tree Ferns than by an artificial shading only. The artificial shading may be wanted as well, but the living leafage is more pictorially satisfactory as a means of representing the subdued light of a tropical forest.

And winter gardens so arranged as to give some such illusion during the five dull months of our northern climate are undoubtedly desirable, and for the best enjoyment of plants should be arranged in a free, informal manner.

There is another class of structure, such as the large Orangeries attached to old houses of the palatial class, that would demand more formal treatment, because the buildings themselves have a distinct architectural value that should be not only recognised but intentionally emphasised. These are nearly all on the same general plan, with one blank wall at the back and one main face pierced with large lights often with arched heads, and between them important pilasters that carry the cornice. And often this face was designed in relation to the adjoining parterre, for its original purpose was that it should be a place for storing the large boxes or tubs of tender trees, such as Oranges or Oleanders, that would stand out on the terraces in summer.

The modern greenhouse, on the other hand, is a thing so hopelessly ugly that I consider it should never intrude into dressed ground or be visible from it. Any attempt at so-called ornament, of turned finials or florid cast-iron ridges, only makes matters worse,

as these things are never well designed, and only
serve to draw attention to what is already sufficiently
unsightly. If it is already there, and cannot be
screened by plantation or any other device, the best
thing is to paint it some quiet colour such as what
painters call Portland-stone colour, made of brown and
black mixed with white-lead.

If I were designing a large range of glass
houses and could "have my head," I would lay it
out as a walled enclosure of say half an acre.
From outside, nothing would be seen but the high
wall or some suitable treatment of it. The houses
for show would range all round inside for a width
of some twenty-five feet; the inner space would be
for the growing or service houses. The southern
side of the glass-garden wall would be in connection
with the pleasure garden, and if the wish of the
owner was for a good piece of formal gardening,
the wall might well be treated as the back of a
cloistered loggia. On the northern face of the
enclosure outside would be the potting shed,
furnaces, &c. One would enter through the
middle of the cloistered wall into a space where
in winter would be placed the tubs of Orange,
Myrtle, Oleander, and white Datura that would
stand out of doors in summer. In shape and
area this might be a double square of fifty by
twenty-five feet. Opposite the entrance would be

a walled passage ten feet wide, with glass roof, passing right across the enclosed space from entrance to potting-sheds, and giving covered access to all the service houses. It would have a flagged walk, and borders against the walls for Camellias, Heliotrope, Myrtle, *Daphne indica, Carpenteria, Clematis indivisa,* the double white *Rubus roscæfolius,* and many another good thing that only wants winter protection. The glass lights of the roof should be taken off in summer.

To return to the entrance enclosure, there would be partitions right and left leading into large "temperate" spaces. Entering the one on the left there would be some main arrangement of noble foliage of Banana, Orange, Lemon, and white Datura, and of lesser growths of the dwarf Palm of the Mediterranean region, and Maidenhair and other Ferns. All these would be planted and growing in the ground; both main groups and ground-covering being so disposed that between and among the permanent plantings, pots of flowering things could be brought in and arranged in wide groupings.

The further enclosures would advance through an intermediate temperature to that of the "stove." The same principle of arrangement would run through all, of main groups of large foliage and of beautiful ground-work, both planted. In the warmer houses, and perhaps in a lesser degree in the temperate region, the wall would in places be the background of

an arrangement of rockwork for the better planting
of Ferns, and temporary placing of Orchids and other
plants on rocky shelves and niches hidden by the
growing greenery.

So many are the lovely kinds of tropical Orchids
that it would be difficult to make a small enough
selection, but it would include some of the noble
Cattleyas whose magnificent blooms show all that is
best in purple and lilac colourings; the best forms of
the free-flowering Cælogyne of tenderest white; the
splendid orange, yellow, and buff of Dendrobium;
some long wreaths of brown and yellow Odontoglossum,
leopard-spotted and tiger-striped; the tender white-
shaded rosiness of Lycaste; the thick ivory-white of
Angræcum, a flower of singular nobility, coming in
the deadest of the winter months; and the stately
Phaius, with its dignified upright bearing, large handsome leaves, and immense spikes of flower of white
and pink and rosy-brown.

In my tropical houses, as everywhere else, the aim
would be to have the most beautiful plants beautifully
arranged.   Nothing would be admitted merely because
it was curious or rare or costly.   There should be no
unbeautiful audacities like *Anthurium*, no evil little
curiosities such as *Stapelia*, no insignificant plants of
unworthy price, such as people crowd to look at at
shows because they are valued at a hundred guineas;
none of the usual commonplace unworthinesses, as
of houses full of the coarse nettle-like Coleus, most

of them of shocking colour; of hundreds of pots
of Calceolaria and Cineraria; no stove half full of
uninteresting *Achimenes*, a family of plants I confess
to disliking; without grace or beauty of form, in
colour either washy or distinctly displeasing, and
needing to be tied up to an infinity of small sticks.
Indeed, except for the red velvet leaf of *Gesnera
exoniensis*, sumptuous under lamp-light, and the fine
colour of one or two Tydæas, I am altogether shy of
gesneraceous plants.

But I would have ropes and swags of the scarlet
Passion-flower (*P. racemosa*), and plenty of that goodly
white-flowered company, *Stephanotis* and *Gardenia* and
Eucharis and *Pancratium*, and the glowing *Hibiscus
Rosa-sinensis*, and the great yellow *Allamanda*. And
with them the large-flowered Oriental Jasmines, and
quantities of fresh-coloured tender foliage of the
beautiful Ferns of the tropics. Here, as in every
other part of the garden, I would avoid the usual
weary inharmonious mixture; I would fight against
the mental slothfulness of easy heterogeneous
agglomeration, and steadfastly resist the common
and irritating jumble of all kinds of irreconcilable
forms of vegetation. Even of distinctly beautiful
plants there are nearly always too many sorts
brought together. Of such things as Croton and
Caladium and Begonia Rex, a dozen plants of one
kind of each will make a handsome group, and two
dozen a still better one, while twelve or twenty-four

all different, can only make a group of no merit
from a pictorial point of view.   And though I
advise this temperate use of plants as a general
principle, I do not presume to lay it down as a law.
For it is just in occasional or even frequent exceptions in the practice of such treatment that the
garden artist can best use his knowledge.   Though
nine plants out of ten may no doubt be best used
in liberal groupings, yet every now and then one
comes upon something that looks best as a single
object, and often in the large groups of one kind
of plant there comes a point where it is desirable
to make some slight variation; for though to make a
good effect there must be moderation and simplicity,
we do not want monotony.   In arranging a group
of say two dozen Caladiums, there may occur some
place where it is desirable to have two or three
whose leaves have some slight difference of colouring or variegation, and a few more may need to be
quite detached from the main group though still
in relation to it.   Some incident or circumstance
belonging to the environment may demand · the exceptional treatment; it is perceived almost unconsciously, the plants are duly placed, and the picture
comes right.

The service houses in the middle space would
grow good things in quantity for all the tempera-
tures, both of Ferns and other beautiful greenery,
and of flowering plants : Orchid, Gloxinia, Begonia,

Azalea indica, Pelargonium, Primula, Cyclamen, Streptocarpus, Hippeastrum, Vallota, Chrysanthemum, and Canna. Then all the best of the bulbs that force well: Tulip, Hyacinth, Narcissus, Nerine, Freesia, Lachenalia; and successions of Mignonette and Lily-of-the-Valley, and those of our hardy plants that will bear a little forcing like hardy Azalea and Solomon's Seal and Funkia. What a pleasure it would be to go to the service houses and choose the plants for the making of the pictures, gathering them together by sorts on a low trolley, where already one could see at a glance that the plants for each group would go well together for colour; and what a satisfaction it would be to be able to show the well-arranged plant-pictures, and how helpful to both employers and gardeners!

I have only attempted to give a very slight sketch of what might be done in an important range of such houses, but I think it desirable to get out of the beaten track not only in the way of arrangement but in choice of plants. How seldom, except in gardens specially given to their culture, does one see enough use made of the lovely and fragrant tropical Rhododendrons, or the delightful *Luculia gratissima*, or of the sweetness of *Boronia*, or noble climbers like *Beaumontia* and *Schubertia*, or gems of purest colouring like *Leschenaultia* ! Even old favourites get forgotten, for though quite easy to

grow in a cool greenhouse and even hardy near our southern coasts, how rarely do we meet with the lovely and fragrant *Mandevilla* !

Two sides of such a square enclosure as I have suggested would probably be enough for the arrangements of tender and tropical flowering plants, or rather a space equal to two sides, extending from one end of the transverse passage, along the inner side of the enclosing wall, till the further end of the covered way is reached. The opposite portion would comprise vineries, peach and fig houses, and any other kind of fruit culture under glass. In the case of the many smaller places where there are but few glass houses or even only one, the same enjoyable arrangements can be made if there be any space, even two square yards, that can be given exclusively to decoration. Some modest dwelling-houses have an enclosed glazed porch with side bays for plants, and an excellent plan it is. Many that have a good-sized built porch might have it arranged for flowers, by knocking through the side walls, leaving a small space of nine inches to a foot right and left to form piers, and turning a brick arch of half a circle, or of a segment of a larger circle, from pier to pier to support the upper part of the wall, and putting up outside such a glass structure as might best suit the space at disposal. Moreover, the brick arch and piers would have the distinct advantage of both acting as a frame to the flower-picture and of hiding a good deal of the upper part of the glazing, while the plants would have the full benefit of the light. If the porch was of fair height and the glass merely a lean-to, giving a space inside of only four or five feet wide by two or three deep, it would still accommodate enough plants to make a pretty show, and I know nothing about a house that offers so bright and kindly a welcome to a visitor.

Such a small space, even without a greenhouse in the background, could be easily dressed with a few pots of Aspidistra and some potted hardy Ferns as a groundwork; then a flowering plant or two, renewed from time to time at very small cost from a nursery or shop or barrow, would be all that is needed to keep it bright.

Wasted opportunities are ever-flowing sources of regret. I feel this every time I pass any of the small villa residences near towns, whose doors face the road; where, for the sake of some form of desire for pretentious display, or some allied motive to me equally incomprehensible, a good proportion of the small garden-space around the house is wasted, and privacy sacrificed, for the sake of a useless drive to the door, with either a pair of gates in and out, or a screwy space where a one-horse carriage can barely turn. How much better to have one door straight on to the footpath, and a glazed passage filled with well-arranged plants. Such an entrance, seven feet wide inside, would allow a three-foot-wide path of plain stone flags, and a space of two feet on each side for pot and growing plants. The wood and glass-work would rest on the outer edge of a nine-inch wall three feet high, the remaining part of the top of the wall still giving space enough within for the standing of small pots. Climbers and some of the main masses of foliage plants would be planted in the borders. There would be no regular staging, but, excepting those that might be placed on the three-foot wall, the plants would be arranged on the ground, standing the pots on pieces of slate or tile to prevent worms getting in, and raising some of the pots, as the shape of the groups might demand, by standing them on empty ones inverted.

Many plants would thrive in such a passage, even without artificial heat, or with a lamp-stove for the coldest nights, at any rate in and below the latitude of London. Fuchsia, *Clematis indivisa* and *C. cirrhosa*, *Cobœa scandens*, *Passiflora cœrulea*, *Physianthus albens*, *Solanum jasminoides*, and *Daphne indica* would be an ample list from which to choose climbers, while Hydrangeas and several kinds of Fern would do planted out, as a groundwork for flowering plants in pots.

If the passage was to have a heating system I would have it wider, not less than 11 feet; and in this case the rows of pipes that would pass along by the walls should be hidden by a thin inner wall built as rockwork in cement, leaving rather large openings both at the side and top, so as not to shut off too much of the heat. I can recommend this plan with the greater confidence because I have myself built and planted such a wall in a greenhouse, and found it to answer perfectly. In it were built pockets for Ferns and Selaginellas, and the whole soon became a mass of beautiful greenery; the openings showing as fern-shrouded caves of mystery.

An ordinary galvanised tank with its regular supply, for dipping, was sunk in the ground, its edge being hidden by slabs of sandstone. Just above it the rockwork rose rather more boldly, and from the rain-water gutter outside a pipe was led through, and passed under a concealing stone into a little rocky channel, which brought in addition any rain water, by one or two rough steps into the tank, pleasantly splashing the neighbouring Ferns on the way.

CHAPTER XV

THE MAKING OF POT-POURRI

" Do tell me how you make your Pot-pourri ? " is a question that comes often during the year; and it is so difficult to give a concise answer or a short written recipe, that I will just put down all I can think of about the material and method that go to its making, in the hope that it may help others who wish to prepare the fragrant compound on their own account. And though any one can make Pot-pourri after a fashion, yet to make it well and on rather a large scale, a good deal of care and a good deal of time are needed, besides suitable space and appliances, and a proper choice of material.

The greater part of the bulk is of Rose petals and Sweet Geranium leaves, then, in lesser quantity, Lavender, leaves of Sweet Verbena, Bay, and Rosemary, prepared Orange peel, and finally Orris-root powder, and various sweet gums and spices.

There are of course the two kinds of Pot-pourri, the dry and the moist. The dry is much the easier and quicker to make, but is neither so sweet nor so enduring, so now the moist is the only kind I care to have. One of the chief reasons why it cannot be done by a fixed recipe is that the materials have first to be got to a certain state—limp and leathery—neither too wet nor too dry; and this state can only be secured by trying, and feeling one's way, and getting to know. When the ingredients are dried to the right degree, they are packed tightly into jars with a certain mixture of salt, which seems to combine with the remaining moisture, and serves both to retain the mass at the right degree of dampness, and also to preserve it from any kind of decay or mouldiness. In my own case, as a considerable quantity is made, I find it best to prepare a jar of each ingredient by itself, and then to mix all together; but when the whole making is small, there is no reason why it should not all go into one receptacle until the time comes for adding the spices. In the whole arrangement the matter that wants most care is the proper preparation of the Rose petals. And the Roses must be in good order. They may be full blown, but must not be faded or in any way injured, and above all they must be quite dry. A Rose is a great hand at holding water. If it has been rained into when first opened, it will still hold the wet in its inner depths two days afterwards. Dew does not seem to go so far in, and is generally dried by noon; but in any case it is safest to gather the Roses on a warm sunny afternoon.

So every two or three days, when Roses are in plenty, we bring them in, perhaps a bushel-basket

Rose Leaves for Pot-fourri

The Pot-pourri Harvest: Cutting Lavender

full at a time. If they cannot be picked over at once, they are laid out, not more than three inches thick, on a rough hempen wrapper about three yards long by two yards wide; if they were left in the basket they would soon begin to "heat" and spoil. The shady, paved garden-court on the north side of the house is the chosen place, and the Rose-cloth is spread where the broad passage upstairs overhangs, so that we can sit below in shelter even in rain. Then at the earliest opportunity the Rose petals are pulled off their hard bases, and carefully sifted through the fingers so as to separate them as much as possible. Sometimes visitors are pressed into the service, sometimes the little nieces come down from their home close by, and often I go and pick them over after dark in the pleasant summer evening. It is just as easy to do without any light, and then one enjoys all the more the wonderful fragrance and the pleasant cool texture; and plunging hands or face into the mass, delicious alike to scent and touch, one calls to mind how such generous measures of plucked Roses played their part in the feasts of ancient Rome.

The separated petals lie on the cloth for two days, or for a longer or' shorter time, as the air may be more or less drying, in order that they may lose a part of their moisture; how much I cannot say, but perhaps half, as they look to be shrivelled to about half their size; and now they are ready to go into their preparation jars. After making shift for some years with various odds and ends of jars, the best of them being a big blue and grey German one and some South Italian oil jars, I had some made on purpose at Doulton's pottery. The material has to be firmly and evenly pressed, as it lies in the jar layer on layer, and as this is difficult to arrange in any vessel of bulging form, my jars were made quite cylindrical, and they answer admirably. They stand twenty-two inches high and have a diameter over all of ten inches, and have flat flanged lids with loop handles. They are of the strong buff stoneware, like salt-jars, glazed inside and out. In order to keep the material well pressed down, I had some leaden discs cast of such a diameter as to go easily inside; these are five-eighths of an inch thick, and weigh fourteen pounds each, and have also handles to lift by.

The Rose petals are thrown in, about two good handfuls at a time, and are made to lie close together by gentle ramming, and have a thick sprinkling (not quite a covering) of the salt mixture. This is of equal parts bay salt and kitchen salt; the bay salt, which comes in hard lumps, being roughly pounded, so that the greater part of it is in pieces the size of peas or smaller. The Rose leaves are put in as before, two handfuls or so, rammed, salted, and so on till all are in, then the leaden weight goes in, and the jar is covered till the next supply is ready.

The process is the same with the leaves of Sweet Geranium, only that they are taken off their stalks before they are dried, and all but the smallest are pulled into three or four pieces. They take about as long to dry as the Rose petals, and are laid out in the same way on the Rose-cloths. Sweet Verbena is of such a quick-drying nature that it only has to be stripped from the stalk and can be put in the jars at once; also Bay leaves, Rosemary leaves, and Lavender; but all are treated alike in that they are put into the jars in moderate layers, lightly rammed, salted and pressed.

Lavender, whether for Pot-pourri or for drying, should be cut as soon as a good proportion of the lower flowers in the spike are out. My friends often tell me that my Lavender smells better than theirs; but it is only because I watch for the right moment for cutting, and am careful about the drying. If it is picked for drying, and is laid too thickly, it soon goes mouldy; it must be laid thinly and turned once or twice till it is dry enough to be safe.

An important ingredient in good Pot-pourri is strips of Seville Orange peel stuck with Cloves. The peel is taken off and cut in pieces from end to end of the Orange, so that each is about half an inch wide in the middle and two inches long; holes are pricked in it, and the shaft of the Clove pressed in so that the heads nearly touch each other. The pieces are then packed into a jar

firmly with the hand—they would not bear ramming—with sprinklings of salt in between and over
the top. This is the first ingredient to be made
ready, as the Oranges are in season from the end
of February to the middle of March; the last
batches of preparation being made towards the
middle of September, of the later pickings of Sweet
Geranium.

The materials seem to be mellower and better
for being left for some time in the preparation
jars, so I put off the final amalgamation till near
the end of October. The jars now hold the produce
of some seven or eight bushels of Rose petals, about
four bushels of Sweet Geranium, and another bushel
of various sweet leaves, all of course much reduced
in bulk by drying and ramming; with this is about
fifty pounds of the mixed salt.

Now we have to get together the spices, sweet
gums, and Orris-root. As an improvement on plain
Orris-root it is advisable to use Atkinson's Violet
Powder; we therefore have—

> 5 large packets Violet Powder,
> 1 pound ground Allspice,
> 1 pound ground Cloves,
> 1 pound ground Mixed Spice,
> $\frac{1}{2}$ pound ground Mace,
> 1 pound whole Mace,
> 1 pound whole Cloves,
> 1 pound pounded Gum Benzoin,
> 1 pound pounded Gum Storax or Styrax.

All the powders are mixed together in a large bowl, and the whole Mace and Cloves are in another bowl, and now we are ready for the grand mixing. A space is swept on the brick floor of the studio just in front of the raised hearth of the broad ingle; the full jars are brought into a wide half-circle; the home children and their elders, and perhaps one or two neighbours, are convened to the Pot-pourri party, with tea to follow; one mixer is posted at each jar or bowl, and the materials are thrown handful by handful on to the floor in the middle space.

When first I made Pot-pourri it could be mixed in a large red-ware pan; as I grew more ambitious the mixing was done in a hip-bath, in later years in a roomy wooden tub; but now the bulk is so considerable that it can only be dealt with on a clear floor space.

The heap rises, and from time to time has to be flattened as the jolly party all round throw on their handfuls. The post of honour seems to be the distribution of the Orange peel stuck with Cloves, but the claim for the supreme dignity of this office is clearly though tacitly contested by the holder of the large basin of "sauce" of sweet powders. The pressed stuff in the jars is so tightly compacted that it has to be loosened by vigorous stabs and forkings with an iron prong, by one whose duty it is to go round and fork it up

so that it can be handled; this official can hardly
get round in time to satisfy the many calls of
" Please give me a stir up." The heap grows like
one of the big ant-hills in the wood, until at last
all the jars are empty, and every one's hands are
either sticky with salt or powdery with sweet spices.
Now the head Pot-pourri maker takes a shovel, and
turns the heap over from left to right and then
'from right to left, and backwards and forwards
several times till all is duly mixed. Then the
store cask is brought forward: a strong iron-hooped
oak cask with a capacity of fifteen gallons. It
looks as if the fragrant heap could never be got
into it, but in it goes shovelful by shovelful, and
again it is rammed, until all is in, leaving only a
bare two inches of space on the top. The cask
has been made on purpose, and has no upper head,
but a lid with a wood-hooped rim that fits over
the edge, and a knob-handle set out of the centre,
the easier to lift the cover by jerking it to one
side.

The full cask is now so heavy that it is a job
to get it back to its place against a farther wall;
it must weigh a hundredweight and three-quarters,
possibly more. If the mixture stays some weeks or
even months in the cask before any is taken out,
by remaining untouched for awhile it seems to
acquire a richer and more mellow scent.

The studio floor is left in a shocking state of

mess. A wide space in front of the ingle shows a
dark patch of briny moisture; footmarks of the same
are thick in the neighbourhood of the site of the
heap, and some small tracks further afield show where
little feet have made more distant excursions; but
it is growing dark, and we must leave it and wipe
our shoes and go in to tea, and there will be a
half-day's work for the charwoman to-morrow.

The foregoing description answers my friends'
questions as to how *I* make Pot-pourri; but it does
not follow that they may not make it in different
and better ways, according to the degree of personal
intelligence and ingenuity that they may bring to
bear on the material they have at disposal.

I have always noted any Pot-pourri recipes that
came in my way, and as the practice that suits my
own conditions was evolved from them I will give
them as they stand, only adding such critical or
explanatory remarks as seem desirable.

" *Pot-pourri* (*Mrs. F. M.*). Put alternate layers of
Rose leaves and bay salt in any quantity you please,
in an earthen pot. Press down with a plate and
pour off the liquor that will be produced every day
for six weeks, taking care to press as dry as possible.
Let the mass be broken up, and add the following
ingredients, well pounded and mixed together:—Nutmeg $\frac{1}{4}$ oz., Cloves, Mace, Cinnamon, Gum Benzoin,
Orris-root sliced, 1 oz. each. Mix well with a wooden
spoon."

The obvious weakness of this recipe is, that it begins by saying Rose leaves and bay salt "in any quantity," and then gives a precise amount of the spice seasoning; an amount which, according to my practice, would be suitable for 1½ gallons of the larger bulk. It is also clearly a considerable saving of labour to dry the Rose leaves to the right degree at once, instead of having to attend to them "every day for six weeks."

"*Pot-pourri* (*Lady F., from an old recipe*). Put into a large China jar, used for this purpose, Damask and other single Roses, buds and blown flowers. Add to every peck of these a large hand-ful of Jasmine blossom, one of Violets, one of Orange flowers, Orris-root sliced 1 oz., Benjamin and Storax 1 oz. each, two or three handfuls of Clove Gilli-flowers, Allspice, pilled Marjoram, and Lemon Thyme, rind of Lemon, Balm of Gilead, and a few Bay leaves. Chop all these and mix them with bay salt, cover the jar, and stir occasionally."

In this recipe I do not see the use of Rosebuds, as the aroma is not developed till the flower is full-blown. "Benjamin" is Gum Benzoin. "Pilled" Marjoram means Marjoram leaves stripped off the stalks. "Chop all these" is a vagueness of instruc-tion only too frequent in the recipe book, for it is evident that a small round hard object like the seed or berry or dried bud, whichever it may be, of Allspice, and resin-like masses of aromatic gums, should be bruised or pounded or in some way more finely divided than could be done by such mere chopping as might serve for the division of more soft and bulky masses of leaf and flower.

"*Pot-pourri* (*Mrs. D. W.*). Gather large Damask Rose leaves and dry them in the sun, also Lavender flowers and scented Verbena, also dried. Bruise a little common salt with ½ lb. of bay salt, ½ lb. Saltpetre, ½ oz. Storax, 6 gr. Musk, and 2 oz. pounded Cloves. Mix all together with the dried leaves and put in a covered jar."

" *Pot-pourri* (*Lady J.*). Pick your Roses when they are quite dry; it ought to be the red single Apothecary Rose. Strip them, being sure to utilise the little seeds from the centre, and have a large earthenware jar. Put in layers of Rose leaves, and between each layer shake in two or three handfuls of bay salt and of powdered Spice, Cinnamon, and Cloves, and on the top pour some Lavender water. You can keep on adding to your jar as it sinks and you get fresh Rose leaves."

"*Pot-pourri.* A thin layer of bay salt at the bottom of the jar, any sort of sweet flowers dried in the shade, with Storax, Gum Benjamin, Calamino Aromatico, and Sandalwood shavings; a very little Musk, Cloves, and some powdered Cinnamon; bay salt must be thrown over the whole. It must be stirred daily."

In these recipes there is the same ambiguity about

the proportion of bulk to that of seasoning, and it
should be made clear that the jar should be either
of porcelain or of strong earthenware well glazed both
inside and out.

"Calamino Aromatico" is no doubt Styrax, otherwise Storax, although the recipe that includes it also
has Styrax. But I read in one of the most interesting
books of reference I have on my shelves, namely,
Mr. Daniel Hanbury's pharmacological and botanical
"Science Papers" (Macmillan, 1876), of "Styrax
Calamites," a term derived from the ancient method
of packing it in reeds.

In ordering these sweet gums for Pot-pourri, it is
well to remember that there is a liquid Styrax as well
as the solid resinous kind. Once, when I had ordered
a pound of Gum Styrax, at the last moment when I
thought all was ready for mixing, there was a jar
of aromatic viscosity like birdlime, quite useless and
unmanageable.

"*Pot-pourri* (*Lady Betty Germain*, 1750). Gather
dry, Double Violets, Rose leaves, Lavender, Myrtle
flowers, Verbena, Bay leaves, Rosemary, Balm, Musk,
Geranium. Pick these from the stalks and dry on
paper in the sun for a day or two before putting
them in a jar. This should be a large white one,
well glazed, with a close-fitting cover, also a piece
of card the exact size of the jar, which you must
keep pressed down on the flowers. Keep a new
wooden spoon to stir the salt and flowers from the

bottom, before you put in a fresh layer of bay salt above and below every layer of flowers. Have ready of spices, plenty of Cinnamon, Mace, Nutmeg, and Pepper and Lemon peel pounded. For a large jar $\frac{1}{2}$ lb. Orris-root, 1 oz. Storax, 1 oz. Gum Benjamin, 2 ozs. Calamino aromatico, 2 grs. Musk, and a small quantity of oil of Rhodium. The spice and gums to be added when you have collected all the flowers you intend to put in. Mix all well together, press it down well, and spread bay salt on the top to exclude the air until the January or February following. Keep the jar in a cool, dry place."

This, on the whole, is the best of these recipes, though, for my own taste, I should leave out the Musk and oil of Rhodium. I have never tried pepper; and though at first it sounds doubtful, it may be worth trying, bearing in mind that the irritating property that makes one sneeze comes from inhaling particles as a dry dust, whereas in the damp preparation, where the atoms would be clogged into the mass, the fragrant scent only would be given off. In this recipe again comes the puzzle of Storax *and* Calamino aromatico. I have not been able to ascertain what difference there is between these two, all that I have as yet found out pointing to their being the same thing. "Spread bay salt on the top to exclude the air;" *to exclude the air* seems a doubtful explanation of the purpose of the salt; the close-fitting cover is to exclude the

air; the function of the bay salt is to retain moisture
and to resist corruption.

In making Pot-pourri by the lazier and less
effective dry process, it is the drying of the Rose
petals that requires the most care. The Roses must
be picked quite dry, the petals pulled apart and
laid thinly on sheets of paper in an airy room till
absolutely dry. They must then smell quite sweet,
without the least taint of mustiness; any batch
so tainted must be thrown away. The Lavender
and Sweet Geranium that will form the greater part
of the rest of the bulk must also be carefully dried,
but in their case the drying is much easier. For
a quantity equal to two-thirds of a bushel the spice
mixture would be—Cloves, Mace, Cinnamon, 2 oz.
each; Coriander, Allspice, Gum Styrax, Gum Benzoin,
½ oz. each; Violet Powder, ¼ lb. The spices and
gums should be in powder or finely crushed.

For any kind of Pot-pourri I am always on the
lookout for sweet materials such as shavings or
sawdust of Sandalwood or Sweet Cedar; all ingredients
that have an enduring fragrance are good and welcome. I do not use any special sort of Rose petals,
but all or any that are in full blow and in good
condition. One of the recipes quoted says "it ought
to be the single Apothecary Rose." I do not know
what the Apothecary Rose is, and as I have asked
a trusty friend, who is a learned scholar and a
careful botanist, and who has made a special study

of garden Roses and their origin, who says he also
does not know what it is; and further, as I find
I can make very good Pot-pourri without being able
to identify it, I conclude that it does not matter.
There also seems to be a divergence of opinion as
to whether the Rose petals should be dried in the
sun or in the shade. This also I think is of far
less moment (though I rather incline to drying in
the shade, as a process slower and more under con-
trol) than that the petals should be dried evenly and
to the right degree.

CHAPTER XVI

PLANTS FOR POOR SOILS

THE natural soil of my heathy hilltop is so excessively poor and sandy that it has obliged me, in a way, to make a special study of plants that will do fairly well with the least nutriment, and of all sorts of ways of meeting and overcoming this serious difficulty in gardening. It is some compensation that the natural products of the upper ten acres of my ground—Heath and Bracken, Whortleberry, fine grasses and brilliant mosses below, and above them a now well-grown copse of Birch and Holly, Oak, Chestnut, and Scotch Fir—are exactly what I like best in a piece of rough ground; indeed I would scarcely exchange my small bit of woodland, especially after some years of watching and guiding in the way it should go, with any other such piece that I can think of.

The main paths through this woodland space are broad grassy ones kept mown; they enable one to get about with perfect ease among the trees, and being fairly wide, about fifteen feet, they incite one to a broad and rather large treatment of the tree-groups near them. But there are smaller paths about four

237

feet wide that pass for the most part through the
more thickly wooded places. They were made for
a twofold purpose, firstly for the sake of having
paths where paths were wanted, and secondly for
obtaining the thin skin of black, peaty earth, the
only soil my ground can boast, that overlies the great
depths of yellow sand and stony strata that go down
for nearly two hundred feet before we come to water.
As the paths were made, this precious earth was
stored in heaps by their sides, and these heaps have
been a precious reserve to draw upon ever since.   In
some places this peaty surface is only an inch thick,
though in some hollow holes there may be as much
as four inches. Below that is an inch or two of
loose sand, partly silver sand; this we also save; then
comes hard yellowish sand and what is called the
"pan," a thin layer of what is neither stone nor sand,
but something between the two. It is like thick flakes
of rotten rust; hard enough for the spade to ring on
when it reaches it, supported by the firm sand below.
In all cultivation for woodland planting it is necessary to break through this pan; nothing thrives if
this is not done.

No part of my copse was broken up except a
space of about forty feet wide next to my southern
frontier, where I wished to plant groups of Juniper,
Holly, Mountain Ash, and Ilex; and a roundish area
about the middle of the ground for Cistuses. Both
are now so well covered with a natural carpet of the wild

THE CISTUS GROUND

Heaths that one would not know they had ever been touched, and I could wish for nothing better, both as a groundwork to what has been planted and as a growth that harmonises with all that is near. Before the present wood grew up—it is all self-sown—the ground was covered with an old plantation of Scotch Fir. This was cut when full-grown, but one or two trees that had misshapen or double stems were left. One of these stands near the Cistus ground, and though its thin old top has been badly battered by storms of wind and snow, yet from several points of view the old tree has much pictorial value.

There can be little doubt that for the poor soils of our southern counties there are no better shrubs than the hardier of the Cistuses. Of those that are hardy south of London the most easy to grow is *C. laurifolius.* It soon becomes a large bush; in sheltered places seven feet high and as much through. It will thrive in almost pure sand if deeply worked. Throughout the month of June it bears a daily succession of its two-inch-wide white flowers; it greets the kindly south-west wind with a lavish outpouring of its delicious fragrance, not only in summer but in the very depth of winter; and as it grows old, and here and there a branch breaks and dies, it has, like Lavender and Rosemary and Juniper and many another good thing, an old age which is neither untidy nor unsightly but is dignified and pictorial.

Cistus ladaniferus, the Gum Cistus, is an even

more beautiful shrub, but it is rather more tender. The manner of growth is not so solid or compact; the long shoots and long-shaped leaves look almost willow-like; but the beauty of the whole shrub is of a high order. So also is that of its wide white purple-blotched flowers of delicate substance, that, poppy-like, retain the mark of the folds of bud-life in the petals' dainty texture during their short span of unfolded beauty. For the only thing to regret about a Cistus is that its flowers are so fugacious. Many expand in the morning to fall at noon, and though some may remain an hour or two later, yet by the afternoon the bushes are nearly bare, and only by the white pool of fallen petals on the ground below them may we know how fair and full was the flower of the forenoon.

These, the two largest of the Cistuses for our gardens, have foliage of a deep green colour and a dull smooth surface, *C. ladaniferus* having the brighter leaf of the two. The foliage of both of them turns to a curious bluish-leaden colour in winter. *Cistus populifolius* and *C. cordifolius* are smaller bushes of lighter foliage; with me they stand all but the severest winters, as also do *Cistus albidus*, *C. salvifolius*, and *C. monspeliensis*. *C. florentinus* is about the same for hardiness. This and *C. creticus* are two of my favourites among those of moderate growth. *C. creticus* has rough leaves of a lively green, while those of *C. florentinus* are of a deep green, very low in tone, that in full summer assume a splendid richness of reddish-bronze, while the long succession of its extremely abundant bloom makes it one of the best of the family for the more important portions of the garden. *Cistus* is so closely related to *Helianthemum*, and their uses are so nearly identical, that the mention of *Helianthemum* naturally follows. They thrive under the same conditions of poor soil and full sunshine; they are mostly lower of stature, the leaves smaller and greyer, and though *H. algarvensis* has an upright way of growth, and against a wall will rise some feet, yet their more usual habit is that of low bushes, some quite trailing. *H. formosum* (as often known as *Cistus formosus*) is a capital plant in my garden. The yellow flowers are large, and so abundant that the whole small bush shows brightly from a distance. *H. halimifolium* has an almost prostrate habit; foliage also grey, and bloom abundant. These are the only ones with yellow flowers, except our small native Rock-rose, that I know well. *H. rosmarinifolium* is a beautiful dwarf bush, suited for a sunny place in the front of the choicest shrub-bank. Its leaves are small and narrow, Rosemary-shaped, and dark in colour; its many small flowers are milk-white, of delicate texture, and extremely fugacious. Then there are the many species and garden varieties of the branches of the family that our common wild one (*Helianthemum vulgare*) may be taken to represent; with flowers of many colours, red, rosy pink,

orange yellow, and creamy white; some with double-
flowered varieties; all good as sun-loving plants in
poor soils.   These, as well as all kinds of Cistus,
are easily raised from cuttings.   As old plants of the
dwarf Rock-roses are apt to get into straggling masses
of matted growths unless judiciously cut-in every two
years, it is well (and indeed wise in any case) to make
a few cuttings from time to time.

Best among all good plants for hot sandy soils are
the ever-blessed Lavender and Rosemary, two delicious
old garden bushes that one can hardly dissociate, so
delightfully do they agree in their homely beauty and
their beneficence of enduring fragrance, as well as in
their love of the sun and their power of resisting
drought.   I plant Rosemary all over the garden, so
pleasant is it to know that at every few steps one
may draw the kindly branchlets through one's hand,
and have the enjoyment of their incomparable incense;
and I grow it against walls, so that the sun may draw
out its inexhaustible sweetness to greet me as I pass;
and early in March, before any other scented flower
of evergreen is out, it gladdens me with the thick
setting of pretty lavender-grey bloom crowding all
along the leafy spikes.

In the island of Capri, as elsewhere around the
Mediterranean, Rosemary is a common plant; but
rambling over its rocky heights I found not unfre-
quently, besides the one of ordinary habit, a dwarf
form, quite prostrate, pressing its woody stems and

branches so tightly to any rock or stone that came in its way that it followed its form as closely as would a dwarf and clinging Ivy. Other plants seem to break into varieties with this way of growing. I hear of the same trick among Junipers in Norway, in plants otherwise the same as those that grow into upright bushes. In my own ground there is a common Juniper that will not grow upright; it is a foot high and four feet across, the branches all growing horizontally, and apparently with a kind of deliberate determination, for the branches grow lower and straighter than even those of its relative, the Savin, whose business it is to grow in this way.

Of Lavender I always arrange to have two hedges of a good bearing age, besides a number of bushes here and there. Every year in early summer we make a good number of cuttings. When rooted these are planted out in nursery lines, and in the autumn of the next year they are nice round little bushes, just at the best size for planting out permanently. Lavender can also be propagated by layering, but the plants are not so well shaped as those grown from cuttings. The year after planting, the young hedge gives a few nice flowers, the next year a good crop, and the third year its fullest yield. After that, with me, the bush deteriorates, and begins to show bare gaps, yielding less bloom. Still in half-wild places I leave it, because though it is no longer so effective as a flowering bush it is distinctly pictorial. But

the Lavender hedges which are in the region where
pleasure garden meets working garden, and the flowers
are wanted as a crop, the bushes are only kept for
three flowering years, after which they are pulled up
and destroyed and a young hedge made, the plants
being put about three and a half feet apart. I always
think it well with all these plants and shrubs of South
European origin to put them out as early as possible,
not later than the middle of October, so that their
naked roots may get hold of the ground while it is
still warm. In places where the soil is stiff enough
to take up growing things with a ball of earth it
matters less, but here and in other poor soils the
earth shakes off entirely, leaving the roots quite
bare.

If the plant has been grown in a pot this
difficulty does not occur, but I have a great dislike to growing hardy plants and shrubs in pots ;
the roots become painfully cramped and distorted,
and the damage done to them, besides the risk of
inefficient planting—for a pot-bound root needs the
most careful manipulation — does not in any way
compensate for the convenience. The Lavender
crop is carefully watched and harvested at the
moment of its best early maturity. This is when
a good number of the lower flowers in the spike
are open, but none of those in the top. We
arrange to have the two hedges that are in bearing in such positions that one is in a rather

warmer aspect than the other, so that the whole
crop does not come ripe at the same time.

Shrubs of the Broom and Gorse tribes are some
of the very best for light soils. The common yellow
Broom (*Cytisus scoparius*) of our sandy wastes is
worthy of garden space ; its bright colouring only
excelled by that of the sparer - flowering yellow
Spanish Broom (*Spartium junceum*). I like to plant
pale flowered bushes of our wild yellow with the
white Portugal Broom (*Cytisus albus*) and with
the sometimes warm - white and often pale straw-
yellow - coloured *Cytisus præcox*. *C. Andreanus*, the
partly red-flowered sport of the common Broom, is
best planted with bushes of the type of rather
deep colour.

The Spanish Gorse (*Ulex hispanicus*) is a beautiful small shrub, very neat and round in habit, and
smothered with bright yellow bloom in early summer.
The double form of our wild Gorse is so well known
that it need not be described; its only fault is its
short life of not many years, but this can be remedied
by careful treatment, and its life much prolonged—
indeed almost indefinitely — by cutting down all or
many of its branches every three years, and by layering
some of those that are outermost. The Brooms also
bear pegging down, and it is a good plan, if a good-
sized group is being planted, to let some in the middle
and at the back of the group grow upward unchecked,
and to plant others between them and rather to

PATH THROUGH BIRCH AND CISTUS

the front, leaning forward or outward the better to prepare them for future pegging.

Among shrubs more suitable to the garden proper, though also good for rough places in the very poorest and hottest soil, is the Jerusalem Sage (*Phlomis fruticosa*); a curious and picturesque plant in all states, the leaves much like those of Sage, but stiffer and whiter, and with a strongly waved outline. Stems and leaves are covered with a woolly coating that feels like a rough-piled velvet; looser and browner on the stems.

At its full growth it is nearly five feet high, and will spread to seven feet, tumbling about in picturesque masses when old. In a roughish place, where such a form is suitable, it is a strikingly handsome plant, but in trimmer garden spaces, if it threatens to invade equally worthy neighbours, it very well bears cutting; in this case it is best to take out whole branches from the bottom, to avoid the stiff, stunted look that a shrub has when pruned all over. There are other kinds of Phlomis, but this one is the best.

The Tree-Lupin is another of our grand plants, growing quickly from seed, and at its third and usually last year quite a large bush. Except from the fact of its short life, for it is scarcely hard wooded, it would be a grand wall plant, covering a space ten feet high by the third year; but though the life may be prolonged for a year or two by clever pruning, the gap it leaves when it dies is so large that it is perhaps wiser to clothe the wall with something more enduring.

The colouring is in varieties of pale yellow and pale purple; the clear yellows are those I like best. Occasionally seedlings disappoint one by coming of a poor muddled colour, a mixture of washy purple and dull yellow and dirty white. I hear of the fixing of a fine white kind, and shall grow it next season in the hope that it may do credit to its advertised character.

Two of the North American thornless Brambles, *Rubus nutkanus* and *Rubus spectabilis*, are capital plants in poor soil. The taller of them is a very handsome thing in late summer. Many of my visitors assume that because my soil is sandy, and there is a thin skin of peat, that it is therefore perfect for Rhododendrons and Azaleas. But such an assumption is much too hasty, and though I do grow these grand shrubs, and even Kalmias, it is only by means of a careful preparation first and a close watchfulness afterwards. Where they were to be, the ground was first deeply trenched, but at every place where a Rhododendron was planted, the trenched soil was taken out two feet deep, and a good barrow-load of the peaty top earth was put in. Then the plant was placed, and its ball covered with a little of the peaty stuff. A good dressing of cow manure was next worked in so that it should be well rotted by the time the growing roots should reach it next year; then the soil was partly filled in, leaving the plant standing in a shallow depression (for economy in watering) over whose surface was spread another good coating of cow manure, and this coating was renewed for several years in succession. Even this careful planting must also be followed up by copious waterings in dry seasons, for all plants of this class are moisture-loving, and though, when they have been growing some years, and have so well covered the ground that it is kept somewhat cool by their own shade, they may do fairly well, they would do very much better if they had the constant comfort of moisture within root reach.

My Rhododendrons are in large clumps, with Auratum Lilies in many of the spaces between them, and hardy Ferns, Andromedas, and some of the Dwarf Rhododendrons filling up the outer spaces between them. But the Azaleas, some distance away, stand unevenly· apart, among open spaces of grass and Heath, and want yearly atten- tion because the grass and weeds so soon invade the richer preparation at their root. I often bewail the waste of these lovely shrubs when I see them planted close together in bare beds of poor soil, or, worse still, mixed up with even more starved and unhappy Rhododendrons. Though all my Azaleas are some yards apart, I sometimes wish they were still more largely spaced, although I like here and there to plant two or three of the same together, or if not the same, of such colourings as approach each other and will make a mass of closely related harmony. Kalmias are almost swamp-plants, and are grateful for any amount of water that can be given them in a dry soil. How I long to have a good patch of peaty swamp and to plant it mainly with Kalmias of different ages, and to have with them a restricted number of things that would enjoy such a place. My first choice would be some patches of Royal Fern and of Lady Fern, with a wide planting of *Epigœa repens* and a long drift of *Cypripedium spectabile*.

All the hardy Heaths are happy in poor, sandy soil simply trenched. There are so many beautiful kinds that it is hard to resist getting a larger number of varieties than look well together. Our own heathy wastes show a good example of how two, or at most three, suit each other's company.

It would be extremely interesting to plant a large space with these Heaths, and though I have more than once seen bold plantations of them, I have never seen them placed quite as I should like. I should always plant them in the long drifts that seems to me by far the most natural and pictorial way of placing most plants in rather wild places, and I would have them so that very few kinds were in sight at the same time. And I would have plants of different sizes, and sometimes a space of bare earth where their seed might fall and grow. And I would allow the finest grasses to grow between; and if the height and spread of the Heath overcame the grass let it do so, as does the *Calluna* of our wild heaths.

In extremely poor soils such as I have to deal with, and of which there are large tracts in the South of England, it is useless to attempt to grow shrubs or the stronger garden plants without a thorough cultivation. If the soil cannot be artificially made—I make all mine nearly three feet deep—let it be broken up or trenched to nearly this depth. It is the only other alternative; indeed it is quite remarkable how things will grow in the poorest soil if only it is deeply stirred, especially in the first year or two. A bank twenty feet deep of pure sand wheeled out of a quarry will grow Birches and Scotch Firs. And with suitable manuring and constant working I have seen such depths of lately-moved sand converted into productive vegetable ground. In extra deep trenching of poor soil, of course the precious top spit must not be buried at the bottom as is done in simple trenching. A system I find to work admirably in my own ground is to open a trench nearly three feet wide and deep, laying aside the top spit and some of the sand close at hand, and wheeling most of the sand from below right away. Two-thirds of the depth is then filled with vegetable refuse from the rubbish heap, or with green waste from any part of the garden. At the rubbish yard we are careful to separate our waste products; only burning that which is absolutely dry, and rotten woody material that would breed fungus. If this stuff is already more than half decayed we fill it in higher, but if still rather green or quite fresh it is rammed down, mixing in some of the sand. The top soil is then returned to the top and the next trench opened. It is surprising how all plants and shrubs will thrive in ground so prepared; the secret of their happiness is that there is a cool medium under them, as well as a vast region of long-enduring nutriment for hungry rootlets to explore.

Let no one think that general gardening is easy in these light lands overlying two hundred feet of dry sand and rock. Unless the things grown are restricted to the few kinds already named, and some of the sand-loving plants to be named presently, the ground must be deeply prepared. But in a great many places it would be distinctly desirable just to grow these things and no others. The restriction to the small number of kinds would be of the utmost benefit in the way of saving the garden from the usual crowded muddle of a multitude of single plants, and it could be made and maintained with the least possible labour, simple trenching and very moderate enriching being all that would be wanted.

No family of plants is more absolutely at home in sandy ground than the Sea-Hollies. If I had some long stretches of bare, unsightly heaps or ridges of sand, how I would plant the noble Eryngiums: the dwarf blue-leaved kind (*Eryngium maritimum*), native of sandy dunes near the sea; the taller blue (*E. oliverianum*), both perennial and long enduring; the grand biennial (*E. giganteum*); giving this lovely so-called Silver Thistle room to sow itself for future years. Such a planting on a large scale would present a picture of rare beauty, especially if approaching the flowers of blue and silver there was a planting of the blue-leaved Lyme Grass (*Elymus arenarius*). I have no such stretches of sandy waste, but knowing how it will do in a place that is poor and dry, I grow it in the end of a shrub-clump, where a large Birch tree robs the ground, and where I think nothing but this fine handsome Grass would be likely to flourish. I believe I may truly say that of all the groups of plants in my garden there is none that attracts so much notice and admiration.

There are families of aromatic plants that do well in the poorest ground; many of them are in pleasant harmony of leaf-colouring of whitish or bluish-grey. Such are many of the Wormwoods, of which the fragrant cottage favourite, Southernwood (*Artemisia abrotanum*), is one. This grows into a dense bush two feet high, and may well be associated with some of the smaller kinds such as *A. nana* and *A. sericea*.

MUNSTEAD GLASSES *(see page 204)*

LYME GRASS (*Elymus*) AND LAVENDER-COTTON (*Santolina*)

Other sand-loving plants with whitish leaves are
Lavender-cotton (*Santolina Chamœ-Cyparissus*) and *Cineraria maritima*. This beautiful plant, with its deeply-
cut foliage of silvery grey, is unhappily not generally
hardy, though it will stand through the milder of our
winters; but it is easily grown from seed.

Light, sandy ground is of a dry, warm nature, and
many southern plants that rot away with damp in
stronger soils survive in it and thrive. *Acanthus* in its
several varieties is grand in full sun, and nothing can
be happier than the beautiful Alströmerias of Chile,
or that finest shrub of comparatively recent introduction, the Mexican Orange-flower (*Choisya ternata*).
The giant Grasses from Japan, *Eulalia japonica striata*
and *E. zebrina*, do grandly, and when after a year or
two they have grown into strong plants, are very
handsome, and combine extremely well with many
kinds of flowers. I have them in the borders of
Michaelmas Daisies as well as in the larger flower
border. The tall white Asphodel of the Mediterranean region is also happy in the warm sand, and
so is the dwarfer yellow kind; and nothing can do
better than the grand Mulleins, *Verbascum olympicum*
and *V. phlomoides*.

The large garden Thistles are magnificent—the
great silvery *Onopordon* eight feet high, and its
relative *O. arabicum* of still greater stature; also
the Milk Thistle (*Silybum Marianum*); they look
their best in rough ground or on sandy mounds, and

The Silver Thistle (*Eryngium giganteum*) (*see page 254*)

when once planted will always sow themselves
afresh.   The pretty lilac-flowered, grey-leaved Catmint (*Nepeta Mussini*) should have been named
among the sand-loving plants with hoary foliage.
It is a capital thing anywhere, but especially on
dry sunny banks ; it groups charmingly with
Lavender bushes, and I like to have near it, for
harmony of flower-colour as well as for its own
sake, and because it also loves our combination of sun
and sand, the pretty little *Sisyrinchium Bermudiana*.
With the Catmint should be associated the handsome herb Hyssop, full of its purple flower-spikes
in early autumn ; a plant that seems to have a
singular attraction for the pale-brown bumble-bees.
Oriental Poppies like the light ground if deeply
worked, and so do the greater number of the flag-
leaved Irises.   These are best divided and trans-
planted every fourth year ; their rhizomes grow fast,
and if left longer, crowd upon one another so
closely that the roots cannot find nourishment ;
they then make known their discomfort by refusing
to flower and by showing starved-looking foliage.

A very pretty plant is *Stobœa purpurea ;* it well
deserves to be better known and more often grown.
It has prickly, silvery, rather Thistle-like foliage,
but the flower, instead of being disappointingly
small in proportion to the plant as in Thistles, is
wide open like a large loose Daisy, and its colour,
the faintest tinge of purple pervading white, is

both lovely in itself and in relation to the colour of the leaves. The radical leaves are rather large and spreading; the flower stems, each bearing from twelve to fifteen of the large blooms, are three feet high and richly ornamented, for they are clothed with a leafy growth, handsomely waved and scalloped and spine-edged, just as if each of the long stalk-leaves grew on to the stem by its mid-rib for half its length or more.

Gaultheria Shallon must not be forgotten among dwarf shrubs that will flourish in sand. It is slow to move when first planted, but like many plants that run underground, it grows and spreads fast when well established. It has the unusual merit of doing well under trees, and will even grow under Scotch Firs, though not perhaps under their deepest shade. And sand-loving is the sweet wild Thyme and its garden varieties, and others of the dwarf sweet-herbs, whose fragrant merit is so great that it should not be wasted by their being grown only in the kitchen garden.

The handsome *Corchorus japonicus*, so well grown in cottage gardens, is also a sand shrub, and so is the pretty Tea-tree (*Lycium europæum*), so good for covering porches and arbours.

Few Roses are natives of sandy places, but we have a grand exception in the Burnet Rose and its garden varieties the Scotch Briers, described in the chapter on Brier Roses. It is true that the two wild Roses,

R. canina and *R. arvense*, grow in our hedges, but only sparingly in comparison with their abundance in chalk or clay lands. But happily, with a moderate preparation, we can enjoy the beauty of the free-rambling Cluster Roses and some of the species, notably *R. polyantha*, which is easily grown to a very large size.

Some of the low-growing *Cruciferæ* are quite happy in poor ground, such as Aubrietia, Arabis, Cerastium, and Alyssum. All these are at their best in banks and loose rock walls, either in sun or shade, where they can either trail or hang over in sheets of pretty leaf and bloom; and with them should be some of the hybrid Rock-Pinks, at home in the same places and willingly growing in the same manner.

CHAPTER XVII

GARDENING FOR SHORT TENANCIES

IT often happens that from some circumstance of life or occupation a temporary home has to be made. A governor or other official has a three or five years' appointment; married officers whose regiments are in camp or garrison take houses in the neighbourhood; a son is at a public school, and his parents wish to be near him. Hence, for these and many such reasons, official residences and other houses are occupied for a short term of years only; but so general is the love of flowers among us, that most of these houses of short tenure are lived in by people who wish to make the most of their gardens.

The question how to treat the gardens of such places comes to me all the more frequently because I live within reach of Aldershot. A letter lately received says "all Aldershot tries to have a little garden," and I feel all the bolder in venturing to offer suggestions, in that the extremely poor, sandy soil of the district exactly matches my own. Therefore it is quite safe to advise, firstly, the deepest possible cultivation. Even if it is nothing but sand, stir up that sand so that the always-beneficial movement of air and water may play through it both up and down, and keep it sweet and wholesome. If there is anything like soil at the top, or even a few-inches-deep top layer stained with "humus" (decayed vegetable matter), trench three spit deep, and keep this top spit in the second layer. Simple technical terms like this one "spit" are a stumbling-block to many. A "spit" in gardening is a spade's depth of any kind of soil, representing a depth of about eight inches. Here, in a typical Aldershot soil, I am not content with a depth of three spit, but go three feet, as described in the chapter on "Plants for Poor Soils," p. 252.

But official dwellers in and about the camp have one grand advantage which I have not, in a vast supply of stable manure. And though it has neither the cooling quality of cow manure nor the richness of pig, yet anything of a nourishing nature in so poor a soil is of extreme value, especially as it also puts into the ground the precious chemical constituents of the decayed straw. And an abundant supply of stable refuse has another use, hardly less important. For supposing the ground to be deeply dug, and a good dressing of manure worked in, and flowering things planted, nothing, in a light soil and a climate with an over-abundance of blazing sun, such as the camp enjoys, can be more valuable than the possibility of applying a generous "mulch." To mulch is to cover the ground with some porous material that will keep the surface cool and open ("open" means not caked

or clogged). Lawn-mowings, half-decayed leaves—
fresh ones would do, but they blow about—cocoa-
fibre refuse, are materials commonly used for mulching, but manure is far the best, for it has the additional
advantage of its feeding power, the rain washing the
nourishing matter down to the roots in gentle doses,
and presenting it in the way most easily assimilated.

It should be remembered that an abundant supply
of richness is also a danger, because it is easy to over-
manure, and plants too heavily manured may be
actually starved, because the food is not in a state
that they can take up. It is therefore important that
manure dug into the ground should not be too fresh,
but partly decayed. The wisest thing is to keep a
good stock of it and let it heat and ferment, turning
it over about once in three weeks. Another good
way is to spread it over the ground and let it lie for
a fortnight before digging in. Or, better still, some
may be had already decayed, when it may go into
the ground at once. Many plants and bulbs cannot
endure fresh manure at their roots; of these the most
impatient I can think of are Pæonies, Hellebores,
Gladiolus, and Tulips. Fresh and decayed stuff is
technically known as "long" and "short." Therefore
it will now be understood that when we read, "Long
stable litter is an excellent mulching material," it
means that it is well to coat the surface of the ground
among plants with fresh refuse from the stables. For

mulching, it does not matter whether it is old or new, but as the decayed or short is the more valuable for putting into the ground, it is a convenience in garden economy to use the long for mulching. So it will be seen that a mulch may be protective only, or it may be both protective and nutritious. Nothing can be better for the surface of a flower border than a mulch a good two inches deep of stable stuff without the straw. The sun soon bleaches it to a pale colour that makes the bare places on borders rather too conspicuous, but by midsummer no ground will be seen and the health and vigour of the plants will soon show the virtue of the treatment.

Mulching is also a great economy of water, for not only does it keep the surface of the ground cool, so that less watering is required, but when water is given, none is lost by running off or wasted by evaporation, but all goes in, carrying with it some of the richness of the protective coating.

So much, therefore, for the necessary operations in naturally poor ground; the same methods being equally applicable to any place where the garden has been neglected.

It is obvious that when a garden is to be occupied for a few years only, it is not worth while to do much in the way of permanent improvement, though my own wish would always be to do some one thing in this way, so that I might leave the garden distinctly better than I found it. So that we may leave out of consideration the planting of slow-growing shrubs and trees, for it is only after from three to five years that these make strong and regular growth.

Let us suppose that the house is taken at mid-summer. No important gardening can be begun then, but it is always well to have a little time before-hand to consider what is best to be done and to see what the garden already contains.

The first thing will be to see what dry rubbish there is, and to clear it away and burn it, keeping all soft rubbish, such as green weeds, leaves, &c., for burying deep in cultivated ground. Then, if the case were my own, I should look over any hard-wooded flowering shrubs; many of them, such as Weigela and Spiræa, want cutting back after flowering; not clipping all over, but cutting out any portions that look old and overworn to let more air and light into the younger wood. Much of this can be done more conveniently in the winter, but not nearly so effec-tively, because the healthy growth of leaves on the younger wood points clearly to what should be kept. The beautiful Weigelas especially call for this help in summer.

If there are any frames and hand-lights they should be repaired and painted, so that they may be in good condition for housing anything rather tender through the winter and for raising seeds in a hot-bed in March and April.

If there is any bare ground, or ground bearing

worthless crops, or flowering things of poor kinds, it had better be all deeply dug and manured so that it is in readiness for autumn sowing. The first seeds to sow will be those of Poppies, about the middle of August; the great double Opium Poppies, Shirley Poppies, and beautiful kinds such as *Papaver glaucum* and *P. umbrosum.* Then in the first or second week of September we can sow Sweet Peas. They should be sown thinly in a shallow trench, say three inches deep at the bottom and sloping out to a width of a foot at the ground-level, and they should stand about four inches high in the shelter of the trench through the winter. Other good things to sow at this time are Nemophila, *Omphalodes linifolia*, tall annual Larkspurs, Pot Marigold, Platystemon, and annual Iberis; then we must try and beg or buy some biennials that were sown last May—Wall-flowers, Pansies, Foxgloves, Mulleins, Canterbury Bells, *Œnothera lamarkiana*, and Sweet-William. If there are any bedding plants worth saving, cuttings should be made in August. The simplest gardener knows how to make cuttings and how to make a hotbed, but any amateurs who wish to know for themselves should have that most useful book, " Johnson's Gardener's Dictionary " (George Bell & Son).

It is difficult to make any one understand how very thinly annual seeds should be sown, and even though I know it well myself and never cease preaching it to others, I confess that I can never sow

Poppy-seed so thinly as to be to my liking. In any case there must be a deal of thinning, for the large Poppies should stand not less than a foot apart, and in the case of autumn-sown Nemophila and Platystemon a single plant will easily cover a yard of space. One often sees annual seedlings coming up like a thick turf, when it is almost impossible to thin them: it is wrong twice over, for seed is wasted and plants are spoiled. But if the sowing is so thin that the little plants come up about two inches apart, the easy thinning of the weaker will leave the stronger undisturbed, the ground is not robbed, and the youngsters grow on thrivingly.

Unless the garden is unusually well stocked and planted, it is best to clear off all " soft stuff" (annuals and tender bedding plants) by the middle of September this first year, so as to have, as it were, the decks cleared for action in good time.

If there are any evergreen hedges of Yew or Cypress that want clipping, or any such trees that need careful pruning or shaping, it should be done in the end of August or beginning of September.

A few hard-wooded shrubs are of fairly fast growth, such as the beautiful Mexican Orange-flower (*Choisya ternata*) and the large-flowered *Ceanothus*, Gloire de Versailles — both liking a warm soil and a warm place; and even for a three years' tenancy it would be worth while to plant some Cistuses—grand plants for Aldershot, as they

revel in light soil and sunshine—and Lavender and
Rosemary. A whole garden could be planted with
these alone to represent hard-wooded shrubby growths;
other plants specially suitable for sandy soils are
described in the chapter already referred to.

In many of these small camp gardens there is a
want of shade and shelter and privacy. A capital
hedge, ten feet high, quickly grown, handsome and
profitable, is made by the ordinary way of growing
Scarlet Runner Beans. Let the occupier of the camp
garden provide a good supply of strong bean-poles,
and a few of the hop-pole size, and he can make
arbour, pergola, and outer screens, and have walls and
bowers and covered ways of magnificent and quick-
growing vegetation. The Gourd tribe alone will make
a summer forest of great leaf and almost greater fruit.
Grandest of all are the *Potiron rouge* of the French.
The Mammoth Gourd is as large a fruit, but to my
eye the taller-shaped is less handsome than the flatter.
I have grown them of more than a hundred pounds
weight; this was over the low-tiled roof of some
garden sheds. The ordinary tiles were unable to
bear the weight, so they were replaced with a very
large and strong tile, and each great fruit as it grew
was provided with blocks to keep it in place. In the
camp garden some of the lower fruits would have to
be given strong seats such as an Army and Navy
Stores case would provide, and higher up in arbour
or trellis some simple bracing of short pieces of pole

GOURDS

would have to be arranged to carry the weight; for the
sudden descent of a fruit weighing a hundred pounds
might be disconcerting, even if not dangerous, to any
one who had sought the repose and shade of the leafy
bower. I always have the seed of the *Potiron rouge*
from that great French firm, Messrs. Vilmorin, Quai de
la Mégisserie, Paris. Vegetable Marrows can be used
in exactly the same way, and there are many pretty
varieties of smaller growing Gourds described in Messrs.
Vilmorin's catalogue as well as in those of our home
seedsmen. All are grown in the same way : sown in
pots in hotbed or warm greenhouse, gradually inured
to a cooler temperature when they have got two pairs
of rough leaves, and planted out early in June with
hand-lights or bell-glasses over them for ten days,
more and more air being gradually given. The seed
should be soaked for twelve hours before sowing, and
where they are to grow, good holes must be prepared
with a barrow-load of manure worked into the bottom
of each, and some of the best mixed soil available, for
the young plants to root into at the top.

I have often thought what a beautiful bit of
summer gardening one could do, mainly planted with
things usually grown in the kitchen garden only, and
filling up spaces with quickly-grown flowering plants.
For climbers there would be the Gourds and Marrows
and Runner Beans ; for splendour of port and beauty
of foliage, Globe Artichokes and Sea-kale, one of the
grandest of blue-leaved plants. Horse-radish also

makes handsome tufts of its vigorous deep-green leaves, and Rhubarb is one of the grandest of large-leaved plants. Or if the garden were in shape a double square, the further portion being given to vegetables, why not have a bold planting of these grand things as a division between the two, and behind them a nine-feet-high foliage-screen of Jerusalem Artichoke. This Artichoke, closely allied to our perennial Sunflowers, is also a capital thing for a partition screen ; a bed of it two or three feet wide is a complete protection through the summer and to the latest autumn.

Other climbing plants of quick growth, just what are wanted for making a good show during a short tenancy, are the blue Passion-flower (bought in a pot at the nursery and planted in spring or autumn), *Eccremocarpus scaber*, hardy in our southern counties, *Cobœa scandeus*, sometimes surviving if well protected, and the annual Japanese Hop. The three last are easily grown from seed, but *Cobœa* and *Eccremocarpus* should be sown in heat. The common Hop is all very well if it is there already, but as it is a strong-rooting peren-nial it takes two years to become established ; then, as it is herbaceous, it has every year to grow afresh from the root, so that it does nothing more to our advantage than the annual one, while its great roots are desperate robbers of our poor soil.

Still thinking of some of the questions of my camp visitors, and also bearing in mind the indefinite way in which the word " herbaceous " is commonly

used, it may be well to explain that herbaceous is a
term in botany meaning that a plant has a perennial
root and an annual top. As there are herbaceous
plants in all parts of the world, many not hardy with
us, it is simpler and at the same time more accurate
to say hardy plants, or hardy perennials if we wish to
exclude the mention of annuals ; and I cannot repress
a feeling of regret when I hear people talk of " herba-
ceouses," when they do not mean to speak of plants
that are actually herbaceous, but of such as are hardy
and suitable for the flower border ; for these include
a good number, such as all the varieties of Broad-
leaved Saxifrage and the Sea-Lavenders, that are
quite hardy but not at all herbaceous.

The camp and other garden of short tenure will
naturally want some good hardy border plants ; and
these must be chosen among those that will make a
good show the first season after planting. Among
these, three families stand out conspicuously ; for in
light soils they require yearly transplanting, with the
accompanying new digging and enriching of their
places.   They are the perennial Sunflowers, the perennial Asters (Michaelmas Daisies), and the Phloxes.
The two first families especially, revel in light soil well
manured.   The Phloxes are happier in a cool strong
soil, but they are so important in late summer that
it will be well to say how they may be grown.   The
fact that they are all plants that increase quickly
(from three to four-fold in the yearly growth), points

to the need of also yearly division and fresh enrich-
ment of the earth. Of the Sunflower, there are six
kinds that I think most worthy, namely, *Helianthus
decapetalus, H. lætiflorus,* two varieties of *H. multiflorus*
(the tall single and the shorter double Soleil d'or), *H.
rigidus,* and its giant variety Miss Mellish. The good
kinds of Michaelmas Daisy, a family that has of late
years been much improved, are now so numerous that
an attempt at a detailed description would be too
lengthy, but any of the good nurseries would send a
selection of kinds if the buyer stated his wishes, such
as for tall or short, early or late varieties. I always
group with the Michaelmas Daisies the handsome
tall white Daisy, *Pyrethrum uliginosum.* Though it is
a plant of a different family, it is of Daisy form and
flowers with the Asters; and as there is as yet no very
large white flowered Aster, it answers to the need in
an admirable manner. Indeed I am not at all sure
that it will not always keep its place as the most suitable companion to the Michaelmas Daisies, for it must
of necessity be a long time before a white Aster can
be evolved that can come into successful competition
with its hardy nature and bounty of large white
bloom. This fine plant also needs yearly division,
and therefore is one of the best for the camp garden.

The whole family of autumn-blooming Phlox is
impatient of drought and hot sunshine. They should
therefore be planted where they are shaded from the
longest and fiercest of sun-heat, and in as cool a place

as may be; then if well mulched and watered they
will do well.

The next group of plants of most importance will
be the flag-leaved Irises, for though they flower rather
sparingly the first year, their bloom is at its best in
the two years following. Other good hardy plants
that bloom well the year after planting are *Anthemis
tinctoria*, the Scarlet Balm (*Monarda*), *Lychnis chalce-
donica*, the Heleniums, the herbaceous Spiræas, includ-
ing the double Meadowsweet—all Spiræas like water
—the fine blue Cranesbill (*Geranium eriostemon*), the
smaller Œnotheras, *Chrysanthemum maximum, Coreopsis
lanceolata, Gaillardia grandiflora, Nepeta, Doronicum,
Galega*, and hardy autumn Chrysanthemums.

These plants, with a certain number of the
cheaper bulbs, such as *Gladiolus brenchleyensis* and
G. Colvillei The Bride; mixed late Tulips, or some
of the cheaper of them in separate colours, such
as *T. macrospeila* and *T. Gesneriana*, both reds;
Golden Crown and French Crown, yellow and red
and yellow respectively; and Spanish Iris, with some
spring-grown hardy annuals sown in place, and a
selection of the best half-hardy annuals sown in
heat, ought to be enough for a small garden.
The half-hardy annuals would be Stocks and China
Asters, Zinnias, French and African Marigolds,
Nicotiana affinis, Maize, and annual Sunflowers, of
which I consider the pale sulphur-coloured one is
much the best. These have to be raised in pans

in heat, and hardened and grown on in a cold
frame till ready to put out early in June. Here
again beware of thick sowing; indeed, unless there
is ample convenience for pricking out the seedlings into boxes of earth, it is better to place
each seed so spaced in the pan that the young
plant may stand and grow without crowding its
neighbour till planting-out time comes.

All this advice, as will be seen, is for those who
have not had much previous knowledge; the kinds
of plants can easily be increased or altered by
those who have already some experience of plants
and gardening.

Hollyhocks may also be grown; plants should
be bought; a good rich hole prepared as for
Gourds will suit them, also Dahlias, but the roots
of these must in winter be kept in some place
that is fairly dry and quite frost-proof.

If the owner of the camp garden is ingenious
he will make flower-boxes and fill them with
Geraniums, bought in June at four shillings a
dozen; then there are the shallow open butter-
tubs to be had of grocers—pretty flower-holders
just as they are, lasting from two to three years,
and longer if painted. For colour of paint for
garden tubs or seats I should advise matching the
grey-green of the sage-leaf.

We ought not to forget the quick-growing
ways of the great Japan Knot-weeds (*Polygonum*),

growing fast and tall, or the pretty Two-flowered Everlasting Pea (*Lathyrus grandiflorus*), a perennial of about the height of the Sweet Pea. This pretty plant is shown at the cottage door (page 75). And then there are the grand Nasturtiums, for hanging down from boxes or for growing up spray, or for clothing the ground with their gorgeous bloom, so splendid of colouring in latest autumn. And a plant that should not be forgotten is the Box-thorn or Tea-tree, often used to cover cottage porches or to make arbours. It is a fast-growing, slightly thorny shrub throwing out long arching sprays. The foliage is neat and the flowers rather pretty though not conspicuous. It will grow in almost pure sand.

People who are handy and ingenious and willing to take trouble can do all sorts of delightful things in the garden. If such a case as the temporary ownership of a small garden in sandy soil had been my own, I should not only have put up trellis shelters and arbour frames, but I should have arranged to cover their winter bareness and provide the garden space with some kind of winter shelter. Where there is a sandy soil there are probably large plantations of Scotch Fir. I should set about finding out if I could get a few Scotch Fir trees—thinnings of a plantation or loppings of lower branches of trees on common lands, and I should cut them up into large branches

and in some cases whole tops, and tie them into
arbour and trellis with osier withes. These materials
are easily to be had in the district I have mostly in
mind, and probably in any other there would be
equivalents. And it does not do to give it up
because the first person asked cannot put one in
the way of finding out. One must ask everybody;
especially country carriers, old country carpenters,
land and estate agents, auctioneers, landlords of
public-houses where numbers of country folk call.
And so I should make my little garden warm
and snug in winter as well as well clothed and
shaded with luscious leafage in summer, and it
would only be in the keen winds of March that the
sheltering branches would turn first pale and then
rusty, and then we would have them down and
make them into a neat stack in the corner where
rubbish is burnt, to use from time to time as the
substructure of the frequent fire-heap.

CHAPTER XVIII

SOME NAMES OF PLANTS

IT is interesting to try and trace some of the ways by which familiar garden plants come by their popular names.

Many of our oldest favourites have names only slightly altered from the Latin; in this way we get Rose, Lily, Tulip, Pæony, Lavender, Rosemary, Violet, and numbers of others. Some of the most familiar names of the sweet-herbs of the kitchen garden come to us in the same way; hence we have Mint, Borage, Fennel, Coriander, Thyme, and Chervil, and the vegetables, Carrot, Cauliflower, and Beet, and some trees, as Elm, Poplar, Juniper, Tamarisk, and Cypress. And all these names are so familiar and have become such good English that we forget how we came by them, and that they are only the Latin names with the corners rounded off. And of the older names these seem to be the most permanent, for though we may retain many of what one may call old English names, such as Canterbury Bell and Snowdrop, Hollyhock, Honeysuckle, and Sweet-William, yet a great number, though still known, have gone out of use.

Nobody now says Gilliflower, though it is a much better name than the vague Carnation; and the pretty Eglantine, though the sound of it is still known, is put away in the lumber-room of things not used or wanted ; and most people have even forgotten that it was the older name for Sweet-brier. And as for all that rollicking company of Bobbing Joan and Blooming Sally and Bouncing Bet, they have long been lost, reappearing only in the more dull and decorous guise of Wild Arum and French Willow and Soapwort.

But let us treasure the best of our old plant-names, Sweet Sultan and Bachelors' Buttons, Eye-bright, Foxglove, Nightshade, and London Pride, and especially those that have about them a flavour of poetical feeling or old country romance, such as Travellers' Joy, Meadowsweet, Speedwell, Forget-me-not, Lads'-love, Sweet Cicely, Love-in-a-mist.

Some of our popular names, as indeed are most of the botanical ones, are descriptive of the appearance of the flower or whole plant, or of some prominent form of the seed-vessel. A few examples are Monkshood, Snap-dragon, Pennywort, Shepherd's Purse, Grape Hyacinth, Cockscomb, Marestail, Dutch-man's Pipe, Hose-in-hose, Gardeners' Garters, Cotton-grass, Hartstongue, Snowdrop, Woodbine.

Some derive names from their economic uses— as Broom, Spindle-tree, and Butcher's Broom—while others are among the oldest words of our language;

pure Anglo-Saxon, many of them coming down to us almost unaltered in sound. Among this roll of honour are the bread-grains, Wheat, Barley, Oats, and Rye, also Flax and Hemp, Hazel, Heath, Bracken and Bramble, Oak, Ash, Yew, Beech and Holly, Daisy, Daffodil, Ivy, Mullein and Teazel, Nettle, Dock, Thistle, Rush, Sedge, Yarrow, Hemlock, and Groundsel. Some plants take their name from the time of year when they are in bloom, as May, Lent Lily, Christmas Rose, and Michaelmas Daisy.

I am afraid we must allow that our ancestors were happier than we are in inventing names for garden varieties of flowers ; for when I look in nurserymen's plant-lists and find such a name as " Glare of the Garden " for a beautiful and desirable plant, I cannot help feeling how painfully such a name contrasts with the more pleasantly descriptive and often pretty ones, such as Parkinson quotes in his chapter on Carnations : Faire Maid of Kent, the Daintie, the Lustie Gallant, the Pale Pageant, the Dainty Lady. The last-named Carnation (then Gilliflower) we still grow, but have corrupted the name into the Painted Lady. It is a pretty kind that should be more grown, with fringed petals that are rosy-scarlet on the face and white at the back. It is not perhaps easy to get, and probably not much in favour in nurseries because " the grass has no neck " ; that is to say, the shoots, instead of spreading outwards with long joints at the base

"One other department of the garden is a source of pleasure, namely a border or ... garden for the sweet-herbs ... not in the kitchen garden only ... Here should be two or three plants each of the Thymes, Basils, and Savouries, Tarragon and Chervil, a bush of Sage, some clumps of Balm, Marjoram and Fennel, Soup-celery and Parsley ... Borage and a little Mint, and within reach a Bay-tree." A decorative herb garden with, in the foreground, a thick growth of Borage.

that are easy to layer, have the joints so short that
the shoots are crowded together into one close tuft.

Sometimes when the botanical name is descriptive,
it is simply translated into the English equivalent, as
Helianthus into Sunflower and *Chrysocoma* into Goldi-
locks.

Some flowers have names referring to Bible stories
or incidents, such as Aaron's Rod, Jacob's Ladder,
Solomon's Seal, and Star of Bethlehem, all still in use,
though others that might be classed with them, such
as Grace-of-God (*Hypericum*), Gethsemane (*Orchis*),
and Hallelujah (*Oxalis*) have been lost.

Though it is undoubtedly desirable to have a
popular name for every flower that has become
familiar, the numbers of fine plants that have been
introduced of late years have been many more than
have as yet found fitting names in our own tongue.
And in spite of vigorous effort on the part of those
who have earned the best right to give English names
to plants comparatively new to cultivation, but now
well established in English gardens, the fact remains
that the names which are used or proposed have to
follow that strange but undoubted law in the progress
of language, that all words belonging to it must grow
and cannot be made.   Sometimes a new name will
be adopted at once ; the good white and yellow
varieties of *Chrysanthemum frutescens* that came to us
from France were very soon called " Paris Daisies " by
the market people, and Paris Daisies they remain.

In this case no doubt the general want of a popular
name was only a part of the reason for one being
quickly found, for to many people " Chrysanthemum "
means only the garden varieties of *C. sinense*, and an
easy English name became necessary in order to
avoid confusion.

But language is like the horse in the proverb,
you may lead it to the water but you cannot make it
drink.   A word that is really wanted may be invented ;
it may be graceful and suitable and placed temptingly
before the public eye ; it may be taken up or it may
be left—there is no saying.

The strangest thing of all is the way some perfectly good, strong, much-wanted words drop out of
use, such as the old English " Sperage " for Asparagus.
Here is a fine old plant-name with its honourable
pedigree written on its face, recalling on the way the
ancient use of the feather-brush-like sprays of the
wild plant in the old Roman churches of Southern
Europe for " asperging " the congregation.   And for
some unknown reason this good old word goes out
of use, in order to revert to the much more cumbersome Latin.

In our common speech many an example may be
found of the same capricious waywardness, that shows
itself in neglecting the good word or in perverting it
from its true meaning, and putting in its place some
other word which is weaker and in all ways worse.
In some cases a whole swarm of poor substitutes only

show the more clearly how much the good old word
is wanted, and yet it is left unused till at last it dies.
These fine old words die first in common speech,
though they may linger long in literature. Why are
we shy of the good word " trustworthy," or why for
once that it is used do we hear fifty times the
weak and ill-constructed " reliable " or the still worse
" dependable " ?

Why do we hover all round the fine old verb to
" thrust " with feebler words like " push " or " poke "
or vulgarities like " shove " ?

What has become of the name of the old virtue
" fortitude," seldom heard in speech and only living
in the best literature ?   What other word can express
the magnificent combination of courage and endur-
ance that we only hear spoken of in terms of school-
boy cant as " pluck," or in those of racing slang as
" staying-power "

In many cases the botanical names of plants have
been so long in popular use that they have actually
become a part of our language. When this is so,
and the Latin or Greek name has become perfectly
familiar, there is no need to cast about for an English
one, especially in the case of those plants whose names
are pretty and pleasant and neither long nor cumbersome. So we have Iris and Ixia, Azalea, Kalmia,
Daphne, Anemone, Clematis, Verbena, and Cistus and
many others. They have passed into the language by
general adoption and approval, and there can be no

need of other names in their places. A few long
awkward names such as Rhododendron have passed
in with them, but as they are generally known they
must also remain.

But among well-known plant-names there are
some curious vagaries, for we commonly call the fine
flowering shrub *Philadelphus* "Syringa," which is the
botanical name of the Lilac, and it is much more generally
known as Syringa than by the English name Mock-
Orange. Another example of the botanical name of
one plant being used as the popular name of another
is that of the family *Tropæolum*. Who can say why
we call it "Nasturtium," which is the botanical
name of the Water-cress?

Sometimes a plant is popularly known by its own
specific botanical name as in the cases of Oleander,
Auricula, and Hepatica. These are botanically *Nerium
Oleander*, *Primula Auricula*, and *Anemone Hepatica*.
But there is a reasonable excuse for this practice,
because they were classed by the older botanists under
those names as generic which are now retained as
specific only; and according to botanical usage, which
by no means disregards the concerns of etymology, this
fact in the plant's history is recorded by the capital
letter being retained in the specific name.

I can only think of one English plant-name that
is made from a true specific name. This is the Tube-
rose (*Polianthes tuberosa*). It reminds me of a dear
old garden friend and true lover of plants, whose

apprehension of botanical names was somewhat vague, but whose use of them was entirely without restraint, who asked me if I had got any of that beautiful "speciosum." Putting my mind into a suitable attitude I answered, " Oh yes, and any amount of the still more glorious ' spectabile ' " !

Considering how much of our language and civilisation came many centuries ago from France, it seems strange how few names of French origin remain among our flowers. There are no doubt others, but I can only think of Dandelion (*Dent de Lion*), aptly named after the toothed edge of the leaf. The much more modern "Mignonette" has a French sound but at any rate now is purely an English name, for the French for Mignonette is always the botanical name *Réséda*. I often ask cottage folk what they call the familiar garden flowers. The answers are not always satisfactory, as, except in the case of those that cannot be mistaken, such as Rose, Lily, Pansy, and Violet, they are apt to apply well-known names rather indiscriminately.

Indeed I have known several cases in which all garden flowers were called " Lilies," and all weeds "Docks." An old woman that we had some years ago to weed the lawn was one of those who held to this broad and simple distinction in botanical nomenclature, for though there was not a Dock in the grass, and her work was to fork up Daisies and Dandelions, Plantains and Hawkweeds; yet whenever one asked how she was getting on, and of what kinds of weeds she found the greater number, her broad brown face would beam her appreciation of the interest shown in her work, and her stout figure would make a sudden subsidence in the good old country bob-curtsey, as she gave the invariable answer " Docks, m'm."

Sometimes the country folk will make a name of their own. I think this must have been the case in a village in the south of Sussex in whose neighbourhood I was often on a visit to a dear friend, now, alas, no longer living. There was a grand growth of *Bignonia radicans* along the front of some cottages, whose occupiers called it by the capitally descriptive name of Flowering Ash. And from the same friend I learnt the most remarkable country plant-name I ever heard; for she told me that one day, asking the mistress of a cottage home what she called the well-known Stonecrop with spreading heads of bright-yellow flowers on six-inch-high stalks that grew on the low old wall in front of the cottage garden, the woman said: " Well, m'm, *we* call it Welcome-home-husband-be-he-ever-so-drunk " !

CHAPTER XIX

WILD FERNS

I am thankful to live in a place where many Ferns are among our wild hedge plants, and above all where there is an abundance of Bracken. For though my neighbourhood is populous, and the hedges of the most frequented ways have been stripped of their Ferns, yet I know the country so well for a good many miles round, that when I want to see any particular Fern I am nearly always able to find it, though it is true that some habitats of rather rare Ferns have been entirely destroyed. In one great swampy hollow, where, when I was a child, I remember the Royal Fern growing high above my head, not an atom now remains. It used to grow in great mounded tussocks, the crowns springing from a sort of raised table of matted black root nearly eighteen inches high. I remember leaning back against one of these and looking up and seeing how bright the sunlit rusty heads of flower looked against the late summer sky. It was then so abundant, and its home so little known, that there was no reason to hesitate about taking some pieces to plant by our ponds.

I have still a strong plant, that, after several
removals, has, I hope, found a final resting-place.
How tough that black root-mass was! no spade,
much less trowel, would divide it; after a first
trial with these feebler implements we had to give
it up and come back another day armed with
choppers. It was no matter of regret, for the
place was full of beauty. Such a wild bog-garden!
Sheets of brilliant Sphagnum covering stretches of
soft black bog that could not be crossed, but whose
edges might be cautiously approached. Quantities
of the wonderful little Sundew clutching its prey;
white plumes of the silky Cotton-grass; tufts of
Bog-Asphodel, neatest of small plants, with its sheaf
of tiny Iris-like leaves and conspicuous spikes of
deep-yellow flower; the pale and shaggy Marsh St.
John's Wort, and, daintiest and loveliest of wild
plants, the tiny Bog Pimpernel, its thread-like stem
carrying the neat pairs of leaves through the tufts
of Sphagnum, and its flowers of tenderest, loveliest
pink looking up to the sun.

Then what stretches of the pink Bell Heather,
with here and there a white one for luck, and the
pink all kinds of pink from pale to quite a rosy
colour. And what a joy it was to find for the
first time, on a rather bare patch that two years
ago some poor commoner had pared for peat, the
Stag's Horn Moss (*Lycopodium clavatum*), with its
bright though deep green prostrate branches pinned

to the dark peaty earth by the wiry white roots. The Northern Hard Fern (*Blechnum boreale*) abounds in the haunts of the Osmunda. Of this plenty remains, as it is abundant on the fringes of the boggy peat ground, and not being generally considered so ornamental as some others, it escapes the random collector. Like the Osmunda, it has also a flowering spike, or rather a taller development of frond which alone bears the fructification ; the smaller and more numerous fronds being entirely barren. Every now and then one comes upon patches of Blechnum upon quite dry ground, but here it is always stunted and bears fewer fertile fronds.

Where the wild heathland has been partly tamed and adjoins cultivation, and ditches have been cut, there is the place to look for the large and lovely Lady Fern (*Athyrium Filix-fœmina*). Clear and fresh of colour, stately of port, admirable in the perfect " set " of the large twice-pinnate fronds and in their grace of carriage, arched as they are with a plume-like bending towards their tips—to the Lady Fern must be accorded the place of honour for beauty among our native kinds. This lovely plant seems most at home when growing at the edge of water with its roots taking up their fill of moisture. To see it thus, with its noble fronds mirrored in the face of the still pool, is to see a picture of fern-beauty that can hardly be surpassed.

The only other of our wild Ferns that in my

opinion comes at all near the Lady Fern in beauty is
the Dilated Shield Fern (*Lastrea dilatata*), slightly stiffer
in form and perhaps all the better for it, for the
only defect of the lovely *Filix-fœmina* is a slightly
succulent weakness of aspect. The broad shoulder and
equality of plane in the whole frond are distinctive
features in this handsome Shield Fern, and the tooth-
ing at the edge has a look of well-finished design
that is vigorous without being over-hard. The fronds
are not many, but are well displayed, and the whole
plant conspicuously handsome.

Here and there throughout the country are large
old woods of Scotch Fir. Two of these adjoin boggy
heathland, and on the shady sides of ditches and
depressions on their outskirts, and even in their hearts,
this grand Fern grows in luxuriance.

The Prickly Shield Fern occurs here and there.
I scarcely wish it to be more frequent, for of all the
larger common Ferns it is the one I least admire. I
always think it uninteresting. The colouring is dull
and heavy, and the fronds stand in a rather upright,
crowded way that to my eye is unsatisfactory. The
Male Fern (*Lastrea Filix-mas*), on the other hand, I
am glad to know is the commonest of all; a fine
cheerful handsome thing, always a welcome sight.
Many a hedge a little way out of the beaten track is
full of it, and in some places in our deep-cut lanes
it defies the collector from its inaccessible position.
It will bear to be in a fairly dry place; the shady side

of a hedge-bank is its most usual home, but it often
occurs in great beds on the flat in hazel copses, and
in these sheltered places will hold the fronds green
into the dead of the winter. Cottagers are fond of
a good tuft of Male Fern in their gardens, and in
my own garden I use it rather largely among Rhododendrons and for many positions at the edge of shrub
clumps next to the grass.

It grows capitally in London in back-gardens,
areas, or pots; indeed I remember reading a few years
ago about the wild plants that had sprung up on a
plot of land in the heart of the City, where buildings
had been demolished, and that for two years had not
been built upon. Among them were some flourishing
tufts of Male Fern.

The most frequent of the Ferns in our lanes is
the Polypody. It seems to love our crumbling sand,
and to establish itself among the roots of trees
and bushes, especially on Hazels. The creeping
rhizome laps over the Hazel roots and "plashed"
stems, so that it is easily detached in a sort of thin
sheet with its accompaniment of short moss and sandy
earth. Not infrequently one finds such a sheet of
the Fern lying fallen at the foot of the hedge-bank,
when the crumbling of dry sand that is always going
on underneath has left it without support. Sometimes whole square yards of ground at the top or
upper part of one of our shaded sandy lanes will be
covered with Polypody. The young fronds come up

fresh and bright in June and stand far into the winter, only perishing with severe frost.

In some places Polypodies will grow on the trunks and branches of rather stunted Oaks. In a wood I used to know in the Isle of Wight, where a thick growth of small Oaks came down to within twenty yards of high-water mark, this was the rule rather than the exception; but in my neighbourhood I have only seen a single case of a wood where the Polypodies grow on the Oaks, and that is only in one sheltered corner at one edge of the wood. If it happens there, I always wonder why it does not occur oftener. There are plenty of stunted Oaks about, and plenty of Poly-podies, why therefore does not the happy combination oftener come about?

The fine Hart's-tongue Fern is rare about here; it wants a strong loamy soil. I remember a few plants of it in the edge of one ditch, but that ditch has long been buried under the raised approaches to a railway bridge. It is fairly plentiful a few miles to the south in the clay lands of the Weald. But I sometimes see it a few courses down the mouth of a well, grow-ing out of the relics of lime in the decaying joint, and its occurrence in a curious way in a railway wall will be described presently.

The Ferns that seem to have least need of water, after Polypody, which is frequent in old walls, are the two other most common of wall Ferns, the Wall-Rue (*Asplenium ruta-muraria*) and the Wall Spleenwort

(*Asplenium trichomanes*).   Common   in   the   moister
climate of the west of England, but rare here, is the
Scaly Spleenwort (*Ceterach officinarum*).   Of old-established habitats in this neighbourhood I only know
two.

Twenty or more years ago a branch line of railway
was built, passing about three miles from where I live,
and running more or less north and south.   There is
a level crossing just at the end of one of the station
platforms, on a road along which I often drive.   Only
a couple of years ago, when on the crossing, I saw
something like a fringe of greenery growing out of
the upper part of the dwarf wall facing the line, that
brings the platform to the level of the carriage foot-
boards.   Going to see what it was, to my delight
there was a tightly-packed little wild Fern-garden, all
growing out of one joint of the brickwork.   The edge
of the platform and top of the wall is formed by a deep
and wide blackish coping-brick, with a rounded edge,
its top surface having a slight fall towards the line, in
continuation of that of the whole width of the platform.
Its upright face next to the line has two courses of
bricks below it, overhanging the lower part of the wall,
which from that point recedes about three inches.
The lowest edge of these overhanging courses is, no
doubt, intended to act as a " drip " for any wet that
runs off the platform, and very likely it does so; but
some of the moisture evidently reaches the joint, and
at this point grows the little Fern-garden, in the one

joint only. Here are no less than seven kinds of Ferns, two of them rare in the district. The list is : Male Fern, Black Spleenwort, Polypody, Wall - Rue, Wall Spleenwort, Hart's-tongue, and Scaly Spleenwort (*Ceterach*). They grow sometimes singly, sometimes in a friendly group of two or three sorts together. I hope this may not meet the eye of any guardian of the line, or that if it does, that he may love Ferns. Of course, they do take to themselves a little of the lime in the company's mortar, but they are content with so little sustenance that I should doubt if any root penetrated more than half an inch ; and meanwhile they adorn the wall with so gracious and beautiful a trimming that to remove them would seem an act of wanton barbarity.

When one sees this one spot where these little plants have found a dwelling, it sets one thinking about the millions of fern-spores that must be everywhere flying about looking for places where they may lodge and grow. In all probability the minute seedspores did not actually lodge in the joint where they took root, for it is overhung by the upper courses of brickwork ; unless they were blown up from below, which seems unlikely. I should think it more probable that the spores landed on the platform and were washed into the joint.

But of all our Ferns the one that is really important in the landscape is the Bracken ; in all its many forms and aspects a thing of beauty and of

highest pictorial value. Growing only a foot high
on the poorest and most exposed of our sandy wastes,
in sheltered woodland its average is six to seven feet,
while in hedges and clumps of forest brake it rushes
up among the taller growths, and shows the upper
ends of its fronds at a height almost incredible. How
delightful it is by the sides of our many unfenced
roads; how it accommodates itself to the conditions
of its position and graces every place. How perfectly
it groups itself with its wild companions great and
small; with the Heaths and fine Grasses of the moor-
lands, with the Brambles and Thorns, Hollies, Birches,
Junipers, and small Oaks of the wild poor ground that
has never known the plough, with the thicker woods
of Fir, where in cooler ground it takes a deeper colour;
while in woodland openings the blue of the heavens
is reflected in the wide-spread sheets of flattened
frond.

Then one thinks with satisfaction of how pleasant
a shelter it is to living creatures, to the deer of park
and forest, and to all the smaller feathered and furry
folk of copse and moorland and roadside waste.

It is not in summer only that the Bracken is good
to see, for in winter its cheerfulness of rusty warmth
is distinctly comforting, as we who live on the sandy
hills well know. For when we visit our neighbours
in the weald or in the valleys, and see the sodden
grass reeking with winter wet, and the leafless trees
dripping, and the cold mists hanging to the ground

Birch and Bracken in wild Woodland

we come back with glad thankfulness to our warm
dry hills with their red Fern-carpet and their well-
clothed Firs; to the silver-barked Birches swaying, and
their crimson spray swishing, in the cheerful breeze
and the clear bright light of the blessed sun.

When I was a child, this neighbourhood, now rather
thickly populated, was very little known. Ferns were
plentiful in the cool lane-banks, many of them deep,
and dark with the shade of old Hazels and Oaks nearly
meeting overhead. Now, alas, with the increase of
population many of our sandy lanes have become hard
roads, and the Ferns have been torn from the hedges;
and though we know of some of the more secluded
ways where they may still be seen, yet there are no
longer the copious fringes of Polypody, and the neat
tufts of black Spleenwort, and the grand shuttlecocks
of Male Fern that were formerly so frequent, and that
added so much to the beauty of the old country bye-
ways.

I think that many people who would be glad to
grow hardy Ferns in quantity can scarcely know how
pleasant and interesting it is to grow them from seed.
Fern seeds are very minute; they are more properly
called spores. A frond of hardy Fern that looks quite
mature and that bears the dark brown seed-masses
on its back should be shaken over a sheet of paper,
when it will give off a fine dust of spores. An old
friend who was a keen gardener and successful raiser
of Ferns wrote out for me his method of growing these

spores, and for the benefit of others I can hardly do better than quote it in full. " Procure a bell-glass, not too flat at the top, but so shaped that the moisture within will trickle down the inner sides and not fall in drops on the surfaces of the small pots, for this would be certain destruction to the young growth, causing mildew. Have a seed-pan of such a size that the bell-glass goes in, leaving a little space all round between the inner side of the pan and the outer side of the glass. This space will be afterwards packed with pieces of perfectly cleansed sponge torn up. Small pots with good drainage, and filled with soil made of loam, leaf-mould, sand, and small fragments of charcoal, should be arranged in a circle on some paved space. Pour quite boiling water quickly into a fine-rosed watering-pot and well water the earth in the small pots, throw a sheet of paper over them and allow them to become stone-cold. The boiling water destroys all the eggs of insects, confervæ, and other hindrances to growth. Having ready all your small packets of Fern-spores, you may arrange them so as to grow *Athyrium* and *Scolopendrium* together, or *Polystichum* and *Athyrium* or any such mixture. By this means you can economise the room in the small pots, and at once see the varieties show themselves as they grow on. They will begin to show after a few weeks, first as a sort of green efflorescence; this changes to small green half-transparent crumpled cups, and finally the first small fronds show them-

selves. When this begins, which will be after some two or three months, you may introduce a trifle of air by placing a bit of broken slate under the edge of the bell-glass, in a few days a bit double the thickness, and so on until you can tilt the edge of the glass a little. The sponge all round must always be kept moist with cold boiled water. The pots should be properly labelled. Be sure, by using a magnifying glass, that you are sowing the actual spores and not the minute spore-cases only. When parting the young Ferns for growing on, it is well to have the pots not too moist, or the young roots will cling together and be likely to get broken; when slightly dry the soil falls easily from the small rootlets. Shade is indispensable."

"But of all our Ferns the one that is really important ... is the Bracken; in all its many forms and aspects a thing of beauty and of highest pictorial value ... how it accommodates itself to the conditions of its position and graces every place ... in winter its cheerfulness of rusty warmth is distinctly comforting."

CHAPTER XX

THE KITCHEN GARDEN

MUCH as I love the flower garden and the wood-land, I am by no means indifferent to the interest and charm of the kitchen garden. For though its products are for the most part utilitarian, they all have their life-histories, and on the rare occasions when I am free to take a quiet stroll for pure pleasure of the garden I often take it among the vegetables. I cannot help thinking of what immense importance in our life and health and well-being are the patiently gained developments of even one alone of the many families of kitchen-garden plants. When I have seen in rocky places on our English and other coasts, a straggling plant with broad glaucous leaves, I have always looked upon it with sincere respect; for this wild plant is the parent of all the members of the great Cabbage tribe. And then I think of the many hundreds of years that it has been patiently cultivated, until little by little it has been driven by careful selection and keen observation into the many forms it now takes in our gardens and on our tables. For not only do the different shapes of Cabbage, of all sorts and sizes—round,

flattened, or pointed—of loose, open shape like a
rose, or tight and hard as a drumhead—come from
this one wild plant, but also the many varieties of
Cauliflower and Broccoli, where the parts most developed are the flower-bud and thickened flower-stalk.
And besides these there are the kinds selected for
their hardiness, and by slow degrees coaxed and
persuaded into taking the forms of the winter Kales,
some nearly smooth of leaf, but often with the
leaf-edges heavily curled. Then another of the
hardiest of these winter green things is the Brussels
Sprout, its stem thickly set with tiny little tight
Cabbages just the size for a doll's dinner-table. A
still more remarkable development of this many-
sided vegetable is the thickening of the base of the
stem into a turnip-like root, as in the Swede. This
concerns the farm rather than the garden, though
a young Swede is well worth cooking. Then there
is the Kohl-Rabi, another capital turnip-rooted
Cabbage, in whose case the bulb-shaped swelling is
a little higher up the stem, so that it is just clear
of the ground, instead of being partly underground
as in the Swede. Kohl-Rabi should be more used,
for when cooked at just the right age it is an
excellent and delicate vegetable. But it is not yet
generally popular in England because it is so often
left to grow too large. If it is brought in at the
size of a billiard-ball, or of a thickness not greater
than an inch and three-quarters, it is excellent, but

is quite uneatable when old and full of a kind of
network of harsh stringy fibre. We have not yet
done with all the forms of the Cabbage, for there
are some kinds cultivated for the sake of the
succulent leaf-stem; and many members of the
whole family have a second life of productiveness,
making top and side sprouts throughout the winter
and far into the spring.

Nearly related to the Cabbage is the Turnip;
sharing with it the botanical name of *Brassica* and
with a clear relationship of flavour. For broad
practical means of distinction it is enough to
remember that all Turnips have full-green leaves
rough with prickly hairs, and that all Cabbages
have smooth ones of a glaucous colour; the only
exception to this characteristic being those of the
Savoy class, whose leaves are of a full and sometimes quite dark green, with a surface that though
smooth as to the nature of its skin, is covered with
raised blister-like prominences that give a rough
look to the leaf. The curly Kales have also a
false look of roughness because their edges are so
tightly crimped and frizzled, but the actual skin
is always smooth.

In a very delightful small book—I wish it were
longer!—entitled "Round the Year," by Professor
Miall, there is a half-chapter about Cabbages and
Turnips of the highest interest. He pictures to himself (and to his readers) how the earliest recognition

of the Cabbage as an article of food may probably
have come about; how the hungry savage, wandering
on the seashore and seeing the rather succulent plant,
tries it and finds it eatable, and by degrees brings it
into cultivation. This picture came home to me all
the more forcibly because I had already, many years
ago, had the same kind of idea about another sea-
side plant in connection with some possibly food-
hunting Ancient Briton, who would find his Sea-kale
with its tender stems blanched, not only by its natural
habit of rooting deeply in the loose sea-sand, but often
to a much greater degree, from the increased depth
over the plants of sand wind-blown, or high-heaped
by the shovelling-power of tide and storm combined.
And so my Ancient Briton would have learnt not
only that Sea-kale was good to eat, but that it was
all the better when, after winter storms, the tender
young growths were pushing up through the over-
loading covering of sand, and so he may have learned
the general principle of earthing-up, such as we
practise with Celery and Cardoons and some of our
winter salads.

I have more than once found how sweet and
tender and how little bitter is the whitened growth
of a wild Dandelion (near relation of the Lettuces)
when it has been blanched and drawn out in length
by having to grow through a mole-hill.

Professor Miall also tells of the immense benefit
that we have received from the Cabbages and Turnips

during the last two hundred years, since their introduction and cultivation as field crops for the winter
feeding of the live-stock of the farm.   For before that
time all sheep and cattle, except those reserved for
breeding, were killed and salted at the beginning of
winter, and the meat-eating population for several
months of the year had salted meat only.   Cases of
scurvy and leprosy and allied disorders were then
frequent throughout the country; but thanks to
Cabbage and Turnip, now in every cottage garden
or allotment, and to their winter use on farms, those
terrible diseases are no longer with us.

Several important occupants of the kitchen garden,
though not so nearly related as Cabbage and Turnip,
come within the great botanical family of the
Cruciferæ—plants that have all four-petalled blooms.
Among these are some of our best-known garden
flowers, such as Wall-flowers and Stocks, Iberis and
Alyssum.   Rape, so much cultivated on the Continent
under the name of Colza, for the oil of its seeds, is
botanically almost identical with Turnip.   Then, again,
Rape and Mustard are very closely connected; the
round " Mustard " seed that we sow for the quickly-
grown seed-leaves, as one of the firm of Mustard and
Cress, is very often Rape seed, which does nearly as
well.   The rank weed Charlock, with rough leaf and
yellow flower, which comes up so freely on waste
ground and on heaps of newly-moved soil, is our
native wild Mustard.

Radishes are also nearly related to Mustard and Turnip; indeed the round white ones, both in leaf and root, are a very fair presentment of a tiny Turnip. All gardeners know that Radishes should be grown as quickly as possible; a slow-grown Radish is like slowly-made toast, hard and tough and distasteful. A learned garden-friend once said to me, " Grow your Radishes in nearly pure leaf-mould." I tried growing them in well-decayed leaf-mould without admixture in late summer in a half shaded place, and kept them well watered; and though the leaves were a little drawn, never did I eat such Radishes for delicate, crisp, wet tenderness.

Within the same family of *Cruciferœ* are the delicious Water-cress, and the Winter-cress or Land-cress—eatable, but to my thinking, uninteresting— and also Horse-Radish.

Sea-kale, already mentioned in its wild state, is so handsome as a foliage plant, that I am using it in prominent places in the flower border. I only found out early this year what a capital table vegetable is the mass of crowded flower-bud, cut when at the most Broccoli-like stage. Indeed I might not have found out at all, but that I thought it well, for the encouragement of further leaf-development in some plants in the flower border, to cut out the whole stalk of bloom with its head of tight bud and thickened stem. And as it happened that green spring vegetables, after a trying drought during the last summer, were ex-

tremely scarce, and as the bud-mass looked tender
and much like a purple Broccoli, I had it cooked. It
proved so good that even when other things are in
plenty I shall not fail to use it again.

The products of the large Pea and Bean tribe are
probably of still more ancient use as human food than
even the members of the Cabbage family. Botanically
they are called *Leguminosæ*. In the flower garden
they are represented by Sweet Peas and by several of
the deep-rooted perennial Peas; by *Lathyrus sativus* of
loveliest green-blue bloom; by the Spring Bitter-Vetch
and the great Orange Vetch, handsome kinds that we
used to know as *Orobus*, but that botanists now class
all together as *Lathyrus*; also by many pretty Alpine
plants under the family names of *Anthyllis, Onobrychis*,
and their allies; and all our garden Lupins, annual
and perennial.

The same family includes the farmer's Clovers,
Tares, and Vetches, Lucerne, Saintfoin, and Trifolium,
the Broom and Gorse of our waste lands, the pretty
rosy Rest-Harrow of the roadsides, and the Dyer's
Green-weed, the true *Planta Genista* of the Plan-
tagenets.

If I had a wide upland meadow and wished to
produce honey on a large scale, I should grow a
quantity of the *Melilotus*, which I believe to be the
finest of all bee-plants; a trefoil of rather tall,
branching habit.

I wish all growing things were as clearly and

distinctively named as the Broad Bean; for I know
no plant that in nearly all its parts and phases and
aspects displays so visibly the quality of breadth.
What pair of seed-leaves are so absurdly broad? and
how broad is the leaf and the pod and the bean
within, and how thick the stem! But as if to redeem
the Broad Bean from a certain stiffness and want of
grace shown by the whole plant, there is the pretty
flower of white and black; the white of the soft
quality that is seen in white velvet, and the black the
richest of brown-blacks, also of a velvety texture.

What a delicious early summer fragrance is that
of a flowering Bean-field, when the sweet scent is
offered up as a grateful gift to the life-giving sun, and
the kindly breeze blows a share of it aside to gladden
the heart of the wayfarer. And then the Clover-field,
delicious also with sun-released, wind-blown sweetness,
less luscious than the breath of the Bean-flower, but
with a modest, honeyed homeliness that bears with it
an even greater charm.

The first tender little green Peas, how delicious
they are; their delicate sweetness makes them
almost more like some dainty fruit than a serious
food-stuff such as comes under the rude general
classification of "green vegetables"; and how good
are the first dwarf French Beans, and what a
staunch friend of late summer and autumn is the
trusty Scarlet Runner,

Elsewhere I have mentioned how useful a thing this is for growing as a temporary screen or arbour. Working people who live just out of London often use it in some such way, or train it up strings to decorate the sides of a window.

One of the prettiest ways of growing Scarlet Runners is by planting three bean-poles fully ten feet long in a triangle, with their bases about two and a half feet apart. They are put in slanting towards the centre of the triangle, and are tied together at such a height (about three feet above the ground) that their tops will spread to between six and seven feet. Three beans are sown near the foot of each pole; they soon run up, and when they are nearly full grown one or two can easily be led across to make garlands from pole to pole. Such groups in a long row some fifteen to twenty feet apart are quite handsome objects. Many years ago I learnt this piece of wisdom from an old cottager : "Gather your Runner Beans while they are straight." As the pod grows large and old they become curly in shape ; any time before this occurs they are nice and tender.

A dish of dry Beans, soaked over-night, boiled and served with hot olive-oil poured over, is the regular main meal of many a poor family in Southern Italy.

Lentil soup is about the most nutritious food that can be eaten ; it is a pity that it is not more

known and used among our own working folk, for
not only has it the finest feeding power, but it is
easily made and very good to eat. The "mess of
red pottage" for which Esau sold his birthright
could have been nothing but Lentil soup.

Every one who has to do with horses knows how
not only nourishing but also how highly stimulating
are some Beans added to the usual feed.

The large botanical order *Compositæ*, that gives
us so many garden flowers (Sunflowers, Michaelmas
Daisies, Chrysanthemums, and hosts of others), is
largely represented in the kitchen garden. All the
varieties of salad of which Lettuce is the type
come within this order, and are themselves nearly
related. They come under a sub-head as the
Chicory group. This includes Lettuces, Endive,
Dandelion, and the kinds of Chicory that we use
for winter forcing. The wild Chicory or Succory,
so frequent by roadsides in chalky soils, has pale
blue flowers of a very delicate and pretty quality;
the stems are extremely tough, and if one wants to
bring home a bunch of the pretty blooms and has
no knife, it is difficult to know how to pick them.

Being confronted with this difficulty on one
occasion, it occurred to me that where there is
chalk there are flints, and that moreover where
there are broken flints a fairly sharp edge may be
found. Luckily there was a whole heap of flints

within sight for road-mending, and it was not
difficult to find one that could be so used with a
sort of sawing action, the stem meanwhile pressed
against another flint of rounded form, as would
compel the Succory plant to give up its flowers.

The French have long cultivated a strong form
of the common Dandelion, a winter salad that should
be more generally cultivated, for it is quite excellent
and very wholesome, and nothing can be easier to
grow. It should be sown in April in an open trench;
by the time the nights are getting frosty in late
autumn it should be earthed up, earthing a little
higher as the tips of the leaves come through. A
good line of it gives an abundant supply throughout
the winter. All the late summer I have been watching the development of one wild Dandelion in a part
of my pleasure garden. It showed such a great
breadth of leaf and such unusual vigour that I am
keeping it to try for salad. As soon as the seed is
ripe, which will be about the end of next April, I
shall sow a line, and if it fulfils its early promise it
will be quite as good as any that I can buy.

I sometimes eat a salad of quite wild Dandelion
in March; for convenience of carrying cutting up
the whole plants, just under the top of the root-
stock. To avoid the greater part of the bitter taste,
which is in the juice of the mid-rib, the green part
is torn off and makes the salad. Dandelion is
Taraxacum, whose tonic properties are well known.

Salsafy, a plant of Spanish origin, comes also within the large order of Daisy-flowered plants, and both of the Artichokes; the Jerusalem Artichoke, of which we eat the roundish tuberous roots, being a near relation of the tallest growing kinds of our border perennial Sunflowers.

The Globe Artichoke and the Cardoon, two plants that botanically are nearly identical, seem to me to be of almost more value in ornamental ground than in the kitchen garden; for excellent though both are to eat, I think them still better to look at. But when they are used as noble foliage plants in the pleasure garden, it should be remembered that if the leaves are to remain in beauty the flower-stems must be cut out. But in a group it is easy to arrange that some of the plants away from the edge should be allowed to bloom, for it is beautiful in all ways, and the mighty Thistle-flower with its extremely bright blue-purple colouring is very handsome in the late summer. In the kitchen garden a fresh plantation of Artichokes should be made every three years, for as the strong-growing crowns get crowded the flower-buds become smaller; but when grown for ornament they can be left longer.

What a prosperous-looking plantation is a well-grown breadth of Beet. For preference I grow the rather small Dell's Crimson, it is so finely coloured all through, never showing those pale rings that give such a coarse look to the cut sections. And I like

its modest size, and the fine crimson of its polished
leaves that take wonderful reflections from blue sky.
The field Beets (Mangel) share the functions of the
Cabbage and Turnip family as winter feed for cattle,
but like their garden relatives they have to be harvested
early, as they are rather tender.   The other kitchen
garden plants that are related to Beet are the quick-
growing annual Spinach, and the more persistent
Orache, also the less often grown perennial Good-
King-Henry.   The leaves of all these are used in the
same way; and there is another plant, the Spinach-
Beet, a kind with bold pale leaves that are cooled
as Spinach, but is less good than the others.

There are not many representatives of this family
in the pleasure garden.   The greater number of them
have rather coarse leaves and loose spikes of greenish
flowers, but the tall annual *Atriplex hortensis atro-
sanguinea* is a fine thing in late summer and autumn,
the whole plant turning to a dull red-purple colour,
of good effect not only out of doors, but when branches
are cut for room decoration.   But it should be remembered that it is unsuitable for use in any glass
vessels, as it dyes the water red.

So many of the succulent plants that grow near
the sea are related to the Beet family that the next
plant that comes to mind is Purslane, an admirable
vegetable that is far too much neglected.   It is a
near relative of the brilliant garden Portulaccas from
Brazil.   It is used in soups, especially in that excellent

milk-soup *bonne femme,* in equal proportion with Sorrel ; also chopped fine and stewed in stock as a vegetable by itself.

The plants that bloom in umbels are well represented in the kitchen garden—Carrot, Parsnip, and Celery being the most important. The wild Carrot has a very thin root, and strangely enough, though it is the parent of our mild red kitchen friend, it has a poisonous quality. It can always be known among the many wild plants whose flowers so nearly resemble it, by the central little flower of the umbel being of a crimson or purplish colour, all the rest being white. In the late autumn one should keep a watchful eye on the Carrot-bed, because some of the leaves turn to a beautiful red colour, that makes them good to arrange with flowers.

Among the *Umbelliferæ* of the kitchen garden are also Parsley, Chervil, Fennel, and Angelica. Many of the plants of this tribe have a pungent and aromatic scent and flavour, strongest perhaps in Angelica and in Caraway-seed ; the relationship of scent clearly traceable in Chervil, Celery, and Parsley; also in that pretty plant, Myrrhis, that for its beauty deserves to be in every garden. It is rather large in size for a plant of spring, and charming with its finely-cut pale-green leaves and really handsome flowers. It is the Sweet Cicely of old English gardens.

Fennel is so handsome a plant that it is well worth

a place in the flower garden; the bold, branching flower-stems are thrown up in such graceful groups among the finely-cut foliage, that when well grown it is really a better thing than the Giant Fennels of North Africa. It is not, of course, so tall or so large all over; but, though I have become intolerant of anything at all rubbishy among garden plants, I think the common Fennel is not so well treated as it deserves. It was only quite lately that I learned how good a thing it is in a cut state, when I saw in a neighbour's house a simple and excellent arrangement of the strong yellow Fennel-flower and foliage of Spanish Chestnut.

Among garden plants we have not many of the *Umbelliferæ*. There is the great Cow-Parsnip (*Heracleum*), a fine thing for a cool or marshy place; and there are the grand Sea-Hollies (*Eryngium*), with flowers arranged in a way quite different to that of the larger number of the class; and but few others. But the *Umbelliferæ* give us one most pestilent weed, namely, Goutweed (*Ægopodium*), looking and smelling like a small Angelica; its quick-running roots, once allowed to invade any piece of ground, are almost impossible to get out.

A good crop of Onions is a joy to the culinary corner of the gardener's heart, and I always think there is something highly pictorial about the great silvery seed-heads of the few we keep for seed, borne

"Much as I love the flower garden and the woodland, I am by no means indifferent to the interest and charm of the kitchen garden. For though its products are for the most part utilitarian, they all have their life-histories, and on the rare occasions when I am free to take a quiet stroll for pure pleasure of the garden I often take it among the vegetables."

high on the tall flower-stalk with its curious swollen base. Shallots stand like soldiers in their ranks, so neatly and evenly do they grow, with their dark-green upright leaves looking like well-to-do patches of Jonquil. Chives is a neat edging-plant, growing in close tufts, the chopped leaves good in salads. A row of Leeks is a pleasant sight, both growing and served in a dish as a green vegetable; the mildest of all the Onion tribe. The wild Garlic is such a pretty plant, with its heads of white flowers and broad deep-green leaves like those of Lily of the Valley, and makes such fine sheets of good green foliage in some of the neighbouring woods, that I am always tempted to naturalise it in the home copse, being only deterred by its extremely rank and unpleasant smell when touched, or even when only stirred by the wind.

There are several Garlics (*Allium*) in garden cultivation, the one best known being the yellow-flowered *Allium Moly*. Then there is the useful *A. neapolitanum*, so much imported as an early market flower; and one very handsome one with a tall stalk and round head of a really good blue (*A. azureum*), a native of Siberia, not at all common in gardens. There are several garden kinds with dull pink flowers, but I do not think them of much importance.

At first sight there does not seem to be much connection between Potatoes and Tomatoes, and yet they are nearly related, and bear the same botanical name of *Solanum,* and come from the same region, the northern parts of South America. But the likeness is shown in the flowers, and a good deal in the leaves, also the round berries of the Potato are not unlike the just-formed fruits of the Tomato. Another of these South American Solanums is the Egg-plant, the *Aubergine* of the French, seldom seen in our country, as even under glass we do not manage to grow it well.

Many of these Solanums have a curious and rather disagreeable smell; it is strong in the foliage of the Tomato, and perceptible in the woody Nightshade (*Solanum Dulcamara*) of our woods and waste places. The leaves and stems of the Tomato have a covering of some kind of soft structure that breaks down and rubs off by even gentle handling. When training Tomatoes one's hands become covered with the clammy greenish moisture that dries upon them in successive coats. When the job is done and hands are washed, the stuff washes off by degrees, dyeing the water a bright yellow colour, and it takes quite four washings before it can all be got off.

Hardy in the south of England and always beautiful, is the far-trailing creeper *Solanum jasminoides;* some of the sprays of foliage turning to a deep bronze-black colour that contrasts admirably with the tender white of the flowers. *Solanum crispum* is a grand wall shrub in our southern counties, loaded in April and May with its many-flowered clusters of

lavender-lilac bloom.   Other Solanums desirable for
the garden are *S. aviculare* and *S. Warscewiczii*, strong
growing annuals with handsome foliage, making important bushy growths that will occupy a cubic
yard of space.   Allied to the Solanums are the
Daturas, of which the splendid *D. meteloides* and its
double variety *D. Wrightii* are some of the grandest
objects either for cool greenhouse, or as tub-plants to
stand out in summer.

In these slight notes suggested by a walk round
the kitchen garden I have only attempted to notice
a few of the more important of its occupants, and to
show how, to me, the interest of every one of my
garden crops is much increased by reflections about
their origin and development, and their relationship
to each other and to our garden flowers and wild
things; but there is another aspect that I always try
to keep in view.   It is that, wherever it may be
possible, they should be grown in ways that are
beautiful and interesting, such, for instance, as the
way described of growing the Runner Beans on poles.
And one class of plants, those of the Gourd tribe,
can be used in many beautiful ways, for covering any
unsightly bank or mound, or to make a temporary
screen, or to train over the roofs of low sheds.
These plants may be either the Vegetable Marrows,
or any of the many ornamented Gourds, great or small.
And one other department of the garden is a source

of pleasure, namely, a border or little garden for the sweet-herbs. Where house and garden are newly made I like to arrange places for these herbs, not in the kitchen garden only, but that there should be also close to the house, and somewhere near the door that gives access to the kitchen, a little herb-garden for the cook, so that any herb can be had at once. Here should be two or three plants each of the Thymes, Basils, and Savouries, Tarragon and Chervil, a bush of Sage, some clumps of Balm, Marjoram, and Fennel, Soup-celery and Parsley for flavouring, Borage and a little Mint, and within reach a Bay-tree.

It is much better for the cook to go out and compose the little *bouquet* for the special flavouring of some delicate soup or sauce, picking the right quantity and proportion straight from the fragrant growing things. Moreover, having them all before her, she has a better chance of getting a knowledge of their natures and separate identities, and the little plants and their ways and uses must necessarily acquire in her eyes a more distinctly living interest.

CHAPTER XXI

THE HOME PUSSIES

MY pussies play an important part in my small home
circle. They are my dear companions both indoors
and out. I love their pretty gentle ways and their
extremely interesting individualities, for though I
always have four or five, no two that I have ever
known have been the least alike; indeed they are
almost as unlike as so many human folk. And when
I meet with people who say they do not like cats, I
always find that they are quite unacquainted with cat-
nature, and have certainly never been on purring
terms with any one individual pussy, but have a
general notion that a cat is necessarily treacherous
and ill-tempered and uninteresting.

I think I may venture to affirm that no one who
has carefully and kindly brought up a kitten from its
birth, could fail to find it first a charming playmate
and then a firm friend. But it must be very gently
and kindly treated, from the time when it makes its
first excursion from its mother's basket, and long before it has any other food than its mother's milk.

It must be taught to know that a hand is a kind
thing. My pussies learn this for their first lesson and

never forget it; so much so, that if they see a hand
lying idle they are very apt to give it a friendly
nudge and to say, "What is that hand doing, not
stroking ME?"

I much prefer cats of the common short-haired kind.
They are stronger and hardier than the long-haired
breeds, and the short fur always looks and feels much
cleaner and brighter, and they can keep it nice themselves without any need of adventitious grooming;
and there are never those long periods—nine months
out of the twelve it always seems to me—when the
owner is apologising for a ragged ruff or a wispy tail.
And then the short coat allows one to see the beautiful structure, and every detail of lithe bound and
lively caper, and all the infinitely varied and graceful
movements that are so pleasant to watch.

Tabby and white is my favourite colouring. I
have two all tabby without white, and dear pussies
they are; but for appearance I like them better with
white fronts and paws; it makes them look so clean
and well-dressed. The word "tabby" has an interesting etymology; coming from an Arabic root, and
always signifying something striped or waved or
brindled, whether of animal's coat or of woven fabric.
Hence also the word "tabinet" for a woven stuff of
striated surface; and doubtless the same word corrupted is the "tabouret" of the modern upholsterer,
the name of a woven silk stuff whose design is always
in stripes. It was much in use at the beginning of

the century, and has been reproduced and now again finds favour.

June 18. It is a perfect summer day, and I sit looking down one of the broad turf rides in the copse and see a dark object slowly approaching. By the solemnity of the stately advance I know it must be Pinkieboy. His movements are more than usually deliberate, for he had a rabbit this morning. He brought it, half-eaten, to show me. Tabby was following at a respectful distance, occasionally licking his lips as if asking for a share, but Pinkie only looked round and gave a short growl, which evidently meant, " Better go and catch a rabbit for yourself."

He is capable of extraordinary activity, and yet often assumes an affectation of pretending that he cannot go fast. For when we walk leisurely through the garden or copse together, he following a yard or two behind, when a bush or a turn of the path hides me from view, he will utter the most lamentable cries, as if begging not to be left behind ; then, when he has pretended enough, he will be up with me in one bound, purring and rubbing and asking if that wasn't a real good joke ?

When we meet after an unusual separation of a few hours, as he sees me coming he prepares himself for a good five minutes of pleasant conversation. Its subject is always the same, namely, unqualified admiration and approval of Pinkieboy. About a yard away he slowly lies down and solemnly

PINKIEBOY

makes a beautiful " tuck-under" to invite a good stroking. I always respond and encourage the pretty trick ; a sort of dive of the head and a half roll over, bringing his beautifully-kept white waist-coat and shirt-front uppermost—a gesture peculiar to a good-natured and well-brought-up pussy. It is an expression of perfect confidence. It always seems to say : " I make a polite bow, and put myself in the most helpless attitude, and offer my finest and softest fur for your kind stroking. You see my paws are half curled inwards, and my claws are all put away in their black velvet pads."

Pinkieboy is a big heavy cat, silver tabby and white; that is to say, the groundwork of his large black tabby markings is a cool silver-grey, not a brownish colour. Part of his face is white, and he has a good deal of white underneath, and white hind-legs and fore-paws.

Tittlebat is a cat of rather lighter build, without any white. Dark tabby as to face and legs, with unusually distinct black markings. The top of his head, instead of having close parallel stripes, is all black, his back is also all black. His ears are of a dark cool umber colour richly shaded to the tips. His sides are curiously marked with a close vertical brindling of black, about three stripes to the inch, on a pepper and salt ground. His coat is the finest and smoothest I ever saw or felt, so that in some lights, reflecting the sky, he looks as if he was coated with a silver-blue polish. But his greatest merit is his charming disposition ; kind and gentle and affectionate. He has the prettiest way of chirruping a welcome. If I pass him without notice he softly says, " Courooroo," which means, " Here I am ; don't forget your pussy." If he wishes to leave the room he goes to the door and says, " Croo-ee " (please let me out). English is a noble language, but certainly the pussy tongue is more concise !

He likes nothing better than to have the charge of young kittens. When there is a little family he takes upon himself the functions and responsibilities of head nurse, grooming the kittens and taking care of them when the mother leaves the nest for food or exercise, and as they grow older playing with them so gently that they are not aware of his greater strength and weight.

When I am busy in the workshop he likes to be given my garden jacket to lie on, and wherever I put it there he remains ; or if I am at my writing-table he likes to have a chair next to mine, so as to be within easy stroking reach ; and whenever I put down a hand I am sure of a kindly rub of his silky head, beginning with a touch of a cool wet nose.

There is a certain age at which a kitten makes sudden rushes across a room in a perfectly straight line, reminding one of the way small fishes dart across a stream. In this dear pussy's case this

habit was so unusually marked that I thought I
would call him after some little fish, hence his
name of Tittlebat.

Patty is the latest importation from the outer
world. She is a small cat and I fear will never
be much bigger, for she had her first kittens when
she was not much more than half grown. I always
like, if possible, to bring up my own pussies from
smallest babyhood ; but to my sincere grief I lost
my dear mother-pussy, Toozle, from an internal
disorder that the doctor told me could not have
been cured. And as I always like to have the
pleasure of bringing up a succession of kittens, I
cast about for one to replace her as the mother
of future broods, and found little Patty close at
hand. She attracted me by being the tabby and
white pattern that I like best, and by her beautiful
great aqua-marine eyes and her pretty way of moving. When she first came she was rather inclined
to bite and scratch, and though still sometimes a
little wild, by much gentle handling and good treatment she has greatly improved, and I hope will
soon be nearly as tractable as one of genuine home
growth.

Her little boy Tommy is my latest pet, and
promises to be a handsome and charming addition
to our pussy-folk. He is with me in the morning
when I open my letters, and is the one who has most
appreciation of the many trade circulars brought by

the early post. Most of them are printed on thin crackly paper, and when loosely crushed in the hand they make nice balls that he butts and tosses and chases all over the room. Or if I throw them into the waste-paper basket, he jumps on its edge, and tips it over and hunts out its ample contents for liberal distribution about the floor. And when we have the usual pussy-parade on the lawn at about seven on summer evenings; when, in turn with the bigger ones, he has had some good runs and jumps at the feather on the end of a whip which is the orthodox plaything, in pure delight of frisk and frolic he executes a *pas seul* on his own account, making a rapid series of monkey-jumps with high-arched back and helm hard a-port.

His mother is instructing him in the art and mystery of mousing, bringing him a mouse a day, and sitting by and watching while he goes through his mouse-drill, and finally eats up the poor little victim.

Cats are generally supposed to keep a house free from mice. We have no mice in the house except those they bring in. A rabbit's or hare's foot or a bit of rabbit-fur is a favourite plaything, or a feather. When Tittlebat was a youngster he had a rather large white chicken's wing that he would always carry about with him. One evening lately Patty came running down the front stairs with (as I thought) her bit of rabbit-fur. She goes up the back-stairs, along the oak-beamed gallery, and down the main stairway which comes straight into the sitting-room. It was after dinner, and I was sitting reading with little Tommy on my lap. Patty came down the stairs at a sharp trot, calling her kitten, who jumped down to go to her. They often have a game of play together between dinner and bedtime, and though the game was rather more active than usual I thought nothing of it, although I did hear some squeaks not quite like the kitten's. The pussies were taken away to bed at ten o'clock, and it was not till the next morning, when they were let in again, and they made straight for the sitting-room, where the housemaid found a grand rabbit-hunt going on, that the unusual squeaks and the extra play of the evening before were accounted for. The bit of rabbit-fur that Patty brought down the stairs had a little rabbit inside it! The poor little beast must have passed a frightened night in a corner of the room, where the pussies found him again, and continued their interrupted hunt. We thought that this time the baby-bunny should be let off, for though they are so mischievous in the garden that we do all we can to get rid of them, yet this one was so young and so pretty, and cried so piteously, that he was given his liberty, and away he scuttled off into the wood.

Each grown-up pussy chooses a different garden region as his special domain. Pinkieboy has his own jungle, a small thicket close to the house, where

there is a young Oak-tree and several Hollies and
Junipers, with an undergrowth of Cistus, Bracken,
and long grass. He makes regular lairs, that retain
their shape, and look like grassy tunnels. The little
nieces call them the Pussy-lie-downs. No other cat
is ever to be seen in one of Pinkie's lie-downs; he
would resent it as an ill-mannered intrusion, and the
others quite understand that it would be considered
a breach of etiquette. Tittlebat's sphere of influence
extends over the Primrose garden and the region of
Yew, Birch, Chestnut, and Bracken that surrounds it.
Tabby, a fine whole-coloured silver tabby, frequents
the nut-walk and pergola, and considers himself the
warden of two gates, the hand hunting-gate through
the Yew hedge and the five-barred gate that crosses
the back road behind the summer-house. Both gates
have wire-netting over their lower halves to prevent
the passing of rabbits; indeed but for this necessity
neither gate would be there. When Tabby and I
are walking near either of the gates he runs on and
mounts one of the posts, and we play the game of
Gate-post. It is an easy game, and we both enjoy
it. Tabby on his post is petted and stroked; I then
execute a rapid passage with my fingers along the
top rail of the gate to the other post. Tabby rushes
along and establishes himself firmly on the second
post. More stroking on my part and responsive
rubbing on his; then back to the first post, and so
on till we have both had enough for the present.

The one thing that mars one's happiness with one's pussies is an ever-present fear, and its, alas! too frequent realisation, of loss by wandering. Sometimes one of them will be away for a day, or for two days, and then comes home again. When this happens, we suppose that a big rabbit has been caught and has provided heavy meals for two days, with long sleeps of satiety in the intervals. The dangerous time is at about a year old, when the cat is at its full young strength and greatest activity. The one most recently lost was not quite a year old, the most active cat I have ever known, and the most bright and frank and fearless. My pretty Mittens! with softest coat of large dark tabby markings on a golden ground, and snowy-white front and paws. I always feared he would go some day, the spirit of adventure was so strong in him. He was like a ray of sunshine about the place, with his pretty bright ways and delicious fearless insolence. Sometimes I would hear a commotion among the driving whips hung up just inside the entrance from the court, and knew I should have no peace till I had taken the pussy-whip with the long lash and the feather at the end and given him a grand racing and jumping on the lawn; when he made a big jump he seemed to be almost flying. One day he performed a feat of agility that I never saw before, and should hardly have thought possible. I was playing the feather over him as he lay on his back, with all four paws extended upwards trying to reach it, and in that position, by some sudden and violent action of the muscles of the back, he jumped himself clear off the ground and forward about nine inches, coming down again in the same position before attempting to " right " himself.

What happens to them when they wander and are lost I know not, but my longest frontier is obviously full of danger, for it adjoins a lengthy stretch of woodland where game is preserved.   I only know that every dear pussy that is lost leaves a sad blank in the house and garden, and a very sore place in our hearts.

I know all my pussies in the dark, not only by the feel of their coats, but by the different tone and quality of their purr.   A kitten's purr is rather hard and rattly, high-pitched and unmelodious.

Pinkieboy's purr is of a grand quality, extremely deep in tone, not loud, but highly musical—a purr of the highest distinction.   The sound of it always reminds me of the deep, rich sound of the whirring wings of the Humming-bird Hawk-moth; indeed the two sounds are so nearly alike that I never hear the one without thinking of the other; it may be that they are upon the same note.

I am sure that cats have a strong sense of fun, and, like children, love the delights of make-believe. Two of them will meet on the lawn, and with ears set back and lashing tails will play at having a mortal combat.   In the fiercest of the fray, when the limbs

of the wrestlers are locked in deadly fight, they will
suddenly stop and lick each other's faces. I had two
own brothers who were specially fond of this fun.
They were the best of friends, were scarcely ever apart,
and slept in the same hay-bed, but the daily mock-
combats were fearful to see. A mother-pussy lashes
her tail for her kitten to play with, looking round
out of the corner of her eye to see if he is taking
notice. A small kitten, just learning to mouse, will
toss up a ball of wool or a bit of fur and make an
imaginary mouse of it. And my pussies always enjoy
the game of Tigers in the Jungle, that we play in a
large group of Bamboos, with a slender stick rattled
among the canes. And any little game that I invent
they understand and adopt at once; and if it is
repeated two or three times they remember, and distinctly beg that it may be repeated. And in all ways
I find them kindly appreciative and grateful for
friendly notice; so that if I pass through a room and
pause for a moment to contemplate an apparently
fast-asleep pussy, I have only to say " Patty, darling,"
and I see the last two inches of her pretty tail just
raised and lowered in courteous acknowledgment, and
hear a few drowsy vibrations of responsive purr.

Last winter I had a visit of a week or two from
my youngest niece, of nine years old. Wishing to
have some small jollification before she went home, I
thought it would be nice to have a pussies' tea-party,
and as the prospect delighted her, we set to work

Miss Jekyll
at home 4 O-clo
Mr Pinkie-Boy

Miss Jekyll
at home 4 O
Mrs Magie
and
Miss Clowy

Miss Jekyll
at home 4 O-clock
Mr Titlebat

Miss Jekyll
at home 4 -O-
Mrs Toosel
and
Master Brindel

Menu
Les Filets de Hareng à la Minette
Les Tranches de Riz en Traverse
Les petites bouchées de Beurre frais
La Crème au Naturel

THE INVITATIONS

to talk it over in earnest. No time was to be lost, for it was to be the next afternoon. So we sat down and seriously considered the items of the bill of fare. After some consultation, we decided that the basis of it should be fish, so we sent for some fresh herrings, and they were boiled and held in readiness.

Meanwhile my little companion proposed to issue cards of invitation, and said that she would write them herself. I asked if she could do them in the proper way, and as she was sure she could, I offered no further suggestions, and waited to see what would appear. So she found some scraps of writing-paper and wrote the invitations, and we went round together and presented them to the pussies, who duly purred their acceptance. They were all indoors, as it was wintry weather.

Next day, early in the afternoon, we prepared the feast. The invited guests were four grown pussies and two kittens, so we got ready four large and two small saucers. First a thick strip of fish was laid right across each saucer; an equal strip of cold rice pudding met it transversely, forming a cross-shaped figure that left four spaces in the angles. Thick cream was poured into these spaces, and the solid portion was decorated with tiny balls of butter, one rather larger in the middle, and two smaller on each of the rays. A reserve of fish and cream was to be at hand to replenish the portions most quickly exhausted.

"No year passes that one does not observe some charming combination of plants that one had not intentionally put together. Even though I am always trying to think of some such happy mixtures, others come of themselves. This year the best of these chances was a group of pale sulphur Hollyhock seen against Yews that were garlanded with Clematis Flammula." Here Clematis Montana Rubens has climbed up through Limonia Trifoliata.

In the middle of the sitting-room we placed a small, rather low, round table; and four stools were ranged round for the bigger pussies. As the hour for the feast drew near, much was the wondering as to how the guests would behave. They were to sit on the stools with their fore-paws on the edge of the tablecloth. We decided not to have flowers, because it would have overcrowded the space, as the two kittens were to be allowed to sit on the table.

At last the hour came, and meanwhile the excitement had grown intense. Five grown-ups were present, all as keenly interested as the little girl. The pussies were brought and placed on their stools, and the kittens, Chloe and Brindle, were put up to their saucers upon the table. To our great delight they all took in the situation at once ; there was only a little hesitation on Maggie's part; she thought it was not manners to put her paws on the tablecloth ; but this was soon overcome, and they all set to work as if they were quite accustomed to tea-parties and knew that nice behaviour was expected.

It was good to watch the pleasure of my little niece. I had expected that she would rush about and scream with delight, but she stood perfectly silent and still, with hands half raised, mouth a little open, and big eager eyes drinking in the scene, as if she thought it would vanish if she made a movement. Meanwhile the small guests were steadily eating away at their portions. Pinkieboy, as became the

oldest and heaviest, finished his first, and after licking
his saucer quite clean, and then his own lips, he looked
round and clearly said, "That was very good, and
please I should like a little more, especially fish and
cream."

When they had all done there was a grand purring and washing of paws and faces before they got
off their stools, and as they dispersed to find cosy
sleeping-places, as wise pussies do after a comfortable
meal, we all thought that our little party had been
brilliantly successful, and had even some thoughts of
sending a report of it to the *Morning Post*.

Many years ago, when Kew was a place of royal
residence, and my father was quartered there with
a detachment of his battalion (1st Batt. Grenadiers),
frequent were his drives with some brother officer
between Kew and London. And to beguile the tedium
of the way they would lay a mild bet on the number
of cats seen, each taking his own side of the road.
But a cat sitting in a window summarily decided the
game in favour of the one on whose side the pleasing
picture was displayed.

And in my father's later years, when I used
to drive with him in the country, at the sight of
a pussy in a cottage window, his face would light
up with a merry twinkle, and I always expected
and never failed to hear the well-known formula,
"Cat in a window's Game!"

I have only once seen a pussy in church. It was not a parish church, but the chapel of one of the great London hospitals. The congregation was assembled and was awaiting the entrance of the chaplain, when a young pussy of an age somewhere between cat and kitten solemnly marched, with tail erect, up the middle gangway. Without hesitation, and as if fulfilling a usual duty, he made for the reading-desk, entered it, and for an instant was lost to view. But a moment later head and shoulders appeared above the desk, and a small wise face looked round with an air of quiet assurance and professional unconcern. I quite expected to see the little paws reverently folded, and to hear a tiny voice say: "Let us purr"!

TABBY. "CAT IN A WINDOW'S GAME"

CHAPTER XXII

THINGS WORTH DOING

THE heading of this chapter might embrace the conclusions of all the deepest philosophies, but none the less has relation to the simplest thoughts and acts of every-day life. Is it worth having? Is it worth doing? These questions form a useful mental sieve, through which to pass many matters in order to separate the husk from the grain. And nowhere have we occasion to use it with more vigour than in matters pertaining to the garden.

When I had less knowledge of garden flowers and shrubs than I have been able to gather through many later years, I got together all the plants I was able to collect; not with a view to having them as a collection, but in order to become acquainted with them, the better to see which I could use on my own ground or recommend to others whose gardens were of different natures. And in this way I have discarded numbers of plants, some because I thought them altogether unworthy, some because the colour of the flower displeased me, others because they threatened

to become troublesome weeds, and others again because, though beautiful and desirable, they were very
unhappy and home-sick in my dry soil, and it was
quite evident that they were no plants for me.
Several of these were natives of the Alps, that
missed the cool shade of the towering rocks, and
the constant trickle of moisture to the root, and
the overhead bath of mountain mist. It is only in
the case of a thing so indispensable as the White
Lily that I go on trying against nearly certain
failure, and hoping almost against hope, and am re-
warded perhaps only one year in seven by a clump
doing fairly well, in spite of having carefully tried
all the recipes and nostrums kindly given me by
my many friends of highest horticultural ability.
Still the White Lily is one of the good things
worth doing, and after all, as a last resource, one
can pot it in loam and lime and so compel it to
live and flower.

But the stores of the rubbish-heap were much
enriched by the many plants that seemed to me
unworthy, or of which better garden kinds could
be had; so all my older clumps of Michaelmas
Daisies found their way there—it was twenty years
ago, before the grand modern ones had been much
cultivated—and a whole set of the oldest of the
garden forms of the albiflora Pæonies, as well as
many other unworthy individuals.

And I found that one thing well worth doing was

to get together as many kinds as I could of any one plant in general cultivation, and grow them together, and compare them at their blooming season and see which was really the best and most beautiful; for in equal or even greater proportion with the growth of critical appreciation, there comes an intolerance of rubbish, and by the constant exercise of the critical faculty the power of judging becomes unconscious, and, as it were, another natural sense. And though I am far from venturing to think that the conclusions of my judgment are infallible, yet I believe that they are soundly based and of good general utility, and therefore fairly trustworthy for the guidance of others.

I think it is a fair test of the genuineness of the profession of the many people who now declare that they love plants and gardens, to see if they are willing to take any trouble of this kind for themselves. For though there are now whole shelves-full of the helpful books that had no existence in my younger days, yet there are many things that can only be ascertained by careful trying in individual gardens.

Now that there is so much to choose from, we should not let any mental slothfulness stand in the way of thinking and watching and comparing, so as to arrive at a just appreciation of the merits and uses of all our garden plants.

It is not possible to use to any good effect all the plants that are to be had. In my own case I should wish to grow many more than just those I have, but if I do not find a place where my critical garden conscience approves of having any one plant I would rather be without it. It is better to me to deny myself the pleasure of having it, than to endure the mild sense of guilt of having placed it where it neither does itself justice nor accords with its neighbours, and where it reproaches me every time I pass it.

I feel sure that it is in a great measure just because this is so little understood, that gardens are so often unsatisfactory and uninteresting. If owners could see, each in their own garden, what is the thing most worth doing, and take some pains to work out that one idea or group of ideas, gardens would not be so generally dull and commonplace.

Often in choosing plants and shrubs people begin the wrong way. They know certain things they would like to have and they look through catalogues and order these, and others that they think, from the description, they would also like, and then plant them without any previous consideration of how or why.

Often when I have had to do with other people's gardens they have said : " I have bought a quantity of shrubs and plants ; show me where to place them ; " to which I can only answer : " That is not the way in which I can help you ; show me your spaces and I will tell you what plants to get for them."

Many places that would be beautiful if almost left

alone are spoiled by doing away with some simple
natural feature in order to put in its place some
hackneyed form of gardening.   Such places should be
treated with the most deliberate and careful consideration.   Hardly a year passes that I do not see in my
own neighbourhood examples of this kind that seem to
me extremely ill-judged.   Houses great and small are
being built on tracts of natural heath-land.   A perfect
undergrowth of wild Heaths is there already.   If it is
old and overgrown, it can be easily renewed by clearing
it off and lightly digging the ground over, when the
Heaths will quickly spring up again.   Often there are
already thriving young Scotch Firs and Birches.

Where such conditions exist, a beautiful garden
can be easily made at the least possible cost, jealously
saving all that there is already, and then using in
some simple way such plants as I have recommended
in the chapter on Plants for Poor Soils.   The presence
of the Scotch Fir points to that being the best tree to
plant in quantity ; and the few other trees that will do
admirably in dry light soils, Birch, Spanish Chestnut,
Holly, and Juniper, will give as much variety as can
be wanted by a sober mind that understands the value
of temperance in planting.

There are many people who almost unthinkingly
will say, " But I like a variety."   Do they really think
and feel that variety is actually desirable as an end in
itself, and is of more value than a series of thoughtfully composed garden pictures ?   There are no doubt

many to whom, from want of a certain class of refinement of education or natural gift of teachable aptitude,
are unable to understand or appreciate, at anything
like its full value, a good garden picture, and to these
no doubt a quantity of individual plants give a greater
degree of pleasure than such as they could derive from
the contemplation of any beautiful arrangement of a
lesser number. When I see this in ordinary gardens,
I try to put myself into the same mental attitude, and
so far succeed, in that I can perceive that it represents
one of the earlier stages in the love of a garden, and
that one must not quarrel with it, because a garden is
for its owner's pleasure, and whatever the degree or
form of that pleasure, if only it be sincere, it is right
and reasonable, and adds to human happiness in one
of the purest and best of ways. And often I find I
have to put upon myself this kind of drag, because
when one has passed through the more elementary
stages which deal with isolated details, and has come
to a point when one feels some slight power of what
perhaps may be called generalship; when the means
and material that go to the making of a garden seem
to be within one's grasp and awaiting one's command,
then comes the danger of being inclined to lay down
the law, and of advocating the ultimate effects that
one feels oneself to be most desirable in an intolerant
spirit of cock-sure pontification. So I try, when I am
in a garden of the ordinary kind where the owner
likes variety, to see it a little from the same point of

view; and in the arboretum, where one of each of a
hundred different kinds of Conifers stand in their fine
young growth, to see and admire the individuals only,
and to stifle my own longing to see a hundred of one
sort at a time, and to keep down the shop-window
feeling, and the idea of a worthless library made up
of odd single volumes where there should be complete
sets, and the comparison of an inconsequent jumble
of words with a clearly-written sentence, and all such
naughty similitudes, as come crowding through the
brain of the garden-artist (if I may give myself a
title so honourable), who desires not only to see the
beautiful plants and trees, but to see them used in the
best and largest and most worthy of ways.

There is no spot of ground, however arid, bare, or
ugly, that cannot be tamed into such a state as may
give an impression of beauty and delight. It cannot
always be done easily; many things worth doing are
not done easily; but there is no place under natural
conditions that cannot be graced with an adornment
of suitable vegetation.

More than once I have had pleasure in taking in
hand some spot of ground where it was said "nothing
would grow." On two occasions it was a heap of
about fifty loads of sand wheeled out of the basement
of a building, in one case placed under some Scotch
Firs, in another under Oaks and Chestnuts. Both
are now as well covered with thriving plants and
shrubs as any other parts of the garden they are in,

clothed in the one case with Aucubas, hardy Ferns, Periwinkles, and Honesty, and in the other with Aucubas, Ferns, and the two grand Mulleins, *Verbascum olympicum* and *V. phlomoides*. It should be remembered that the Aucuba is one of the few shrubs that enjoys shade.

Throughout my life I have found that one of the things most worth doing was to cultivate the habit of close observation. Like all else, the more it is exercised the easier it becomes, till it is so much a part of oneself that one may observe almost critically and hardly be aware of it. A habit so acquired stands one in good stead in all garden matters, so that in an exhibition of flowers or in a botanic garden one can judge of the merits of a plant hitherto unknown to one, and at once see in what way it is good, and why, and how it differs from those of the same class that one may have at home.

And I know from my own case that the will and the power to observe does not depend on the possession of keen sight. For I have sight that is both painful and inadequate; short sight of the severest kind, and always progressive (my natural focus is two inches); but the little I have I try to make the most of, and often find that I have observed things that have escaped strong and long-sighted people.

As if by way of compensation I have very keen hearing, and when I hear a little rustling rush in the

grass and heath, or in the dead leaves under the trees,
I can tell whether it is snake or lizard, mouse or bird.
Many birds I am aware of only by the sound of their
flight.   I can nearly always tell what trees I am near
by the sound of the wind in their leaves, though in
the same tree it differs much from spring to autumn,
as the leaves become of a harder and drier texture.
The Birches have a small, quick, high-pitched sound;
so like that of falling rain that I am often deceived
into thinking it really is rain, when it is only their
own leaves hitting each other with a small rain-
like patter.   The voice of Oak leaves is also rather
high-pitched, though lower than that of Birch.
Chestnut leaves in a mild breeze sound much more
deliberate; a sort of slow slither.   Nearly all trees
in gentle wind have a pleasant sound, but I confess to a distinct dislike to the noise of all the
Poplars; feeling it to be painfully fussy, unrestful,
and disturbing.   On the other hand, how soothing
and delightful is the murmur of Scotch Firs both near
and far.   And what pleasant muffled music is that
of a wind-waved field of corn, and especially of ripe
barley.   The giant Grasses, Reeds, and Bamboo sound
curiously dry.   The great Reed, *Arundo Donax*, makes
more noise in a moderate breeze than when the wind
blows a gale, for then the long ribbon-like leaves are
blown straight out and play much less against each
other; the Arabs say, " It whispers in the breeze and
is silent in the storm."   But of all the plants I know,

the one whose foliage has the strangest sound is the
Virginian Allspice (*Calycanthus floridus*), whose leaves
are of so dry and harsh a quality that they seem to
grate and clash as they come together.

As for the matter of colour, what may be observed
is simply without end. Those who have had no training in the way to see colour nearly always deceive
themselves into thinking that they see it as they know
it is locally, whereas the trained eye sees colour in
due relation and as it truly *appears to be*. I remember
driving with a friend of more than ordinary intelligence, who stoutly maintained that he saw the
distant wooded hill quite as green as the near hedge.
He knew it was green and could not see it otherwise,
till I stopped at a place where a part of the face, but
none of the sky-bounded edge of the wooded distance,
showed through a tiny opening among the near green
branches, when, to his immense surprise, he saw it
was blue. A good way of showing the same thing
is to tear a roundish hole in any large bright-green
leaf, such as a Burdock, and to hold it at half-arm's
length so that a part of a distant landscape is seen
through the hole, and the eye sees also the whole
surface of the leaf. As long as the sight takes in
both, it will see the true relative colour of the distance. I constantly do this myself, first looking at
the distance without the leaf-frame in order to see
how nearly I can guess the truth of the far colour.
Even in the width of one ploughed field, especially

in autumn when the air is full of vapour, in the farther part of the field the newly-turned earth is bluish-purple, whereas it is a rich brown at one's feet. On some of those cold, cloudless days of March, when the sky is of a darker and more intensely blue colour than one may see at any other time of the year, and geese are grazing on the wide strips of green common, so frequent in my neighbourhood, I have often noticed how surprisingly blue is the north side of a white goose. If at three o'clock in the afternoon of such a day one stands facing north-west and also facing the goose, its side next one's right hand is bright blue and its other side is bright yellow, deepening to orange as the sun "westers" and sinks, and shows through a greater depth of moisture-laden atmosphere.

Many years ago I had a wooden painting-room, for convenience of drawing and painting animals. I had always great pleasure in painting white horses (the pearly colouring about the head of a well-bred grey and the blue of his muzzle are something delicious), and as a kind neighbour had a stable full of greys of a well-known breed, I was never at a loss for a sitter. One day when old "Sampson," quite white with age, was dozing at his post, and I happened for some time not to be looking at my model, on again looking up I was amazed by the sight of a blue horse with a large orange spot on his

flank.   I never can forget the sudden shock of that
strangely-coloured apparition.   A knot had dropped
out of one of the boards, and a round spot of warm
afternoon sunlight came straight through on to the
horse's white coat that was blue-lighted from the
large north window.

The way colour is applied in brilliant flowers is
the subject of a never-ending and always delightful
investigation.   All painters know how difficult it is
to get a brilliant colouring of clear, unmuddled
scarlet.   It can only be done, especially in watercolour, by running the scarlet over a preparation of
clear strong yellow.   This is exactly how nature
gets over the same difficulty in flowers of that
colour.

It always seems to me that one of the things
most worth doing about a garden is to try to make
every part of it beautiful; not the pleasure garden
only, but some of the rougher accessories also, so
that no place is unsightly.   For the faggot-stack
can be covered with Gourds or Vegetable Marrows,
or quick growing rambling things like the wild Bind-
weed (*Convolvulus*), or the garden variety with still
larger white bloom; and the sides of the coke-
enclosure, built of posts and upright oak slabbing,
can have hardy Chrysanthemums below and a happy
tangle of wild Clematis above; and sheds that would
be otherwise unbeautiful can be adorned with rampant
Vine and Jasmine and the free-growing Clematises

and Virginia Creeper. For my own part, I wish I had more of such places in order to have a wider scope for such plantings; while in other gardens I groan in spirit to see the many opportunities wasted, and unsightliness reigning supreme where there might be pictures of delightful beauty. And to get into the habit of considering and composing such arrangements, and to worry out the way of doing them, is by no means one of the least of the pleasures of a garden.

All sorts of pleasant things may be done by training down shrubs like Laburnums; I regret that I have no place to make a Laburnum hedge, planting them about three feet apart and arching them over one after the other and fastening the head of each to the arched back of the next. Often one can alter the place of a young tree a few feet by bending its head down gradually till it touches the ground, and then pegging it underground till it roots and the old stem can be cut away. I am doing nearly the same thing to some young Scotch Firs (bad to transplant) that are a few feet too near a path. But in this case they will not be rooted at the heads, only gradually drawn down and the head fixed firmly to the ground or near it. In time it will rise and form a tree at that place, and the original stem, lying along the ground, will be so well covered with Heath and Bracken and Moss that in a few years no one would know where the root really was. I planted a few

White Beam trees in the copse; they were nursery trees, and though common native things, they had been grafted, after some law of nurseries that I fail to understand, upon stocks of Mountain Ash. After my standard White Beams had been growing a year or two there was a brush-like growth of Mountain Ash from the root. I therefore pulled down the heads, and by degrees brought them to the ground and pegged them, so as to have the White Beams growing clear of the stocks. When rooted, the old stem is cut clear away at both ends, and I have both trees separately rooted a few yards apart. Many good shrubs are easily propagated by layering, and all the free-growing Roses. Indeed, by repeated layering on the same side, I could make a Dundee Rambler walk from one end of the garden to the other!

No year passes that one does not observe some charming combination of plants that one had not intentionally put together. Even though I am always trying to think of some such happy mixtures, others come of themselves. This year the best of these chances was a group of pale sulphur Hollyhock seen against Yews that were garlanded with *Clematis Flammula*; tender yellow and yellow-white and deepest green; upright spire of Hollyhock, cloud-like mass of Clematis, low-toned sombre ground of solemn Yew. Another good mixture is that of Crinums, tall Cannas, and *Funkia grandiflora*. Others that I always delight in are of Rosemary and China Rose, and of China

Rose and Tree Ivy ; of Jerusalem Sage (*Phlomis*) and
Mullein (*Verbascum phlomoides*) ; of London Pride and
St. Bruno's Lily, as shown in the illustration at page
111; of Gypsophila and Globe Thistle; of dark-flowered
Honesty and the large, handsome variety of *Megasea
cordifolia*. Then there are the many associations of
bluish and grey-leaved plants, as of Lyme Grass and
Lavender-Cotton and Catmint, and these also with
Lavender and its dwarf dark variety and the pretty
Sisyrinchium Bermudiana. All these, and the many
others that will occur, are well worth looking out for
and worth doing.

In many matters it is only by study and observation and comparison that one can arrive at such a
judgment as may be safe to adopt in one's own practice or to advise for the guidance of others, but as far
as I have seen there are a great many cases in which
a beautiful way of tree-planting is misused or mis-
understood. In planting an avenue of trees as an
approach to a dwelling, the question of due proportion
would seem to be of the first importance. They
are so very often planted much too near the roadway
and much too close together, and the proportion
most frequently forgotten or misjudged is that of
length. A certain length will give the utmost dignity, and every yard in excess will tend to deteriora-
tion and monotony. If an avenue is a mile long
the trees should be set back two hundred yards from
the road ; but for the truest beauty and dignity, as

far as I am able to judge, it had better be of no
greater length than from four hundred to five hundred yards, with the trees set back quite fifty feet
from the roadway. In many cases a second row of
trees, showing through and behind the first, is much
to be advised.

I am using the word " avenue " in its usual
English sense of an approach to a house bordered
by trees planted in straight lines, not in the
sense that I believe is usually accepted in Ireland,
and perhaps Scotland, as an approach to a house
only, and without any reference to trees.

From what I have seen I should say that the
noblest tree of all for avenue planting is the Elm ;
the Common Elm first, and then the Wych Elm.
Next the Beech, then the Lime and the Spanish
Chestnut and the Hornbeam—a noble, large tree
that by no means deserves the neglect it usually
receives.

Oaks are so much more suitable for informal
planting that I should scarcely reckon them among
avenue trees, neither should I favour Horse Chestnuts, because, though they are noble trees, their
drooping boughs hide too much of the bole, which
I think should always be visible.   But they are
admirable in formal planting in large parks.   The
Spanish Chestnut has also much the same habit of
growth, but it bears trimming up better than the
Horse Chestnut.

The shorter avenues of grand trees leading to
houses have usually seemed to be the best because
the whole thing can be seen at once, and forms one
complete picture, just as there is always a pleasant
Dutch-picture-like look about a short avenue of
Pollards.

The very long lengths of formal planting are
only suitable for large parks that have palatial
houses of a certain class. The fashion of planting
trees in this way came from Holland with William
III., and prevailed for many years. The examples
that remain from those days have now acquired all
the beauty of a more than mature overgrowth; and
though this kind of tree-planting is by no means
the most delight-giving, yet one cannot help re-
gretting the destruction of the many fine examples
that had no sooner attained to a splendid young
maturity, than, in obedience to the rule of the next
wave of fashion, they were ruthlessly swept away.

In private roads, such as those through parks,
one often sees a quite unnecessary width of roadway. Except in cases where it is cut in the side
of a hill, there is no need for the road to be of
greater width than suits a single carriage; where
two have to pass, there is no harm in having to
drive over the edge of the grass; indeed even in
the case of uneven ground, if the way is levelled
so as to include grass verges, it does equally well,
and saves a large amount of expensive road-making.

There is a distinctly pretentious and therefore vulgar look about an extremely wide roadway leading to a small private house ; it seems to come within the same classification as an avenue I was once told of, extending for a length of two miles, and planted with variegated Sycamore and Copper Beech placed alternately ! The idea of such a mixture, and of such a long-drawn weariness of direly-monotonous continuity, is like a nightmare ; I did not gather whether the thing was only in contemplation or had really been perpetrated, but can only hope that no such unhappy avenue is really in existence.

CHAPTER XXIII

LIFE IN THE HUT

WHILE my larger cottage was building I lived in the tiny one just across the lawn that had been built a couple of years before. And had I not been burdened with the cumbersome accessories of many beloved industries, and with the wish to house and enjoy my books and pictures and my many "things," and to be able to have the joy of receiving friends under my own roof, I should scarcely have wished to live elsewhere or in anything larger.

The Hut is mostly ground-floor. There is one rather large room with a big window to the east, a room good to paint or work in, but for the time-being more or less filled with stored furniture. It has a handsome ingle-nook and the usual "down" hearth. When on winter evenings there is a great log-fire blazing, and hot elder-wine is ready for drinking and nuts waiting to be cracked, and some good comrades are sitting, some on its inner fixed benches and some facing the fire's wide front, singing "*Craignez de tomber*" or "*Let's have a peal*," or other familiar rounds and catches, it is a very cosy and cheerful place. Great oak beams stretch overhead, tying the

walls; and the double-curved braces above them help
to stiffen the roof. This room has an outer door of
its own leading to a few square yards of paved court
that is bounded on two sides by the cottage, and on
the other two by box-edged garden filled with Roses,
Lavender, Pæonies, and many simple cottage flowers.

The other and more usual entrance to the Hut
is by a paved path through a short tunnel of Yew.
The door opens into a square entrance with the
lowest steps of the stairs in the further right-hand
corner. There is space for a large oak cupboard in
front against the stairs, an oak wardrobe against the
right-hand wall, an eight-legged table with one flap
down under the window that ranges with the door,
a tall clock, and a large rush-seated arm-chair. A
square of cocoa-matting is in the middle space, with
the well-kept brick flooring showing all round. It
looks well furnished without being crowded. Immediately to the left on entering is my little bedroom, next beyond it the sitting-room; straight on
is the kitchen. Upstairs are two bedrooms and a
roomy landing, one room for my servant, the other
stored with furniture and things in use.

The floors downstairs are all of brick, the walls
of unplastered brick white-washed. It is handy to
have no plaster, as one sees at once where to knock
in a nail to hang a picture.

The outer walls are of nine-inch brickwork, coated
with rough-cast; all is sound and tight; the little

cottage does not let in a drop of wet. My bed
stands on the brick floor, there without carpet, and
is against two outer walls and under a part of the
roof that has no room above. As I love to hear
the sound of rain falling on a roof, here, when it
comes at night, I can enjoy it to the full. I had
never noticed before that the first drops of rain
falling on dry tiles have a clear, musical, tinkling
sound, changing to a duller note as the whole surface
of the tile becomes wetted. Though the simple ways
of living in the Hut may sound as if bordering on
the ascetic, yet there was no feeling of hardship,
and the whole way of life was evidently wholesome,
for during the two years that I occupied the cottage
I was never a day ill and only had one slight
cold.

Before I had occasion to live there myself I
had lent it to an old cottager friend, a woman of
the true old country type now, alas, nearly extinct.
In her day she had been a fine hard worker, but
rheumatism and heart-trouble put a painful restriction
on her ability to do the work that her brave old
heart made her unwilling to give up. I had hoped
when I wanted the cottage for my own use to be
able to keep her there as my servant. Her beautiful
cleanliness and ready cheerfulness, her bright, kindly,
apple-cheeked face, her delicious old caps and plain
dress of old-world pattern, were so exactly in keeping
with the simple little cottage that I was unwilling

to let her go, but after a few weeks it became clear
that her strength was not equal to keeping the house
for both of us, and as her knowledge of cooking was
less than rudimentary, I had to find for her a home
in the village and for myself a more able-bodied
helper. Dear old soul, what delicious, inconsequent,
good-natured gossip she used to pour forth; a little
difficult to follow, because as a rule all nominatives
were omitted; and as I could not by intuition keep
up with the discursive workings of her brain, nor at
once grasp the identity indicated by "She," with a
fling of the head or jerk of the thumb towards some
distant farm; and as the disjointed fragments of
narrative ran into one another, or rather flowed out
of one another in a constant flood of small digression,
the end of the story left me much where I was at the
beginning.

But I wish I could remember all the odd tricks
of speech and local manner of wording. There was
one story of a woman who met a toad coming downstairs. The toad bit the woman in the arm—I
could not bear to spoil the story by telling her that
toads have no teeth: "And her arm got *that* bad
—there—it *was* bad, that it was! She had to have
it off, she did!" This wonderful story came up one
day when I came in to tea and found a fine, handsome toad sitting on the raised brick hearth. It is
strange how the country folk still believe in the
venom of toads.

One day I found her groaning in the kitchen, and asked what ailed her. "It's my rheumatics; they do crucify me that crool!" And then she told how she had often worked in the fields in wet weather, topping and tailing turnips and suchlike work, soaked through and through, and on one worst day of all in thin boots: "My thick ones was gone to be mended."

Somebody belonging to her had been in the army, and my boots were blacked on the doorstep with a small old soldier's kit boot-brush. She had also picked up some military technicalities, for I remember one day when I sat down to dinner, and she had just finished setting the table by putting on the salt and mustard, that she smiled with an air of conscious satisfaction as of all duties happily completed, and said, "There! now you've got all your *acuterments.*"

It is one of the perennial griefs of the garden that it cannot grow the White Lily. It is a lime and loam-loving plant; yet one patch in the narrow border between the front of the Hut and the stone-paved path always does well. When the border was made I gave that end a good deep dressing of lime rubbish, both for the sake of the Lily and of its next neighbour, the Knaphill variety of *Pyrus japonica*. This grand form of an always good shrub cannot be too highly praised. The flowers are splendidly rich in colour; they are so large, and the petals of

ENTRANCE TO THE HUT

such good substance, that I never see them without
being reminded of those handsomest of red Camellias
that are only half double, and whose petals stand
up with a certain freedom that makes them so much
more truly beautiful than those that have them
laid flat and exactly evenly arranged. The rest of
the little border has two China Roses, some Lady
Fern and Musk, and next the door the sweet French
Honeysuckle (*Lonicera flexuosa*). Just to the right of
the short tunnel of Yew at the Hut entrance—the
tunnel becomes hedge only, for daylight's sake, for
the three yards nearest the door—is a Holly of rather
upright shape some twenty feet high. Before the
cottage was built I planted near its foot a *Clematis
montana* and a Dundee Rambler Rose, and as they
grew, trained them to run up through its branches.
The Clematis went up quickest, and for two or three
years made a fairly good show, but has not done very
much since; but the Rose now fills the top of the
Holly, and the picture gives some idea of the way
the flowery ends come tumbling out, though no
representation in black and white can show the
charming way that the tender, pink-tinged masses
of the little Rose-clusters are seen upon their ground
of the prickly shining Holly leaves and of the softer
sombre Yew.

Dear little Hut! how sorry I was to leave it, even
to go to the better house that I had long looked forward to as that most precious possession, a settled

home for life. How I loved the small and simple
ways of living, the happy absence of all complications,
the possibility of living close down to nature—I know
no better way of saying it—that seemed to leave one
more freedom to think and to do! Though it is now
nearly bare, only sparely fitted with rough shelves
and benches for seed-drying and other such uses, I
often find myself thinking of it, furnished as it was
when I was in it, especially my cosy little parlour and
the pretty kitchen.

How deliciously simple it all was, how small and
few the bills—a pound a week paid the housekeep-
ing. It was the same in everything. Even in a
matter like the sweeping of chimneys : instead of
having to call in a professional, a lad on a ladder with
a bunch of Holly on the end of a rope and a stone in
it, swept the chimney in good old country style in a
few minutes. I have heard of old farmers doing it
with a live duck ; but I hope never with a beautiful white
Aylesbury ! And then the comforting conviction that
drains could not possibly get out of order, for the good
reason that there were no drains ; at least no long
hidden drains, only one short bit from the kitchen
sink, open at both ends and easily raked with a long
stick.

If it were possible to simplify life to the utmost,
how little one really wants ! And is it a blessing or a
disadvantage to be so made that one *must* take keen
interest in many matters ; that, seeing something that

one's hand may do, one cannot resist doing or attempting it, even though time be already overcrowded, and strength much reduced, and sight steadily failing? Are the people happier who are content to drift comfortably down the stream of life, to take things easily, not to *want* to take pains or give themselves trouble about what is not exactly necessary? I know not which, as worldly wisdom, is the wiser; I only know that to my own mind and conscience pure idleness seems to me to be akin to folly, or even worse, and that in some form or other I must obey the Divine command: "Work while ye have the light."

INDEX

ACANTHUS, 51, 256
Acorns, 50
Adze, 15
Agapanthus, 122
Alchemilla alpina, 152
Aldershot, 261
Allium, 318
Althæa Frutex, 120
Alyssum, 137, 260
Amaryllis, 122
Angelica, 315
Annuals for autumn sowing, 266
Anthemis, 274
Anthericum liliastrum, 112, 122
Arabis, 137, 260
Architect, and builder, 30
Arenaria balearica, 150
Arnebia, 146
Aromatic plants, 254
Artemisia, 139, 254
Artichoke, 270, 313
Arum, wild, 40, 70; leaves for cutting, 200
Asphodel, 138
Aspidistra, 206
Atriplex, 314
Aubergine, 319
Aubrietia, 137, 260
Aucuba, 349
Avenue of trees, 356
Axe, 176
Azalea, 249, 250

BAMBOOS as cut foliage, 187
Bambusa Metake with Lilies, 129

Bean, Broad, 309, flower of, 309
Beeches, in lane-banks, 60; injured by Honeysuckle, 84
Beet, 313, 314
Begonia metallica, 205
Birch, 135
Bog-Myrtle, 135, 137
Book-room, 24
Bowls, arranging flowers in, 188
Bracken, 237, 295
Bridges, old, 82
Brier Roses, 22, 92 and onward; Austrian, 97; Stanwell Perpetual, 98, 295
Broom, 246
Burdock, 47

CABBAGE, 302
Calla, 122
Caraway, 315
Cardamine trifoliata, 144
Cardoon, 313
Carpenter, country, 25
Carrot, 315
Catmint (*Nepeta*), 258
Cats, 322; tea-party, 334
Ceanothus, 267
Celery, 315
Cenotaph of Sigismunda, 106
Cerastium tomentosum, 56, 138, 155, 260
Charlock, 306
Chervil, 315
Choisya ternata, 256, 267
Cineraria maritima, 256
Cistus, 95, 118, 138, 240

370

Clover, 308; scent of, 309
Cobæa, 271
Colour in woodland in April,
42, 43; scheme in Wall-
flower garden, 56; of Briers
in winter, 99; arrangement
in flower-border, 126; in
large rock-planting, 139; of
cut flowers in relation to
rooms, 196, 198; of paint
for garden tubs and seats,
275; of distant landscape,
351; of white geese, 352; of
white horse , 352; how
applied in flowers, 353
Combinations of plants, 355
Compositæ, 311
Conservatories, 205; ill-
arranged, 206
Convallaria, 122
Corchorus, 259
Corydalis capnoides, 56, 147
Cottagers, 76, 362
Cottages, old, 70; pavements,
74
Crinum, 122
Cruciferæ, 306, 307
Cuckoo-flower, double, 56,
148; way of increasing, 150
Cultivation, deep in poor soil,
252
Cupboards, 26
Cut flowers, 179; preparing
for packing, 179 and
onward; in varied aspects,
199; under artificial light,
199

DANDELION as salad, 305,
311; culture, 312
Daphne pontica, 156
Datura, 320
Delphinium with Orange
Lily, 126

Dog's Mercury, 40, 46
Dog-Violet, white, 147
Donkey, old road-man's, 76
Dryas, 144
Dundee Rambler Rose, 366

Eccremocarpus, 271
Egg-plant, 319
Elder, 103
Electricity, 159
Elymus (Lyme Grass), 254
Embroidery materials, 28
Endive, 311
Eryngiums, 254, 316
Eulalia, 256
Everlasting Pea, 124, 276

FENNEL, 315, 316
Ferns, Polypody, 68;
Blechnum, 68; Hart's-tongue
as pot-plants, 192; wild,
288; Lady Fern, Royal Fern,
134, 143, 145
Flowering Rush (*Butomus*),
134
Footpath to house, 20
Fords, 82
Foundry, 158
Funkia grandiflora, 206

GALLERY, oak, 25; cupboards
in, 28
Gardening for short tenancies,
261
Garlic (*Allium*), 318
Gate-post, game of, 331
Gaultheria, 137, 143, 156, 259
Geological planting, 137
Ghost of a horse and cart, 20
Gilding, 162
Glasses for cut flowers, 204
Glass-houses, their external
ugliness, 209
Glazed passage-entrance, 218
Good-King-Henry, 314

Gorse, Spanish, 246; wild,
246
Gourds, 268, 270, 320, 353
Goutweed, 316
Grass paths, 237
Grouping of cut flowers, 194
Guelder Rose, 118

Haberlea, 144
Half-hardy annuals, 103
Hazel, old, 41
Heaths, 94, 99, 134, 137, 139,
237, 251
Helianthemum, 118, 138, 242
Helianthus, 273
Hellebores, 102
Heracleum (Cow Parsnip),
316
Herbaceous, a term often mis-
used, 271
Herbs, for flavouring, 321
Herring-Lily, 124
Hibiscus syraicus, 120
Hieracium, 146
Holly, 46; its affinity for
Blechnum, 68, 135, 238
Honeysuckle, 83 and onward
Hop, 271
Horse-radish, 270
House, how it was built, 13;
how planned, 34
Humming-bird Hawk-moth,
sound of flight, 333
Hut, the, 360
Hutchinsia, 144
Hydrangeas in tubs, 22
Hyssop, 258

ILEX, 238
Internal house fittings, 14
Iris stylosa, 106; cristata,
146; reticulata, 106;
tuberosa, 106; oncocyclus,
106; pumila, olbiensis,
Chamæiris, Cengialti,

albicans, florentina, pallida,
108; flavescens, variegata,
amæna, neglecta, aphylla,
squalens, 109; lævigata,
sibirica, orientalis,
lusitanica, Pseud acorus,
fœtidissima, 110; in borders,
274
Italian decoration, 163

JAPANESE way of arranging
flowers, 194
Jerusalem Sage (Phlomis), 248
Johnson's Gardener's Diction-
ary, 266
Juniper, 135, 238, 244

KALE, 303
Kalmia, 249, 251
Kitchen-garden, 302
Kitten as chaplain, 340
Knaphill variety of Pyrus
japonica, 364
Kohl-Rabi, 303

LABELS, ugliness of, 140, 142;
how to hide, 143
Laburnum, 354
Lathyrus grandiflorus, 74
Latour-Marliac, Monsieur, 123
Laurels, old, 48
Lavender, 138, 243, 244, 268
Lavender-Cotton, 139, 256
Leguminosæ, 308
Lentils, 310
Lettuce, 311
Lilaceæ, 120
Lilies of France, 117; of
Florence, of-the-Valley, St.
Bruno's, Arum, African,
Cape, Amazon, Belladonna,
122; Water, Scarborough,
White Lily, 123; Tiger, 126;
Auratum, 128; Orange Lily,
124

372

Linaria pallida; hepaticæfolia,
144
Linnæa, 134, 144
London builder's work, 15
London Pride, 114
Lonicera flexuosa, 366
Lycium, 259
Lycopodium, 289

MAIZE, way of rooting, 129
Marsh plants, wild, 289
Melilotus, 308
Menziezia, 134, 156
Miall, Professor, 304
Midsummer, 101
Monks' Rhubarb, 180
Mossy Saxifrage, 137, 145
Mountain Ash, 135, 238, 355
Mulching, 262
Mulleins, 102, 103, 256, 349
Mustard, 306
Myrrhis, 315

NAMES of plants, 278
Nasturtiums, 276
Nightshade, 319
Nymphæa alba, 122

OAK, timber-work, 15; gallery,
25; table, 29; growth in
lane-bank, 60; summer
shoots for cutting, 204;
beams in the Hut, 360
Observation, 349, 356
Omphalodes linifolia, 114
Onion, 316
Orangeries, 209
Othonnopsis, 138, 146

PACKING flowers, 184, 185
Pansy and Violet, 147
Parsnip, 315
Pea and Bean tribe, 308
Periwinkles, 50, 51
Phlomis, 138

Phlox, 273
Picking flowers in the hand,
188
Pigot, 172
Pinkieboy, 106, 324
Planta Genista, 308
Planting in long drifts, 137,
145
Polygonum, 275
Poor soils, plants for, 237
Poppies, autumn sown, 266
Porch, glazed, for plants, 217
Potato, 318
Pot-pourri, materials, 221;
preparation, 222 and on-
ward; mixing, 228; old
recipes, 230 and onward
Pottery, collection of, 169
Prophet-flower (*Arnebia*), 146
Purslane, 314
Pussies, 322
Pyrethrum uliginosum, 273
Pyrola, 134
Pyrus japonica, 364

RABBIT-BURROW, well placed,
47
Radish, 307
Railway fern-garden, 294
Rain after drought, 103; on
foliage, 102
Ramondia, 133, 144, 152
Rape, 306
Rhododendron beds, Lilies in,
128; alpine, 143, 156, 249,
250
Rhubarb, 271
Road-man, the old, 76
Roads in private ground, 358;
in woodland, 78
Roadway, old disused, 45
Rock-garden, large, 133;
small, 142
Rock Pinks, 260
Rock-rose, 242

Rodgersia, 144
Room decoration with flowers, 187
Rosa rugosa, 98
Rosemary, 138, 243, 268
Roses and Lilies, 117; Rose of England, 117; of Sharon, 120
Roses, different forms of; climbing; training down, 130
Rubus nutkanus, spectabilis, 249
Rubus rosæfolius, 192

ST. BRUNO'S LILY, 112
Saxifraga aizoides, 133; peltata, 144; mossy, 145
Scarlet Runner Beans, 268, 309
Scotch fir, in crumbling bank, 66; tracks among, 80, 346
Scythe, 176
Sea Buckthorn, 135
Sea Kale, 270, 307
Shallott, 318
Sitting-room, 22
Skimmia, 156
Solanum, 319, 320
Soldanella, 133
Sound of leaves, 350
Sounds, of building, 36, 37; of wind in Scotch fir, 41
Southernwood (Artemisia), 254
Sower, 176
Special gardens, 54, 92
Speedwell, wild, 155
Spinach, 314
Spiræa, shrubby, 265
Spores of ferns, 295; sowing them, 298
Spruce fir plantation, 43, 44
Stairs, 24
Stobæa, 258

Stratification in rock-work, 137
Swedes, 303
Sweet-brier, 99
Sweet Cicely, 315

Taraxacum, 312
Tea Roses as cut flowers, 200
Theatre, model, 160
Things worth doing, 342
Thistles, giant, 256
Thorn-trees, 135
Thrift, 155
Tittlebat, 326
Tomato, 318
Tools, 166; their kinship, 173
Tradition in building, 16, 72
Tree-Lupin, 102, 138, 248
Trees, in lane-banks, 59 and onward; tree-felling, 176; sound of, 350; suitable for avenues, 357
Trenching, deep in poor soils, 252
Trientalis, 134
Trillium, 136
Turnip, 304

Umbelliferæ, 316

VARIETY, 346
Vegetable Marrows, 270, 320
Verbascum phlomoides, 102
Veronica prostrata; satureioides, 144
Vilmorin, Messrs., 270
Vinca major; minor; acutiflora, 51
Viola cucullata, 147
Violets, 147

WALL-FLOWERS, 51 and onward; alpine, 55
Wall Pennywort, 134

374

Water-cress, 307
Water Plantain (*Alisma*), 134
Weigela, 265
White Beam tree, 355
Whortleberry, 137, 237
Wild flowers for cutting, 186
Windows, 24; window-boards, 24
Winter gardens, 208

Winter house-decoration of foliage, 202
Woodland in April, 38 and onward
Wood-Sorrel, 44
Workman, dexterity of, 36
Workshop, 157; its lessons, 161

The Antique Collectors' Club

The Antique Collectors' Club has 12,000 members and the monthly journal (not August), sent free to members, discusses in more depth than is normal for a collectors' magazine the type of antiques and art available to collectors. It is the only British antiques magazine which has consistently grown in circulation over the past decade.

The Antique Collectors' Club also publishes a series of books on antique furniture, art reference and horology, together with various standard works connected with arts and antiques. It also publishes a series of practical books, invaluable to collectors, under the general heading of the Price Guide Series (price revision lists published annually).

New titles are being added to the list at the rate of about ten a year. Why not ask for an updated catalogue?

The Antique Collectors' Club
5 Church Street, Woodbridge, Suffolk, England

Other books by Gertrude Jekyll published by the Antique Collectors' Club

Wood and Garden
8½ins. × 5½ins./22cm × 14cm. 380 pages, 71 black and white illustrations, 32 in colour. The first book Jekyll wrote takes the reader through her gardening year month by month. Also included are her practical and critical thoughts on the herbaceous garden, woodland, large and small gardens, and other gardening topics.

Colour Schemes for the Flower Garden
8½ins. × 5½ins./22cm × 14cm. 328 pages, 120 black and white illustrations, 32 in colour. Generally thought to be the author's best book. Her sense of colour, thoughts on 'painting' a garden and imaginative ideas on planting arrangements make this book a joy to read.

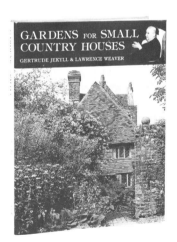

Gardens for Small Country Houses
by Gertrude Jekyll and Sir Lawrence Weaver
11ins. × 8½ins./28cm × 22cm. 260 pages, 387 black and white illustrations. This book is respected by generations of gardeners who continue to find in it inspiration in planning their own gardens, big or small, for the principles the authors expound are both fundamental and practical.